UNDERDOGS TO WONDERDOGS

Fresno State's Road to Omaha and the College World Series Championship

UNDERDOGS
TO
WONDERDOGS

Fresno State's Road to Omaha and the College World Series Championship

Chuck,
You service to
our country and to you
fellow veterans inspires me.
With Gratitude,
Paul Loeffler
PROVERBS 3:5-6

by Paul Loeffler

Craven Street Books
Fresno, CA

UNDERDOGS TO WONDERDOGS
Fresno State's Road to Omaha and the College World Series Championship
by Paul Loeffler

The author and publisher are grateful for the assistance of both the NCAA and Fresno State.

"Underdogs to Wonderdogs" is a registered trademark of California State University, Fresno. "Road to Omaha" and "College World Series" are registered trademarks of the National Collegiate Athletic Association.

© 2009 Paul Loeffler
Cover Design: Jim Goold
Book Design: Carla Green

35798642

ISBN 13: 978-1-933502-27-4

Printed in China

Library of Congress Cataloging-in-Publication Data

Loeffler, Paul, 1976-
  Underdogs to Wonderdogs : Fresno State's road to Omaha and the College World Series championship / by Paul Loeffler.
    p.   cm.
  ISBN 978-1-933502-27-4 (cloth : alk. paper)
  1. California State University, Fresno--Baseball. 2. College World Series (Baseball) (2008)
  I. Title.

GV875.12.C34L64 2009
796.357'630979483--dc22   2008040141

A Craven Street Book

Linden Publishing Inc.
2006 S. Mary
Fresno CA
www.lindenpub.com
800-345-4447

This book is dedicated to all the players, coaches, and fans,
past, present, and future, who understand
what it means to be part of the Bulldog baseball family.

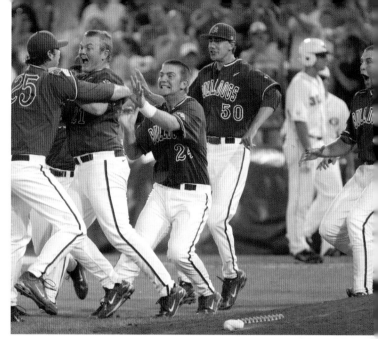

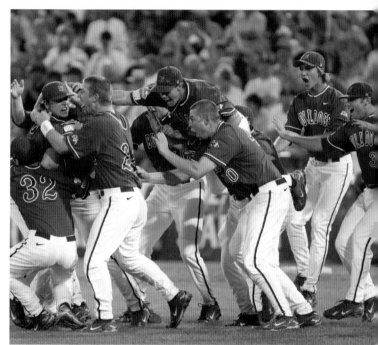

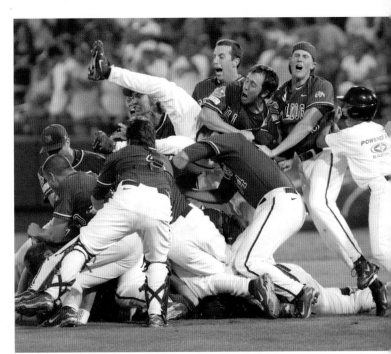

TABLE OF CONTENTS

> "Each new baseball season is a book not yet written."
>
> —Bob Bennett, former Fresno State coach, from *1,302 Winning Quotes for Coaches*
>
> Minorwhite Studios/Fresno State Athletics

ACKNOWLEDGMENTS

If I tried to thank every person who, in one way or another, had a hand in giving me the privilege of calling Fresno State's magic moment on the radio, I can sincerely say that the list would not fit on this page. You know who you are, I'll thank you personally, and I continue to thank God for the way He has used you to bless my life. The 2008 Diamond Dogs proved that the team is far greater than the individual, and without the following three teams, this book would not be sitting in your hands.

The Book Team:

Kent Sorsky, Paul Ladwig, Clarence Chiong, The Dugout Club, the 2008 Bulldog players and coaches, and all the contributors you'll hear from in Chapter 10, my favorite chapter of the book.

The Radio Team:

Skip Essick, Patty Hixson, Todd Lawley, and the beach bum who first hired me at KMJ, John Broeske. Also John Scheideman, Mark Holste, and Steve Gonzalez, the behind-the-scenes babysitters of our broadcasts. Chris Basham, Rych Withers, Joe Mauk, Jim Leedham—you can't have radio without engineers.

Scott Robbs, Marcas Grant, and the guy I grew up listening to on KMJ, Bill Woodward, who all filled in for me during the 2008 season. You will find quotes of some of their radio calls, in addition to some of mine, as you flip through the pages.

Ray O'Canto and his big Bulldog heart; and Steve Hosey, who taught me quite a bit about baseball and life in the years we worked together. Thanks also to Steve Schaack, Steve Weakland, and Fresno State Media Relations.

The Family Team:

Tonia, my beautiful, brilliant, and understanding wife. Avery and Mallory: if they can make Coach Batesole smile, imagine how many smiles they give me every day.

The Bernier, Dibiaso, Paulus, Foshee, and Bohnen families.

Corrie, Beverly, and Karl—I'm proud to be your brother.

My mom, Linda, and my late father, Bobby, both epitomizing "walking the walk."

My most loyal radio listeners over the years, grandparents Bette and Dr. Robert Loeffler. "Gramps" left this earth May 21st, 2008, so when I hear people point to there being some divine intervention behind the Bulldogs' improbable run to the title, the timing of it all makes him a prime suspect.

FOREWORD

by Brandon Burke

"What did you do this summer?"

I don't know how many times I've been asked this question, but it has never meant as much to me as it does now. Most of my summers consist of working, going to the beach a lot, hanging out with friends, and making various road trips. But nothing I learned from any day at the beach has been quite as valuable as what I learned in the summer of 2008.

In August 2007, my teammates and I arrived at Pete Beiden field on a typical 100-degree Fresno afternoon. This was my fourth time attending the annual arrival meeting where we normally get the low-down on team rules and learn what is expected of us on and off the field. This meeting, however, was unlike any of the three previous meetings. Coach Mike Batesole stood in front of his team for the first time with one hand covering his mouth and the other firmly grasping a clipboard full of notes. As our coach gathered his thoughts, I couldn't help but look around and make my first assessments of my new teammates. I thought to myself how intimidated all the freshmen seemed, but that came as no surprise.

At that moment Batesole put his clipboard on the ground as if to say, "This team does not need a lecture." He made sure to make eye contact with every one of us before uttering his first word: "Omaha."

The meeting we had that day did not lay down ground rules or say a word about what was expected of us, because we knew all that. It was day one but we were already ahead of the game. When most teams were trying to learn each other's names, we were

setting goals. The ultimate goal was to finish the year on the bottom of a dogpile at Rosenblatt Stadium. Little did any of us know exactly what sort of an emotional rollercoaster we were about to be strapped into, but every one of us was anxious for the ride of a lifetime.

In Omaha we were called the underdogs, we were called Cinderella, we were David and all seven of the other teams represented Goliath. But in our minds we were teammates, we

Brandon Burke celebrates the final out of the 2008 College World Series.
Minorwhite Studios/Fresno State Athletics

were best friends, we were brothers, and we were Bulldogs. But this isn't your typical college sports glory story because there was much more about that team than anyone could have ever known. We may have battled inside the white lines, but outside of them we had more fun than a 6-year-old at Disneyland.

Holden Sprague, Jake Hower and I would have competitions to determine who could make the funniest faces at the ESPN cameras. Justin Wilson and Jason Breckley had invisible tennis matches that consisted of loud grunts and bodies flying across the dugout at the speed of light. And who could ever forget Kris Tomlinson's skullet that even a retired hockey player would be envious of? All of the coaches tried to contain us, but we were past the point of no return.

In spite of all the fun and games, every one of us learned exactly what we needed to do to be successful as a team. There aren't words to describe the selflessness that I was lucky enough to witness in the summer of 2008—twenty-five guys not pulling for each other, but pushing for each other. We all had a small piece of a giant puzzle, and by the time we figured out where to put the last piece, we were the 2008 NCAA Champions.

INTRODUCTION

They did it. They *really* did it. Movie producers would laugh this script off as too hard to believe, even for Hollywood. But this isn't some melodramatic, feel-good fantasy—this actually happened—and it's hard to imagine any team ever overcoming longer odds to claim an NCAA championship trophy. The same squad that had to rally to finish fifth in a six-team field in its own tournament in March, somehow ended up as the last team standing at Omaha's Rosenblatt Stadium in June. Along the way, the

Bulldogs bid adieu to a preseason all-conference shortstop, saw an injury sideline one of college baseball's most overpowering pitchers, and survived what turned into a six-week road trip that saw the team stare elimination in the face six times.

As twenty-five California kids discovered the power that arises from a true team-first focus, they energized a student body, electrified generations of alumni, and galvanized an entire geographic region in the San Joaquin Valley. Words like "impossible," "in-

surmountable," and "unimaginable" were rendered a little less daunting once these "wonderdogs" pumped hope into the underdog spirit so many of us share.

With each improbable victory making the next one a little easier to fathom, the Bulldogs made believers out of us all. To accomplish that, they first had to make believers out of each other. If wall-magnet Steve Detwiler can hit three Omaha homers with a thumb flopping down below his wrist, then why shouldn't Jake Hower be

Here's how Ray and I watched all the magic unfold in Omaha. *Jim Leedham*

able to shut down Georgia's offense in his first outing in more than a month? If Tommy Mendonca's dislocated fingers can locate and lasso any ball hit within fifteen feet of him at third base, then why shouldn't Clayton Allison be able to squeeze six innings out of an arm he was icing the night *before* he faced North Carolina? And if Kris Tomlinson can be a lights-out lefty throughout the postseason, then why wouldn't Justin Wilson want to prove his southpaw superiority with the performance of his life on college baseball's ultimate do-or-die stage?

In less than two months, Fresno State went from playing mediocre baseball in front of sparse-but-spirited Beiden Field crowds, to capturing the attention of millions around the globe. The team that wasn't supposed to be there became a cause célèbre, inspiring fans everywhere who found themselves dreaming vicariously through two-dozen ballplayers who believed they could win it all, and were determined to have fun doing it.

Justin Wilson told the second-largest television audience in college baseball history, "We are over Cinderella, we're Bulldogs!" Those six words underscore an important distinction. While Fresno State entered the NCAA bracket ranked 89th in the country and had to eliminate half of the top ten on its way to the title, this program is no overnight success story. Only eight schools have made more NCAA appearances than Fresno State, and since Pete Beiden arrived on campus six decades ago, *forty* Bulldog teams have finished with better winning percentages than the 2008 squad.

Beiden's 1951 team might have been the nation's best, but never got the chance to prove it, denied the opportunity to battle USC for a spot in Omaha. His 1959 Bulldogs lost a coin flip that would have put them in the national title game. Bob Bennett's 1,302 victories included an eye-popping thirty-two in a row in 1988, but neither that record-breaking bunch nor his 1991 squad could finish the job in Omaha.

Mike Batesole became the heir to a half-century of championship dreams when he succeeded Bennett in 2002, but not even Batesole could have looked in his dugout after losing the first half of a doubleheader in Sacramento on May 17 and imagined that his four-games-over-.500 ballclub was about to embark on an unprecedented run to baseball immortality. It was over that twenty-game stretch that the diehards of the Dugout Club would witness the magical metamorphosis from underdogs to wonderdogs.

The pages ahead will capture that transformation through the eyes of the players and coaches and their families, fans who rode the wave from Long Beach to Tempe to Omaha, and from someone who remains as delightedly dumbfounded as anyone by this storybook ending: your humble play-by-play announcer.

Long before that dangerous dogpile at Rosenblatt (read on to see who ended up with a black eye), I considered it a great privilege to be part of the Bulldog baseball family. If there is a program in America with more pride, tradition, and sincere alumni support and involvement, I have yet to come across it. What a blessing it was to saddle up next to Ray O'Canto, who had played at different times under the tutelage of both Pete Beiden and Bob Bennett, and try to paint a picture for the listeners at home that would do justice to the way Mike Batesole's Bulldogs fulfilled their diamond destiny. Whether you were in Omaha, listening on KMJ, or watching on TV, it's my hope that this book will help you relive that magical month-and-a-half over and over and over again.

THE SEASON BEGINS: HIGH EXPECTATIONS, MIXED RESULTS

Two hundred and ninety-six schools play Division I college baseball. Each team's media guide invariably lists the current season's schedule on the back cover, with the last three lines reserved for "NCAA Regionals," "NCAA Super Regionals," and "College World Series." For all but eight of those schools, that last line is nothing more than wishful thinking; but as Mike Batesole entered his sixth season as Fresno State's head coach, he wasn't afraid to utter the word "Omaha."

The pieces to the puzzle were in place. One of the most accomplished hitters in school history, Steve Susdorf, had turned down the Detroit Tigers and returned for his senior season. A preseason All-Conference shortstop, Todd Sandell, was paired up with one of Beiden Field's all-time fan favorites, Erik Wetzel, whose presence Batesole often likened to having another coach on the field. At the corners, Tommy Mendonca and Alan Ahmady had shown flashes of stardom as freshmen and were poised for breakout sophomore seasons.

The greatest source of optimism? The pitching staff. With the preseason WAC Pitcher of the Year (Clayton Allison), the reigning conference ERA champ (Justin Wilson), and a projected first-round draft pick (Tanner Scheppers), the Bulldogs coaching staff saw the requisite foundation for a deep postseason run. It wasn't a se-

cret either—Baseball America ranked Fresno State 18th in its preseason poll, Collegiate Baseball pegged the Bulldogs 21st, and they checked in at #29 in the National Collegiate Baseball Writers Association poll.

Anticipation grew as opening weekend approached, with extra buzz generated by the news that Bulldog greats and longtime big leaguers Dick Ruthven (#17) and Tom Goodwin (#1) would have their jerseys retired. With college baseball's new universal start date rule pushing the season back a month, it gave Diamond Dog fans even more time to rev up their engines. The stage was set. The season had finally arrived. And then Mother Nature and U.C. Davis conspired to rain on

the Bulldogs' proverbial parade. Don't confuse this with the actual parade—you'll have to keep reading for a while before we get to that.

Heavy rains leading up to the Friday night debut turned what would have been a solid season-opening crowd into a scattered assortment of longtime fans and players' family members. A U.C. Davis squad, led by a pair of San Joaquin Valley natives, quieted those who stuck around. With Merced High School product Eddie Gamboa striking out seven Bulldogs in five innings, and catcher Jake Jefferies (Buhach Colony High School, Atwater) coming through with four hits, the Aggies took the season opener 4–2. The next day, Jef-

Tom Goodwin at the Beiden Field ceremony to retire his number. *Jack Porter/Valleypix.com*

Dick Ruthven at the Beiden Field ceremony to retire his number. *Jack Porter/Valleypix.com*

feries delivered three more hits, driving in two, and the Aggies opened a doubleheader with a 3–1 victory over Fresno State.

The Bulldogs needed a pick-me-up, and they needed it in a hurry. Before the second game of the doubleheader, the players watched from the dugout as Ruthven and Goodwin, surrounded by old teammates who had come to share in the celebration, received the program's highest honor. Ruthven shared stories about his dominating days as a Diamond Dog, and also his role on the 1980 World Series champion Philadelphia Phillies. Goodwin, who won an Olympic gold medal after playing in the 1988 College World Series, and went on to play fourteen seasons in the big leagues, was about to take a minor league coaching job in the Red Sox organization. I had the privilege of emceeing the ceremony on the field, and I figured I'd give Goodwin a head start on his coaching

duties by asking what one piece of advice he would like to share with the student-athletes who hoped to one day follow in his footsteps.

"The most important thing, if you're trying to do something as a team," Goodwin said, "is that you have to *be* a team. That's the one thing that we had at Fresno State, we *were* a team. Not everybody was on the same page all the time, but we knew that once we took this field, there was one goal in mind, that was just to go out there and give it whatever you had, win, lose or draw."

As some of his old Bulldog teammates nodded in agreement behind him, Goodwin continued: "The bottom line was, I had to get his back, he's got my back, and you just go out there and play your butts off." Goodwin had starred on the 1988 Fresno State team that won a school-record fifty-six games, reached #1 in the rankings, and advanced to the College World Series. But he told the cur-

rent players that achieving a true team-first mentality could carry them to even higher goals. He dared the teams in both dugouts to dream "to one day be in Omaha, and bring that championship trophy back home." Then, turning his attention strictly to the third base side, Goodwin said, "For you Bulldogs over there, we couldn't do it, but you *can* do it, so let's get it done."

It's clear, in retrospect, that Goodwin's exhortation did not fall on deaf ears. The players had heard their coaches talk about being unselfish, trusting each other, and becoming a team as opposed to a collection of individuals. But hearing it from a guy so many of them had seen make those highlight-reel catches and steal bases at will, a player who had sat in so many major league dugouts and played under so many different managers, it couldn't help but lend a little more credence to what their coaches were trying to hammer home.

By the time the second game of that Saturday doubleheader commenced, a different Bulldog attitude was evident. It also helped to have the rocket right arm of Tanner Scheppers on the mound for the first time in 2008.

The 6-foot, 4-inch flamethrower was probably more threatened by the salivating scouts in the stands than by the Aggies' bats, scattering four hits over seven scoreless innings, while striking out ten. Senior shortstop Todd Sandell homered and drove in three, and the Bulldogs picked up their first victory of the season, 7–0.

Fresno State would continue that momentum the next day, scoring four times in the first inning and enduring a two-hour rain delay before beating the Aggies 6–3 to salvage a split of the season-opening four-game series. At the time, splitting with U.C. Davis didn't sit all that well with Diamond Dog fans, but that split would look better and better as the season went on.

Aggies' catcher Jefferies became one of the toughest players in the country to strike out, and would end up being drafted higher (3rd round, 78th pick) than any player in school history. In their first year of eligibility for the Division I tournament, the Aggies would wind up in an NCAA regional at Stanford, where a complete game from Gamboa would fell the Omaha-bound Cardinal in the first game.

Looking back, splitting with U.C. Davis was nothing to sneeze at, but at the time it felt like the first dose of adversity for this determined team. Dose number two wasn't far behind. Up next on Fresno State's schedule was a trip to San Diego for a tournament that represented the Bulldogs' toughest four-game stretch of the season. Three of their four opponents (San Diego, Cal, and San Diego State) were ranked in somebody's Top 25, and the fourth, Cal Poly, had beaten Fresno State ten times in a row dating back to 2004.

The Bulldogs were still ranked 24th in the country by Baseball America, but that disappeared almost as quickly as the 3–0 lead they held over Cal after a half-inning. The Golden Bears got to left-hander Justin Wilson for five runs on nine hits, chasing him in the fifth, and going on to a lopsided 14–4 victory. It wasn't going to get any easier the next day as Fresno State faced San Diego south-paw Brian Matusz, who would go on to become the fourth overall pick of the 2008 MLB Draft. Matusz, who would finish his Torero career with a 26–8 record, had been roughed up by the Diamond Dogs in Fresno in 2007, but he wasn't about to let that happen this time. Eleven strikeouts later, Ma-

tusz had outdueled Scheppers in a matchup of two of the nation's best hurlers.

The 5–2 San Diego victory also gave family bragging rights to USD center fielder Kevin Muno, whose younger brother Danny went 0-for-4 in that contest, playing right field for Fresno State. A few months later, Danny would have his chance to even the score, but, at the time, he and his teammates were just hoping they could knock off Cal Poly the next day.

Clayton Allison pitched well enough to beat the Mustangs, allowing just one run in seven-and-one-third innings. But Cal Poly starter Derrick Saito was even better, striking out nine in six scoreless innings, and D.J. Mauldin followed that with three hitless innings of relief. A 2–1 loss to the Mustangs meant Cal Poly had now won eleven straight in the series and, even worse, it dropped Fresno State to 2 and 5 on the season, raising ques-

tions about an offense now averaging just over three runs a game.

If losing the first two games to U.C. Davis had been a wake-up call, this was a fungo bat on the back of the head. Fresno State's national ranking was a distant memory, and the Bulldogs would need to defeat San Diego State to avoid a winless trip. So how would Batesole try to fire up his troops? To understand the answer to that question you must first understand what makes Batesole tick, and unless you're extremely intuitive, you won't gather that from a first impression.

Batesole: Peace and Passion

The Mike Batesole I know now is a man characterized by focus, discipline, devotion, and consistency. What I recognize now as one of his greatest strengths is that he is not overly concerned with what other

At the ceremony to retire his number, Tom Goodwin told the Bulldogs they could "bring the championship trophy back home." *Jack Porter/Valleypix.com*

people think. He lets his convictions chart his course and rarely, if ever, allows that course to be altered. Why did I employ the word "now" twice in as many sentences? Because like quite a few members of the Bulldog baseball community, it took me a while to get to know the new coach when he was hired in 2002.

It's never easy to replace a legend, and Batesole was taking over for Bob Bennett, who had just retired as the seventh-winningest coach in NCAA history. Bennett had played at Fresno State under the legendary Pete Beiden, had succeeded Beiden as head coach, and held that position for 34 years. For twenty-six of those seasons, Mike Rupcich was Bennett's right hand man, and Bennett had publicly and unequivocally endorsed Rupcich as his successor. Rupcich, a gracious man with a constant smile, was a finalist for the job, but then-athletic director Scott Johnson passed him over in favor of Batesole, who had just won the Big West championship with Cal State Northridge. Bennett was not pleased the school had hired someone with no previous ties to the program, and it quickly became clear that this would not be a seamless passing of the torch. Batesole did choose to retain one of Bennett's assistants, Matt Curtis, but that did nothing to quell the tension that filled the air around Beiden Field.

Change is never easy, and this was a pretty dramatic change. Bennett, a child of the Dust Bowl, had spent the lion's share of his 68 years in Fresno and had developed deep connections in the community as he, both literally and figuratively, built a stadium, a program, and a brand. It was extremely important to him and his loyal supporters that tradition be honored and momentum maintained.

Batesole, 30 years his junior, was coming in with an eye on overhauling a program that hadn't been to the College World Series since 1991. He had met with a large degree of success early in his career, even earning National Coach of the Year honors when he was just 34 years old. He had his own ideas, his own drive, and he wasn't soliciting suggestions. He was all business, all the time.

On game days, Batesole's intense focus would take over, and trying to get a smile or a chuckle out of him was like trying to find a fresh Fresno fig in February—it just wasn't going to happen. That gruff exterior might have intimidated a few, and I'll include myself in that bunch, but I soon realized that Batesole is just one of those people whose trust you have to earn. Once he gets to know and respect someone, he is as warm and as loyal as anyone. With him, that was a process that required a little time. It would take a while for the coach to grow on the community, and vice versa. Here's how Batesole explains those trials of transition:

"There are so many people in the Fresno community who want to have a say in Fresno State baseball. It took time to work through which ones were in it for themselves, and who was in it for the kids. Who wanted rings at all costs, and who wanted degrees first, then rings. Respect and loyalty are earned. When they are earned, there is trust. Trust is the most important aspect of any relationship. It is earned from being where you are supposed to be, when you're supposed to be there, doing what you are supposed to be doing, and doing all that consistently over time. When we took over the program, that kind of trust did not exist. Players didn't trust players, players didn't trust coaches, and players did-

n't trust the system. And how could they? True trust takes time. We had to get players in here who fit, and who believed in our system. You can't run a run-and-shoot offense with a bunch of tight ends, and you can't run a pro-style offense with a bunch of wide receivers."

Growing pains were certainly visible on the field, as Batesole's first three teams had to battle to finish above .500. It took the biggest pitch of David Griffin's life to ensure a winning record in 2003. The lefty had to face Rice star Vincent Sinisi with the bases loaded in the ninth in Houston, but he induced a game-ending double play that delivered a 2–1 win over the 2nd-ranked Owls and allowed Fresno State to post its 27th consecutive winning season, finishing with 30 wins against 29 losses.

Technically, that streak ended in 2004 when the Richie Robnett-led Bulldogs needed to win their final five games just to finish 29–29, making it 28 years without a losing record. In 2005, a 30–29 finish reflected more mediocrity, but something that happened that season set the tone for the run of success that would begin the following year.

Batesole had always put in as many hours as a coach can. He had formulated his own system for evaluating players' effectiveness, and he had the kind of plan he knew could make Fresno State successful. It just wasn't happening on the field, and that inescapable reality was eating at him. The obsession consumed him to the point that it jeopardized his health. In March 2005, Batesole had to be hospitalized and missed two games. The medical specifics were kept private, but it became clear that the health scare gave Batesole pause to reexamine his priorities.

Don't get the wrong impression. The coach didn't "go soft"—he remains to this day as focused and driven and demanding as ever. But what those who know Batesole well have seen in the years since is a continually growing measure of peace. Buoyed by his relationship with God and the support of his wife Susie, whom he first started dating when he was 15 and she was 14, Batesole has tried to lead by example, hoping to motivate and inspire players as much with his actions and his demeanor as with his words. The intensity still flashes, and the passion is ever-present, but the coach has been increasingly defined by the kind of cool, confident comfort that comes from having the courage of one's convictions, and doesn't waver with the ebb and flow of wins and losses.

Coaching at the Division I level was a very demanding job—there was no question about that—but baseball needed to be fun. He had to recapture the joy of that kid growing up in southern California with the posters of George Brett and Earl Campbell on his wall; the young man who went from a Junior Angel watching Nolan Ryan work his magic, to starring at third base for Oral Roberts while his brother Bobby was putting up big numbers at USC. He had to refocus his attention on the example that had been set, in word and deed, by the first real baseball coach he had—his father, Gary.

"The one thing that my Dad really helped me with is he always kept my brother and me humble," Batesole said. "He worked at Rockwell International for 36 years. Punched the clock at the same time every day, took lunch at the same time every day, took breaks the same time every day, and every spare second he got he spent at the baseball field. And that was the

Mike Batesole is all smiles after the conclusion of the 2008 season. *Eric Sorenson*

best advice he ever gave me—go to school, get your degree, get your master's degree, so that you can do what you enjoy."

What's the point of all that hard work over all those years if you're not having fun? The fun would come, and so would the victories. He never stopped believing in his system, and he never stopped believing that one of his teams would really get it, and be in the right place at the right time. He just decided that he wasn't going to let it eat him alive when things didn't go according to plan, and wouldn't you know it, he can look back after six seasons and truly say the reality has surpassed the dream.

"It came together soon enough—our first recruiting class did things never done before at Beiden Field, and our second recruiting class brought home National Championship rings. What I'm most proud of is they did it the right way: nine of nine seniors graduating on time or plus one se-

mester, 2.8+ GPA, an APR that will be in the 970 range, and 100 percent eligibility points, all while playing a record seventy-eight games. It all comes down to degrees and rings."

The Mike Batesole I know now is equal parts peace and passion. You can feel his love for the game in his handshake, his grip programmed into a slight curl from all those years of squeezing a bat in his hands. He is a student of the game, attuned to the finer points that sail right on by most of us. Those qualities are evident, but the more time you spend around "Bates," as his players know him, the more his rough edges dissolve to reveal the "people person" inside. A glimpse of his heart emerges every time you see him around young children, and anyone who's been on the receiving end of a Batesole bear hug can vouch for its sincerity.

Throughout his time at Fresno State he has steadily sharpened his focus on what matters most. He wants to win, and he wants to win big, but most of all he wants to make his mark as a molder of men. He has come to understand that the best way to spur growth and development in a team is to provide a solid foundation of fundamentals, emphasizing team over self; to clearly define the rules and stick to them; and to then give the players enough room to build trust in each other, hoping that the purity of the game will take precedence over stat-watching and one-upmanship. Simply put, when a player can trust each one of his teammates unconditionally, it depressurizes the atmosphere and frees him up to get back to baseball's most basic tenet: playing the game should be fun.

A Classic Approach

Let's return now to early March at Tony Gwynn Stadium in San Diego. How could Batesole inject some life into an offense that managed just four hits against Cal Poly? How could he get his team's attention, and produce a small measure of redemption with a win over the 22nd-ranked Aztecs? The approach was classic Batesole: let them know how you feel, then let them marinate in that motivation while you back off and demonstrate that you trust them to push themselves.

It started on the bus ride back to the hotel after losing to Cal Poly. Coaches kept the position players on the bus for an extra thirty minutes, for what Batesole calls a "priority readjustment." To a struggling Steve Susdorf, Batesole asked, "Is this what you came back for?" To strikeout-prone Tom Mendonca, it was: "I could walk over to Buchanan High School right now and find nine guys who can strike out half their at bats." San Diego to Clovis would have been a pretty

lengthy walk, but the point came through loud and clear, and so did the new edict that the squad's kangaroo court would be happy to enforce:

"We had been talking too much about Omaha in March, when we should have been talking about March in March," Batesole recalled. "We were not going to say the words 'Omaha,' 'Super Regional,' or 'Regional' again."

So the players had all of that to sleep on, and they'd had almost a full day to motivate themselves and each other by the time they returned to the diamond to face San Diego State. If the players in that third base dugout were keeping a close eye on Batesole, they had to take note of the first thing they saw when the coach headed to home plate to exchange lineups with Aztecs' coach Tony Gwynn. They saw a wry smile on Batesole's face as he mouthed something to the Padres Hall of Famer, who in turn threw his head back in laughter. This was the first time Batesole, known for his obsession with every small detail involved in the mechanics of a baseball swing, had ever had a meaningful conversation with Gwynn, one of the greatest pure hitters in baseball history. It had to send a message of trust when the Bulldogs saw that, even after the "priority readjustment," their coach was loose and comfortable enough to greet the living legend with a joke, which turned out to be an anecdote from the days Batesole spent as a teammate of Gwynn's brother Chris in the Dodgers' farm system.

Whether or not that pre-game scene had anything to do with it, the early signs of trust and teamwork began to emerge. On the offensive side of the ball, nothing reflects unselfishness and trust more than two-out rallies and two-strike hits. Team struggles make it easy for a player to

try to do too much, to feel like he has to take matters into his own hands because no one else is producing. When he believes in the guys hitting behind him, he can focus on winning the battle of each at bat or each pitch, not worried that he needs to try to win the whole war with one big swing. The building blocks of that belief in each other began to take shape in the top of the third inning that Sunday in San Diego.

With two outs, Erik Wetzel singled, then Danny Muno kept the inning alive with a single of his own and stole second before Alan Ahmady drove both Bulldogs in with a single of his own, giving the Bulldogs a 2–1 lead. The Aztecs tied it in the bottom of the inning, only to see another two-out outburst from the Bulldogs in the fourth. Mendonca made sure to show Batesole something he wouldn't find at a Buchanan High School game—the sophomore's first home run of the season was a majestic blast of at least 450 feet, sailing well over the giant SDSU Wall of Fame in right field. And it was just the first of five consecutive two-out hits.

"Hitting is contagious," is an old baseball adage that proved itself true that day, with Fresno State more than quadrupling its hit total from the day before. The Bulldogs defeated the Aztecs 9–2, ending their three-game losing streak. "They came out and played mean," Batesole said, "Where had that team been?"

Batesole would be putting out the APB soon enough, because the ups and downs were just beginning. After losing a heartbreaker in Santa Clara when the strike zone disappeared and Brandon Burke walked in the winning run in the bottom of the tenth, the Bulldogs rebounded with back-to-back wins at home over Indiana, building some momentum for their 30th annual Pepsi Johnny Quik Classic, a tournament they were expected to win, as they had sixteen times before.

Opening the tournament against New Mexico State, a team they would face eight more times in conference play, the Bulldogs committed five errors and lost 13–8. The next night, the frustration intensified as the offense went into hiding again, managing just five hits in a 3–2 loss to a Portland team that would go on to finish last in the West Coast Conference. Next up was the same Indiana squad the Bulldogs had beaten twice over the weekend, but just when you thought the bats couldn't be any quieter, Fresno State mustered only four hits in an 11–1 loss to the Hoosiers that ended any hope of a tournament title.

The Bulldogs were now a season-worst four games under .500 (5–9), their preseason ranking was a distant memory, and fans were starting to wonder if the Diamond Dogs would even win a single game in their own tourney. If the Bulldogs were going to turn things around, someone would have to step up and lead by example, and junior right-hander Justin Miller

was up to the challenge. Miller had come to Batesole's program after two seasons at Bakersfield College, where he played for former Fresno State player and assistant Tim Painton. With good velocity on his fastball, and a slider with the kind of break that could make right-handed batters look silly, Miller had been a bright spot during the rough start, and he would be downright dominating against Gonzaga. Carrying a no-hitter into the sixth, Miller would settle for combining with two relievers on a one-hitter. The 10–1 victory over the Zags also included a 5-for-5 performance from senior shortstop Todd Sandell. That's five hits from one player, when the entire team only produced four hits the night before.

Again the Bulldogs had answered the bell, and they didn't want to stop there. Tanner Scheppers posted his third double-digit strikeout game of the young season in a 10–0 undoing of Utah, and even though the Dogs would be playing in the fifth-place game of their six-team tournament, they had a chance to finish their stretch of eight games in eight days on a little bit of a roll. A 12–3 payback

pounding of Portland accomplished that, and a pattern was beginning to emerge.

Three weekends in a row now, Fresno State had backed itself into a proverbial corner, only to come out fighting and finish each weekend on a winning note. Naturally it was time for the pendulum to swing back in the other direction: a 13–8 loss at San Francisco, then a 4–0 defeat in the Western Athletic Conference opener at Hawaii, despite eleven more strike-outs for Scheppers. Jared Alexander went the distance and allowed just four hits in that shutout, and again following the trend, the next game was even worse for Fresno State: just two hits off of Nicholas Rhodes in a 2–0 Rainbow win. So the two-time defending conference champs were now 0–2 in the WAC, back to four games under .500 overall (8–12), and just 1–7 away from Beiden Field. It was another one of those "put up or shut up" moments, and two senior leaders were ready to ride to the rescue.

THE BULLDOGS TURN IT AROUND
(SUPER SUSDORF FINDS HIS PHONE BOOTH)

Through the first twenty games, pre-season WAC Player of the Year Steve Susdorf's offensive numbers were quite Clark Kent-esque. He had almost as many strikeouts (18) as hits (20), he hadn't hit a single ball out of the park after launching 26 over the previous two seasons, and his average was a disappointing .256. This wasn't the kind of senior season Susdorf envisioned seven months earlier when he made one of the most difficult decisions of his life.

After a junior season in which he set career-highs in average (.340), RBI (68) and stolen bases (12), and earned first-team all-conference honors for the second year in a row, Susdorf was drafted in the 27th round of the major league draft by the Detroit Tigers. Coach Mike Batesole, as he does each June, was following the draft online, and felt strongly that his left fielder deserved to have been chosen sooner.

"I still remember the second I saw '27th round' and 'Susdorf' pop up on the screen at the same time. I was doink, doink, doink," Batesole says, mimicking the motion of his finger on a cell phone keypad. The coach recalled the ensuing conversation proceeding like this:

Batesole: "Dude, are you kidding me? Here's what we're gonna do, you're gonna wear number 27 next year, so every single game, every single scout in the stands is gonna see that 27 on your back and remember that they missed out on you."

Susdorf: "Dude, that would be pretty intense."

Batesole: "Yeah, it's intense, and watch what happens."

Susdorf decided to put his professional baseball career on hold, rejecting the Tigers' $50,000 offer and returning for his senior season, with his sights set on leading the Diamond Dogs to the College World Series. He had worn #13 as a freshman, #8 as a sophomore, #9 as a junior, and now had a very special reason for wearing #27. The two previous Bulldogs to wear #27, Beau Mills and Richie Robnett, had both been All-Americans, but Susdorf wasn't looking to piggyback off their good fortune—he was motivated to manufacture his own. Batesole looks back now and sees that

Steve Susdorf's Statistics
First 20 games (through March 21) vs. Final 58 games (March 22 on)

	Avg.	2B	HR	RBI
First 20	.256	6	0	12
Final 58	.375	27	13	76

Steve Susdorf by the numbers.
Minorwhite Studios/Fresno State Athletics

draft-day conversation as a moment that sharpened Susdorf's focus and further fueled his drive.

"Every single day, every practice day—and Susdorf takes more swings than anybody else," Batesole said, "I don't know if he didn't take a swing without a purpose from that moment until we won the national championship. I think every single swing he took was with a purpose. Nobody deserves that [championship] more than he does."

Purpose hadn't quite translated to production yet when the Bulldogs arrived for a doubleheader at Hawaii's Les Murakami Stadium on March 22. This was by far the biggest day of the young season, a pivotal Saturday that could end with the Bulldogs sitting anywhere from 0–4 in WAC play to 2–2.

Susdorf doesn't wear spectacles, "phone booth" has become an anachronism, and capes conflict with baseball's uniform code, but that Saturday in Honolulu was without question the moment that Susdorf shed his Clark Kent statistics and started swinging a super stick once again. With Fresno State leading 2–0 in the top of the eighth inning, Susdorf stepped to the plate with one out and two runners on. He had gone 1-for-3 against Rainbow starter Josh Slaats, but was now facing right-hander Harrison Kuroda.

"First pitch (ping!), there's a ball hit deep to right field, forget about it! Van Doornum looks up, GOOD-BYE! Three-run home run for Steve Susdorf over the right field wall, and it's now a five–nothing Fresno State lead."

— *Scott Robbs, filling in on play-by-play*

Senior Clayton Allison pitched a complete-game shutout against Hawaii.
Fresno State Athletics

Later calling that Saturday "a big relief," Susdorf would go 4-for-8 in the doubleheader, and hit .375 over the remainder of the season, as he reconfigured countless columns in the Fresno State record book. If you were paying close attention, you'll recall I said *two* Bulldog seniors were ready to save the day on March 22. Just as important as Susdorf snapping out of his slump, if not more so, was the powerful pitching performance of Clayton Allison.

Fighting Fire with Fire

Remember, Hawaii had tossed back-to-back shutouts against the Diamond Dogs. If there was going to be a shutout in the third game of the se-

ries, the preseason WAC pitcher of the year was going to make sure the goose egg was in the Rainbows' run column. Clayton Allison had spent the offseason fighting wildfires in Oregon, melting 20 pounds off his 6 foot 5 inch frame in the process. While Susdorf had felt snubbed by his Round 27 selection, Allison had been dealt a bigger draft-day slight. He wasn't picked at all after winning ten games for the Bulldogs in 2007. So he had entered the season with something to prove, and as he took the mound that Saturday afternoon in Honolulu, he knew he was better than his 0–2 record and 5.40 ERA might indicate.

One hundred twenty-two purposeful pitches later, Allison had delivered the most dominating performance of his career. Relying heavily on a split-fingered fastball that, like one of those white-crested waves Hawaii is famous for, came crashing down sharply at the last possible instant, Allison navigated his way to a complete game, four-hit shutout. The Bulldogs won that contest 5–0, then made it a doubleheader sweep when Susdorf's double set up Alan Ahmady's tenth inning triple in a 4–2 victory that secured a split in the four-game series.

Flying back to the mainland on Easter Sunday, the Bulldogs had plenty of time to reflect on resurrecting their record to respectability. Two more victories could get them to the .500 mark, but the opponent for those Tuesday-Wednesday games was Cal Poly. Yes, the very same Mustangs who had beaten the Bulldogs for the eleventh straight time just three weeks earlier. The fact that Fresno State hadn't defeated Cal Poly since 2004 was tough enough for fans to swallow. Making it even less palatable was the way the Mustangs had done it, with players coach Larry Lee recruited from under Batesole's nose in the San Joaquin Valley. The Bulldogs were the ones with the big green "V" for valley on the back of their helmets, but the Mustangs' "Valley boys" had seized the upper hand in the longtime rivalry.

When looking back at the 2008 season, there are quite a few games that spring more immediately to mind than those two matchups with the Mustangs in late March, but hindsight also reveals this pair of thrillers as a microcosm of the season. Every time the Bulldogs found themselves reeling on the brink, they battled back to become the last team standing.

Cal Poly led 2–0 on March 25 when the Bulldogs staged one of their signature two-out rallies in the bottom of the third. Bakersfield native Jared Eskew got the second out for Cal Poly when he struck out Erik Wetzel with the bases loaded, but Susdorf was there to bail Wetzel out. Displaying the kind of trust in his teammates that would eventually become the hallmark of this team, Susdorf did not try to do too much, instead working a walk that brought home the first run. Ahmady reinforced that trust with a two-run single through Eskew's legs to give the Bulldogs a 3–2 lead. Gavin Hedstrom was due up next.

"Eskew off the third base edge of the rubber, sets, and delivers—Hedstrom swings, drives it in the air to right center field. That ball's hit well! Lee going back, will not get there, it is *over* the fence! A home run for Gavin Hedstrom, and this crowd is going crazy at Beiden Field!"

That was the first home run of Hedstrom's three-year Bulldog career, and it pushed the lead to 6–2. Starting pitcher Tanner Scheppers would give up a home run to Clovis High School product Wes Dorrell, but still exit after six innings with an 8–3 lead. It was right about that time that Fresno State football coach Pat Hill had stopped by Beiden Field after a long night of spring practice. After watching the action for a few minutes, he ambled over to our broadcast booth and donned a headset, filling in the gaps between pitches with updates about his team. There was plenty of ground for Hill to cover, and he's always very accommodating, but as it turned out, Hill's visit coincided with a monstrous Mustang comeback. By the time Bakersfield native Brent Morel blasted a three-run homer to left to get Cal Poly within one, I was ready to make Hill the scapegoat.

"It's now 8 to 7, Coach, you're giving up the lead, we're gonna have to go to the lefty out of the pen here!" To which Hill replied, "I better get out of here, I've been booed a few times walking up that ramp, I might get booed walking down the stands today." Hill wanted to see that half-inning through, though, so he stuck around and witnessed a balk called on Jake Hower, bringing in the tying run from third base.

"If they get the lead, Coach, I'm gonna have to kick you out," I jokingly said, but moments later another one of Cal Poly's "Valley boys," Kyle Smith (Buchanan High School, Clovis) delivered the go-ahead single. It was a six-run rally that carried Cal Poly to a 9–8 lead, and as a stunned crowd stood up for the seventh inning stretch, Hill rose to leave and delivered this parting shot: "We are gonna get the lead back, the Dogs are gonna win this one."

Given the team's ups and downs to that point in the season, and the fact that the Mustang Monkey had been riding their backs for four years, I don't know how many of our listeners expected Hill's words to come true, especially as the game headed to the ninth with Cal Poly still ahead 9–8. Fresno State had its back to the wall, and as we all know now, that is the kind of situation that time and time again brought out the best in the 2008 Diamond Dogs.

Leading off the bottom of the ninth was Erik Wetzel. What most of the 1,702 fans at Beiden Field that night didn't know was that Wetzel had attended a funeral service for his grandfather earlier that day in Paso Robles, about 120 miles away. His teammates weren't even sure he would make it to the ballpark in time to play. It's a good thing he did, because he connected on D.J. Mauldin's 0–1 breaking ball, chopping it over the head of Morel at third and down the left field line for a double.

Susdorf moved him over to third with a groundout, giving Alan Ahmady a chance to tie the game with a sacrifice fly. Ahmady could not pull the trigger on a 2–2 fastball on the outside corner, taking it for a called third strike. The Bulldogs were down to their final out, and Cal Poly second baseman Pat Pezet was about to get his chance to extend the Mustangs' dominating streak to twelve.

> "Hedstrom has had a great day. He's driven in four, with a homer and a single. Breaking ball, swung on, chopped up the middle. Pezet charging, MISSES THE BALL! Wetzel scores the tying run, Hedstrom safe at first, and the Dogs aren't dead yet."

The next batter, freshman Trent Soares, would walk, moving Hedstrom to second base and keeping the inning alive for sophomore third baseman Tom Mendonca.

> "First pitch to Mendonca [ping!] — hit on the ground right side, off the glove of Dorrell, trickling into right. HERE COMES HEDSTROM TO THE PLATE! He will score and the Bulldogs have won it!"

It was another early season example of what would become their signature style. The Bulldogs had danced dangerously close to defeat, but somehow found the grit and determination to prevail. It was the first time any of the Fresno State players in that dugout had beaten Cal Poly, but in his post-game interview, Coach Batesole insisted he was unaware of the Mustangs' streak. "You know, until somebody told me about it, I had no idea," the coach told us, laughing, "I guess I better clue in a little bit." One thing he was definitely aware of was the courage and focus of his standout second baseman, who had come through in the clutch just hours after saying good-bye to his grandfather.

"This kid Wetzel, boy, you gotta love him," Batesole said. "He had one heck of a day today. He scrambled to get all the way up here, and he didn't get up here until about a half-hour before game time. What an emotional day for him, and what a special, special kid. We're pretty lucky to have him." You won't find anyone who would argue with that statement, but if you look hard enough, you might find a comical clip from one of Fresno's local TV newscasts that night. Video from the early stages of this back-and-

Sophomore third baseman Tom Mendonca prepares to swing. *Fresno State Athletics*

forth ball game was accompanied by the disappointing announcement that the *Mustangs had won the game, 9–8.* Oops! File that one away with "Dewey beats Truman."

A Rollercoaster Ride

A victory the next day would return Fresno State's record to the .500 mark for the first time since the opening weekend of the season, and the Dogs were hoping to avoid cutting it as close as the night before. Steve Susdorf continued the hot streak he started in Hawaii with two home runs, and the home team took a 10–3 lead to the seventh inning. The seventh inning? Yes, the top of the seventh inning was once again a nightmare, and this time Pat Hill was nowhere to be found.

Cal Poly scored eight runs on eight hits in the seventh, coming all the way back to take an 11–10 lead; but this time, the Bulldogs did not wait until they were down to their final out to snatch that lead back. With one on and one out in the bottom of the seventh, Trent Soares stepped into the batter's box. His dad, Todd Soares, had played on the 1984 Diamond Dog squad that won fifty-four games, a school record at the time. Trent had heard all about Todd's magic moments with the bat at Beiden Field, and now he was ready to produce one of his own.

"Left-handed batter's average stands at .210 for the year after a pair of singles tonight, he's driven in two runs already. The 1-0 pitch, swung on, hit well, center field and deep. Schafer going back—he will WATCH IT LEAVE THE YARD! Trent Soares has given the lead right back to Fresno State with the first home run of his Fresno State career!"

A 13–11 win pushed the Bulldogs' record to 12–12, and they would never again fall below the .500 mark. The fashion in which they won those two rollercoaster rides against Cal Poly was a reinforcement of the basic themes the coaches were hoping would sink in: play hard all 27 outs, every pitch is important, don't get down when things aren't going your way, and always believe in your teammates.

Returning to conference play that weekend against a Nevada squad that entered atop the WAC at 4–0, the Diamond Dogs would catch up to the Wolf Pack in the standings, winning three out of four while outscoring Nevada 37–12 in the series. The roll the team was building took some sting out of the departure of senior shortstop Todd Sandell, who had been a preseason all-conference pick. Benched in favor of freshman Danny Muno after hitting .221 in 19 starts, Sandell finally got into the first Nevada game as a pinch runner, only to be lifted for a pinch hitter once that spot came back around. Sandell was seen leaving the stadium while the game was still going on, and the next day he was off the team.

To his credit, Sandell stayed in school, and was even spotted in the stands at Beiden Field later that season cheering on his teammates. The message to the remaining players was clear: rules would be enforced, and the team must *always* come first. It was the latest in a series of events that reestablished the players' priorities and contributed to the chemistry that would eventually prove so crucial to their success. That homestand ended with a 7–6 victory over 9th-ranked Long Beach State, in which freshman

Jake Floethe earned his first career win, and senior right-hander Brandon Burke picked up his first save of the season. Fresno State had won eight of its last nine games, and had a chance to prove its mettle the very next day against 7th-ranked Cal in Berkeley.

Justin Wilson shut out the Golden Bears for five innings, but in the sixth shortstop Danny Muno couldn't handle what would have been an inning-ending double play ball. Cal would take advantage of the mistake and score five times—capped off by Blake Smith's grand slam—propelling the Bears to a 5–4 win. An 8–5 loss to Cal Poly in San Luis Obispo dropped Fresno State's record away from Beiden Field to 3–9, but then the Bulldogs got to come home and face Louisiana Tech.

Tech had been picked to finish second in the WAC behind Fresno State, and was going to host the WAC tournament, but lackluster play had some wondering if they would even qualify for the six-team tournament. With seven teams in the conference, one squad would be left out, and Fresno's Bulldogs weren't going to feel guilty if they helped bury Ruston's Bulldogs in the cellar. Game one of the four-game series saw Justin Wilson set a career-high with eleven strikeouts in just six-and-two-thirds innings in a 14–5 win. In game three, it was Tanner Scheppers setting a career best, fanning a dozen in a seven-inning 11–1 run rule victory. And in the fourth game, Justin Miller punched out nine, which was the top number of his short Bulldog career, and combined with Brandon Burke on a five-hit shutout as the Bulldogs prevailed 8–0.

Dominant pitching performances notwithstanding, the most crucial game of that series, and in retrospect one of the most telling and pivotal games of the season, was game two, the opening half of a Saturday doubleheader.

Battling Bulldogs Create Comeback Credentials

After the 14–5 blowout on Friday night, Louisiana Tech was reeling. Coach Wade Simoneaux's Bulldogs, who had expected to challenge Fresno State for the conference title, had lost four straight to fall to 2–9 in WAC play and back to the .500 mark (15–15) overall, and they'd laid a pretty ugly egg in that series opener, committing four errors and striking out a total of 14 times. They came out on Saturday ready to turn their season around, and when freshman catcher Clint Ewing broke a 1–1 tie in the fourth with a grand slam, the first home run of his career, it appeared that Tech had finally found its magic.

Albie Goulder added a two-run bomb in the fifth, and all of a sudden the visitors were out to a 7–1 lead. So far in 2008, Fresno State had not been able to overcome that large of a deficit to win a game. The Dogs knew they still had another game to play that day, and it would have been easy for the players to start focusing on that. Not these Bulldogs, not this season.

In the bottom of the sixth, Soares led off with a single, Wetzel followed with another hit, advancing to second when the throw went through to third. Susdorf brought Soares home with a sacrifice fly, with Wetzel aggressively taking third on the play. That allowed Ryan Overland to produce a sacrifice fly of his own two batters later, and Fresno State was back within four. Jake Hower had pitched a scoreless sixth inning and he held Tech scoreless in the top of the seventh, too, giving the offense the op-

portunity it was waiting for. Leading off the bottom of the seventh was Steve Detwiler, who at this point still had two fully functioning thumbs.

🎙️ "Detwiler swings and CRUSHES one, high and deep to left field, the scoreboard won't even catch it! Well over the scoreboard and rolling out toward Cedar Avenue. A monstrous home run for the sophomore Steve Detwiler, and the Dogs are within three. It's 7 to 4."

My broadcast partner Ray O'Canto likened that longball to a hot air balloon in the Napa Valley, going up, up, and away. I compared it to a John Daly drive, rising until it almost

Freshman outfielder Trent Soares waits in the batter's box.
Fresno State Athletics

disappeared beyond the scoreboard. Whichever analogy you choose, the big fly would chase Tech starter Jericho Jones. Jones stayed in the game as the DH, with Simoneaux summoning southpaw Jamey Bradshaw from the bullpen.

After walking Danny Grubb, Bradshaw allowed a pinch-hit single by Hedstrom, then walked Wetzel to load the bases with one out for Susdorf. Everything was set up perfectly. The Bulldogs had their best hitter representing the go-ahead run at the plate. But Bradshaw would rise to the occasion, blowing two fastballs past a swinging Susdorf, then striking him out with a curveball breaking down and away from the left-handed batter. Fresno State had missed a golden opportunity to get closer, but the bases were still loaded for Alan Ahmady, and in all likelihood the outcome of the game rested on his at bat. Much like the ninth inning in that first win over Cal Poly, what followed would reinforce another oft-quoted baseball adage: "Put the ball in play, and you never know what might happen."

"So now the right-handed bat of Ahmady. Alan, 1-for-2 this afternoon. Bases loaded, two outs, bottom of the seventh, tying runs on base for Fresno State. First pitch, fastball, swung on, driven in the air to center, Cobb going back, still going back, reaches up and DROPS THE BALL! He dropped the ball in front of the warning track! One run is in, two are in, here comes Wetzel to the plate, Ahmady diving in safely at third. Fresno State has tied this ball game, and Adam Cobb wants to run and hide in center field."

Longtime Louisiana Tech announcer Dave Nitz later told me that he had never seen the senior center fielder drop a ball before. Never. But this one wasn't over yet. Bradshaw got Overland to fly out to left to end the inning, stranding Ahmady at third and keeping the score tied at 7–7. Brandon Burke pitched a scoreless eighth for Fresno, Bradshaw did the same for Tech. In the top of the ninth, singles by Jericho Jones and Chris Kersten had men at first and second for Patrick Thomas.

"Burke sets, and delivers the 1–0, pulled on the right side, Ahmady dives, can't get it. It's through into right field, they're sending the runner. Detwiler's gonna have a shot at him, the throw to the plate, Grubb *misses* on the tag. Safe at home is Jericho Jones, and Louisiana Tech has the lead!"

It was an impressively athletic move by the 6 foot 5 inch 205-pound Jones to lunge below the baseline and slide around the tag by an inch or less, after what had been a near-perfect throw from Detwiler in right. So after fighting all the way back from six down to tie the game, the Bulldogs were behind again, and the visitors were still threatening with two outs and men on the corners.

"8 to 7 La. Tech now, and another runner ninety feet away. Third-to-first fake, they got him at first! Out at first base is Thomas, he fell for that third-to-first fake, the same

Sophomore first baseman Alan Ahmady at the plate. *Fresno State Athletics*

move that won a game for the Bulldogs two years ago in the regionals against San Diego when Brandon Burke ended a game with that very same move."

It happened that fast. Before Burke even threw a pitch to Matt Combs, Thomas was out at first. You'll read more about Burke's unique pickoff move later, but its appearance at this point did two things: It kept Fresno State within one run, and it injected a little energy into the Bulldog dugout as the team faced a do-or-die bottom of the ninth.

Danny Muno, a left-handed batter, would lead off. But instead of sticking with the southpaw Bradshaw to get a lefty versus lefty matchup, Wade Simoneaux brought in his right-handed closer, 6 foot 7 inch Aaron Lorio, hoping the senior could overpower the Bulldogs' freshman shortstop. It had been a bit of a rough day for Muno. He had singled his first time up, but then it was his error in the fourth that had opened the door for Ewing's two-out grand slam. In a plate appearance that would foreshadow the moxie Muno would display in May and June, the rookie took a ball and a strike, and then sliced a 1–1 fastball past the third baseman Kersten and down the left field line for a leadoff double. Gavin Hedstrom came up next and singled up the middle, moving Muno to third with no one out. Up next, Erik Wetzel:

"2 and 0 the count, Lorio's pitch, fastball, swung on, hit towards second, could be two. Winn to second for one, Grunenwald to first, threw it away! The tying run scores, obviously, and now Wetzel's gonna get second base."

The tying run would have scored whether Louisiana Tech turned two or not, but the second costly error of the day for the visitors had changed what would have been a two outs, bases empty situation into a one out, winning run on second scenario. After Susdorf was walked intentionally to set up a potential double play, Louisiana Tech had all three outfielders play very shallow against Ahmady, hoping to have a chance to throw Wetzel out at the plate on a line drive single.

"Ahmady ready, now Lorio's ready. The big right-hander deals. Breaking ball, swung on, lifted in the air, left center field, Cobb racing back, won't get there, it'll fall, Wetzel will score... and the shallow outfield comes back to bite Louisiana Tech. Ahmady gets it deep enough to get beyond the reach of Cobb, and that is a game-winning single. Fresno State walks off with a 9 to 8 come-from-behind win in game one of the doubleheader."

Bulldogs Comeback

It was a game, like those battles against Cal Poly, that would come to epitomize the season. Unswayed by their opponent's momentum, the Diamond Dogs maintained their focus and intensity, pitch by pitch, until it was over. Not only did it put one more in the win column for Fresno State, help the Dogs overtake Sacramento State for the WAC lead by week's end, and give the team a comeback track record to draw on for similar uphill battles in the future, this game looms even larger, with hindsight, because of its impact on Louisiana Tech. A win for Tech would have snapped its losing streak at four and perhaps spurred

a recovery in the WAC race. Instead, the loss only intensified the team's downward spiral, becoming the fifth of what would become thirteen consecutive conference losses, a skid that ultimately prevented the team from playing in the WAC tournament on its home field.

But I don't want to get ahead of myself—there was still plenty of regular season left after Fresno State's four-game sweep. After a 10–7 non-conference loss at Cal Poly that dropped Fresno State's away/neutral site record to 3–11, the Bulldogs really needed to prove to themselves that they could win on the road, and Las Cruces, New Mexico was the perfect place to do it.

"Tommy Mendonca, 1 for 3 on the day [ping!]. Swings and hits it high and deep to right center field, Lucero will stop, and that ball ain't coming back. Tommy Mendonca, have yourself a day! A two-run home run, and the Bulldogs are out to a 10 to 1 lead."
— Marcas Grant, filling in on play-by-play

Fans heard quite a few moments like that, with Mendonca and Hedstrom going deep three times apiece in a weekend that saw nine Fresno State homers. Playing at altitude (4,000 feet) and in front of sparse crowds (200 on average), the Diamond Dogs outscored New Mexico State 59–22 in a four-game sweep (24–6 in the finale alone), giving them ten consecutive wins in conference play and a three-game lead over second place Sacramento State.

Many coaches will say that to really appreciate the sweet aroma of success, you have to experience the bitter disappointment of defeat, and the Dogs would get a refresher course on that two days later against Santa Clara. Those midweek games often represent a chance for younger players to get their feet wet. Coaches still want to win, but they see these breaks from conference play as an opportunity to develop talent for the future. Jake Johnson launched his first career home run and fellow freshman Nick Hom doubled in a run, as the Bulldogs built an 8–3 lead. That's when things got ugly.

Santa Clara would score two in the fifth, including one when Jake Hower walked three batters in a row, and then two more in the sixth thanks to two hits and a hit batsman. The ninth inning would be the worst. Entering the frame with an 8–7 lead, it was as if the Bulldogs served the game up on a platter for the Broncos. A leadoff walk, the eleventh of the game issued by Bulldog pitchers, a passed ball, a rare throwing error on Susdorf when his throw hit the runner racing home, followed by an error by Muno, all added up to a three runs and a 10–8 lead for Santa Clara. There was no bottom-of-the-ninth magic this time, as Mark Willinsky retired the Bulldogs in order.

It was the first time all season that Fresno State had carried a lead into the ninth inning and failed to emerge victorious, and it was underscoring a frustrating trend: while they had won their last ten conference games on the weekends, the Diamond Dogs had now lost four midweek games in a row. Erik Wetzel summed up the puzzling dichotomy when he told one Dugout Club member, "We never win the games we should, but we always win the games we need to."

There would be plenty of those "need to" games to come, but the next day's battle against San Francisco wasn't really one of them. It wasn't a conference game, and if you ran down the list of the seventy-eight games the Bulldogs ended up playing in 2008, it wouldn't crack the top twenty in terms of importance. I mention in it here though, because, in my opinion, that game contained the most exciting and incredible play of the entire season.

As fans, we're impressed by home runs and strikeouts, clutch hits and diving catches. We would get more than our fair share of those over the next two months, but, as an announcer, the only single play that

came close to approximating the same "unbelievable" factor as the end result of the Diamond Dogs' season, was a play Steve Detwiler made in the top of the ninth inning against the Dons.

The Bulldogs had scored twice in the bottom of the eighth to turn a 3–2 deficit into a 4–3 lead. Now USF was trying to do what Santa Clara had done in the ninth the night before. With one out, Joey Railey singled to center off of Brandon Burke. The next hitter was freshman Connor Bernatz. As my good friend Tom Sommers, who was filling in for Ray O'Canto that night, said as Bernatz stepped up, "If you're Fresno State, you don't want Bernatz to be the hitter, because we have not gotten him out. If you're San Francisco, he's the right guy at the plate for you." Sommers was dead on. Bernatz was 4-for-4 on the night, and about to be 5-for-5, but unfortunately for the Dons, Detwiler was the right guy for the Dogs in right field.

"Brandon Burke's ready, the senior's 1–1 with the runner going—swung on, lined into right, on one hop, played by Detwiler. Railey, racing around second, headed for third, this is

Three examples of the celebratory scream Steve Detwiler calls "the Tiger Woods." *Minorwhite Studios/Fresno State Athletics*

the Bulldogs would be sitting at home. Keep reading to find out where Fresno State ranked in the RPI once the college baseball season was over.

Justin Wilson wasn't thinking about the RPI when he trotted out to the mound at Long Beach State's Blair Field. As opposed to the park the Bulldogs were coming from in Ruston, Blair Field was a pitcher's paradise: 400 feet in center, 387 in the alleys, and 348 down the lines, all underneath the heavy marine air of Long Beach; and to top it off, the wind was blowing in. Wilson wasn't one of the "eight seniors" Mike Batesole talked about so often, but as a junior who expected to be drafted in just a few days, he knew this game could be his last.

After watching Big West Pitcher of the Year Andrew Liebel retire the Bulldogs in order in the top of the first, Wilson matched him, striking out the side with just one walk mixed in. Steve Susdorf led off the second by getting hit with Liebel's 3–2 offering, then took second on a wild pitch. Next up, the RBI machine himself, Alan Ahmady, brought Susdorf home with a double down the third base line. Tommy Mendonca followed with a single up the middle to plate

Ahmady, and the Bulldogs had a 2–0 lead. In the bottom of the second, Wilson struck out one, then hit a batter, followed by another strikeout, and then a walk. A wild pitch moved the runners to second and third, meaning Dirtbag catcher Travis Howell could tie things up with a base hit. Instead, Wilson froze Howell with a 1–2 breaking ball on the outside corner, giving him six strikeouts in the first two innings, and keeping momentum on Fresno's side.

Singles by Danny Muno and Gavin Hedstrom would set the table for another run in third, driven in by Ahmady with a sacrifice fly. The bottom of the third was the frame that threatened to derail the Bulldogs' hopes. With one on and one out, Jason Corder chopped one over the head of Mendonca at third. Always reacting quickly, Mendonca leapt in the air, but upon landing injured four fingers in his right hand and had to leave the game.

Not only had the Bulldogs lost one of the best defensive third basemen in the country, they were now trading the hot bat of Mendonca (9 hits in his last 19 at bats) for freshman Trent Soares, a .202 hitter on the season who took over in center while

Hedstrom moved to third. Employing the by now familiar lesson that it takes an entire team to get the job done, the Bulldogs made sure they wouldn't lose their composure or their lead.

Wilson did allow a two-run single off the bat of Brandon Godfrey, but got out of the inning with Fresno State still ahead 3–2. Two more strikeouts in the fourth gave Wilson nine for the game, and back-to-back doubles by Erik Wetzel and Susdorf in the fifth upped the lead to 4–2.

The longer the game went on, the more anxiety permeated the crowd of close to 2,000 in Long Beach. A strikeout apiece in the sixth and seventh gave Wilson a career-high tying 11, but with his pitch count up to 118, Batesole didn't want to go too much further with him. A few runs could make the decision a lot easier, and the offense was ready to help. Susdorf led off the eighth with his 28th double of the season, tying Derek Feramisco's single-season school record. Then Ahmady reached on an infield single. Soares made his opportunity count, battling Liebel to a 2–2 count before bringing Susdorf home with a sacrifice fly to increase the lead to 5–2. Steve Detwiler doubled over the head

Tom Mendonca writhes in pain after dislocating his fingers (below), then is helped into the dugout by trainer Kristen O'Connell (right). *Eric Sorenson*

of Corder in right, bringing Ahmady home, and then Jordan Ribera singled Detwiler in.

A 7–2 lead with six outs left in a cavernous park made Batesole comfortable enough to lift Wilson, and Holden Sprague took over for the bottom of the eighth. After the Dirtbags closed the gap to 7–3 with a run in the eighth, Sprague worked a perfect ninth, and once Detwiler wrapped his glove around a Jonathan Jones fly ball in right, the Bulldogs had notched their most significant victory of the season.

"That's when I knew we could play," Batesole reflected. "You beat Long Beach in Long Beach, in *that* important of a game, you can play baseball. The season could have been over for me at that time. Truly on the inside, that's what you really want to know as a coach—that the system works, and your guys can put it into play. To win that game, it was real. That's all I needed to know. I didn't need a ring, that was it. I could have gone home that night, there was nothing that could have topped that. To me, that game was the highest level of Division I baseball, and we won."

That may have represented the pinnacle for their skipper, but the Diamond Dog players weren't quite ready for their rollercoaster ride to end.

The Toreros' Kryptonite (May 31, 2008)

Saying Fresno State surprised a lot of people in 2008 is a bit of an understatement, but there was one team that knew all too well what the Diamond Dogs were capable of doing in the postseason: the San Diego Toreros. Fresno State had eliminated USD from the Fullerton regional in 2006, and in 2007 the Toreros were

the #1 seed that #4 Fresno State knocked off to open the regionals. San Diego was deserving of a #1 seed again in 2008, having spent the entire season in the top ten in the rankings, and if the school had put in a bid to host a regional, the Toreros probably would have been a #1 seed. Why didn't USD want to host? Fresno State is partially to blame for that.

San Diego's Cunningham Stadium doesn't meet NCAA regional standards, so when the Toreros hosted a regional for the first time, in 2007, it was at San Diego State's Tony Gwynn Stadium. After losses to Fresno State and Minnesota knocked the Toreros out, coach Rich Hill decided that playing in a rival's ballpark didn't really give his team an advantage, and he vowed not to bid until he could truly "host" a regional on his own campus.

What was the domino effect for Fresno State? It meant the Diamond Dogs wouldn't have to face Brian Matusz, the aforementioned super southpaw who would open the regional by striking out ten Cal Bears in a complete game three-hit shutout. Instead, they would *only* have to square off with two-way star Josh Romanski, another left-hander whose record for the season was a perfect 9–0. In contrast, Bulldog starter Clayton Allison entered the contest with a disappointing record of 2–5, and had gone two months without a victory before getting the win against San Jose State in Ruston. With his mother Sharla sitting in the stands and his father Buddy pacing anxiously in the aisle, Allison, a California kid with a hint of a cowboy drawl in his voice, came out with guns blazing. Three up, three down. Three more, no score.

After three innings, Allison and Romanski had both faced the minimum nine batters. The only hit was

Muno's single to center, which was picked up by his older brother Kevin, who would then watch Danny fall victim to Romanski's pickoff move. Talk about pacing! Buddy Allison had nothing on Anne Muno, who had to alternate cheering sections as her two boys brought new meaning to "sibling rivalry" on the diamond.

After Allison retired the side in order in the top of the fourth, Romanski finally showed some vulnerability in the bottom half of the inning. With one out, Hedstrom walked, and Batesole wanted to make sure that baserunner didn't go to waste. Playing in that cavernous park, on a night where the dueling hurlers were mowing hitters down, the Bulldogs' coach figured it was about time to employ a little "small ball." The coach had noticed that Romanski's left-handed follow-through had him falling off toward the third base side. Wetzel, whose bat control rivaled anyone Batesole had ever coached, would be the hitter, and Batesole quickly got in Wetzel's ear with the idea of shooting a bunt past the pitcher on the right side.

"Romanski doesn't have many weaknesses," Batesole said, "so when you spot one you better attack it, and no one loves to find little cracks like that and exploit them more than 'Wet.'"

Wetzel took a ball and a strike, then caught the Toreros off guard, pushing the bunt perfectly to the right side, getting it past Romanski and forcing second baseman Kevin Hansen to race in and pick it up. Hansen had no chance to throw Wetzel out, but he tried anyway, sailing it past first baseman Jose Valerio and giving Fresno State two men in scoring position with just one out.

Then Batesole tried to catch San Diego off guard again. With Susdorf, the Bulldogs' all-time RBI leader at the plate, no one would have expected a safety squeeze; but as Romanski delivered the pitch, Susdorf squared around, with Hedstrom waiting for contact to break from third. Instead, Romanski's fastball struck right between the 2 and the 7 on Susdorf's back, sending him to first and keeping the game scoreless. Changing speeds in the fashion that made him a second-team All-American, Romanski dodged disaster by striking out Ahmady on four pitches. In the dugout, Batesole reinforced the need for contributions from every member of the team. "It can't be Ahmady every night," he told the hitters.

Detwiler would make sure Romanski didn't get off the hook, especially when the southpaw made the mistake of missing too far inside. Absorbing the first pitch with his front shoulder, Detwiler gladly wore the pain that brought Hedstrom home with the game's first run.

If there was one thing the Bulldogs had developed during their seven-game win streak, it was a knack for turning one small mistake by their opponent into a really big inning, and that's just what Mendonca had in mind when he stepped up. X-rays at a local hospital had revealed that while two fingers were dislocated, and two more bruised, the third baseman didn't have any broken bones. Batesole wasn't sure Mendonca could play, but "nothing broken" sounded like a green light to the spirited sophomore, which would come as no surprise to his tight-knit Portuguese family.

Mendonca's great-grandfather came to the United States in the early 1920s, settling in Stanislaus County as part of a wave of immigrants from the Azores Islands who would establish dairies up and down the San Joaquin Valley. As a boy, Tommy spent many a day on that Turlock dairy farm,

feeding animals, irrigating crops, and learning how to drive tractors.

"He could always find rocks or fruit to toss around to develop his throwing skills," his grandfather Leonard recalled, "Broken shovel handles were put to use as bats to dispatch the rocks and smash the fruit." Rob Mendonca, Tommy's uncle and his coach for the Bulldogs of Turlock High, said he even has a history of dislocating fingers.

"One thing I remember about Tom as a little kid," Rob said, "was when he jumped on a pickup tailgate after a softball game his dad and I were playing in. He was pretty little, and he dislocated his finger to where it was pointing the wrong direction at the knuckle. His dad just yanked the finger back into place and within a matter of minutes Tom was back to normal."

Some things never change. The family farm is no longer a dairy—the Mendoncas now grow corn, oats and alfalfa for neighboring dairymen— but Tommy still possesses the same

kind of toughness when it comes to dislocated fingers. Ignoring the pain as he settled into the front of the box for a rematch with the unbeaten southpaw who had struck him out his first time up, Mendonca was ready to swing something a little more potent than an old broken shovel handle.

🎙 "The pitch, swung on, and hit deep to right field. WAY back, and off the top of the fence! It bounces back into fair territory, one run scores, two runs score, three runs! Tommy and the Bulldogs bust it open here in the bottom of the fourth inning!"

If you measured the magnitude of that moment by the level of excitement in Woodward's voice, it would be in the same ballpark as his call of Fresno State's 1983 N.I.T. championship, the Bulldogs' 1992 Freedom Bowl win over USC, or the overtime victory over Virginia in the 2004 MPC Computers Bowl.

Kevin and Danny Muno with their mother, Anne. The brothers would also meet up on the field. *Muno Family*

9-year-old Tom Mendonca practicing his swing on the family farm.
Mendonca Family

Tom Mendonca as a 10-year-old All-Star in Turlock. There would be a larger trophy in his future...
Mendonca Family

Throbbing fingers and all, Mendonca had narrowly missed a grand slam, his three-run double giving Fresno State a 4–0 lead through four innings. "I've been doing this a long time," Batesole said afterwards, "and he's one of the toughest kids I've ever coached."

Allison made sure USD wouldn't answer that surge in the fifth, recording yet another perfect inning to make it 15 up and 15 down. Victor Sanchez spoiled the no-hit bid with a single in the sixth, but Allison put another zero in the run column. The Diamond Dogs made it 6–0, adding two more runs in the bottom of the sixth, with Susdorf and Mendonca driving in one apiece. The rest of the task would fall on Allison and the defense.

Fresno State was now just nine outs away from clearing the hurdle that had tripped up the Dogs in each of the previous two years, when they won their regional opener, but could not prevail in that pivotal second game. With his split-fingered fastball and its trap door-like drop inducing groundout after groundout, Allison would finish what he started, needing

only 92 pitches to record his second complete game shutout of the season, and moving his team within one win of finding that 1-in-144 ticket to the Super Regionals.

Allison's effort drew high praise from Batesole: "That's how you command a ball game, there. Whatever a gem is, that was it. He could have gone a couple more innings." Said fellow pitcher Justin Wilson: "Clayton threw outstanding tonight, that was awesome to watch. It's our tournament to lose now."

Indeed it was, but if there was any team in the country that had Fresno State in the crosshairs, it was San Diego, determined not to be bounced by the Bulldogs for the third consecutive year. Over the last three seasons, USD was now 2–6 (.250) against Fresno State, while posting a record of 117–53 (.688) against everyone else. The Toreros would earn their shot at a rematch by eliminating Long Beach the next day, 5–1.

Blair + Blair = One More Game (June 1, 2008)

Everything was going Fresno State's way. The Dogs had won eight straight, their longest winning streak of the season, and they were a win away from the Super Regionals. Plus, it was Sunday. Sundays had been good to the Bulldogs. A 9–2 record in Sunday games, with both of those losses coming by just one run, made Sunday, statistically speaking, the team's best day. But don't tell Justin Miller that.

Facing a parade of bats still warm from the win over Long Beach State, which ended just over an hour before this game began, Miller struggled with his control and surrendered one run in the first, four more in the second, and another run before exiting with two outs in the third. To top off

Tom Mendonca at the Long Beach Regional, with his parents Ray and Tami.
Mendonca Family

what was happening on the scoreboard, the Toreros made it personal for the Bulldogs when Romanski, trying to steal third, was caught in a rundown, and bowled over Wetzel trying to get back to second.

Mendonca quickly came to Wetzel's side, ready to further dislocate those fingers if need be. The players were quickly separated, but the tension lingered. Meanwhile, Kyle Blair was pitching as if the ballpark belonged to him. It was Blair Field, after all, and San Diego's freshman right-hander looked right at home as he struck out five Bulldogs in the first three innings.

The Toreros picked up three more runs in the fifth against reliever Sean Bonesteele, making it 9–0. Fresno State broke up the shutout bid in the seventh when Danny Muno, who went 2-for-2 on the day while his brother went 2-for-3, drove in Mendonca from second with a single to left. That was the only run Blair would allow, striking out nine in seven innings while giving up just four hits.

This was clearly San Diego's night, and that was underscored when Batesole emptied his bench, giving freshmen like Jake Floethe, Gene Escat, and Nick Hom a taste of post-season play. Scoring five more in the bottom of the eighth, the Toreros hoped to send a message with a 15–1 shellacking that forced one final do-or-die game in Long Beach. Would the Bulldogs return the next day intimidated by that two-touchdown defeat that ended their eight-game winning streak?

Mike Batesole knew his team better than that. "We've had our backs to the wall for the last eight or nine games," the coach said, "so this is nothing new. Our guys are very resilient."

Tom Mendonca comes through with the big hit against San Diego. *Dennis Simpson*

"I knew Romanski was 9–0. After the fifth inning, that's all I was thinking about." — Clayton Allison on his motivation against USD. *Dennis Simpson*

While the Toreros would have star closer A.J. Griffin and the All-American Matusz available in the relief the next day, Batesole saw the freshness of his bullpen as a strength. "Breckley and Burke have pitched a lot for us over the last three years, and they haven't thrown a pitch in this regional. We have Holden Sprague starting tomorrow, so I like our chances when we put the ball in the hands of any one of those guys."

A Chance to Make History, with Hedstrom's Help (June 2, 2008)

While Fresno State had been to the College World Series three times (1959, 1988, 1991), all three trips came before the 64-team format of 16 four-team regionals leading to eight best-of-three super regionals. Fresno State had never advanced to a Super Regional. In fact, 2008 was the first time the Diamond Dogs had been within one win of a Super Regional. With his parents and sister in the stands, his grandparents and uncles and cousins listening on the radio, Sprague was determined not to see that opportunity go to waste. Sprague had been one of Fresno State's most valuable and versatile pitchers all season long. A glance at his stats for the year showed a 3–2 record and 3.62 ERA, but that didn't tell the whole story.

Used primarily out of relief, the junior right-hander from Fresno's Bullard High School would be starting for the ninth time in 2008. In each of his previous six starts, including the WAC Tournament championship game eight days earlier, the Bulldogs had emerged victorious.

Kevin Muno led off the game for San Diego by popping one up into shallow left field, where his brother Danny ranged back from his short-

stop position to snag it. The next hitter, Romanski, would test the younger Muno again, and this time Danny bounced a throw past Ahmady after fielding the grounder. Muno didn't have much time to dwell on his mistake because the other Danny on the diamond bailed him out on the very next pitch. Junior catcher Danny Grubb, living up to his reputation, delivered a strong and accurate throw to second to catch Romanski stealing. It had to give Wetzel a little satisfaction to slap the tag on the guy who had barreled into him the night before.

Sprague put up a zero in the top of the first, and USD's Sammy Solis matched him in the bottom of the inning, giving up just a single to Hedstrom. Sprague would leave the bases loaded in the third, Hedstrom would single again in the fourth, but the goose eggs kept piling up on the scoreboard, and the game remained scoreless going to the top of the fifth.

Logan Gelbrich led off with a shallow fly ball to center—Hedstrom raced in and dove for the ball, but came up just short, and Gelbrich ended up with a double. After a strikeout, followed by a fly ball to right which moved Gelbrich to third with two outs, Romanski walked to put men on the corners for shortstop Sean Nicol.

Swinging at the first pitch, Nicol lined it right back up the middle, ricocheting off Sprague's leg. As Gelbrich scored, Sprague tried to throw to first but Ahmady could not stop the ball, and as a result the runners ended up at second and third. James Meador was walked intentionally to load the bases, bringing up Kevin Hansen, who had doubled off of Sprague earlier in the game. This was the most crucial situation Sprague had faced in his three years at Fresno State. Another hit by Hansen, and a 1–0 deficit might turn into 3–0 or 4–0 hole.

Location had been Sprague's strength all season long. As his teammate Clayton Allison put it, "He's a strike thrower. He can hit the glove wherever you put it." Sprague couldn't afford to let that change now. A 1–1 fastball went right where Grubb wanted it, in on the hands of Hansen, who grounded out to Wetzel to end the inning, the second time in three innings that Toreros left the bases loaded. Now it was time for Fresno State to mount a response. With the sore-fingered Mendonca stepping in to face Solis, the 6 foot 5 inch freshman fired a fastball inside. Mendonca tried to get his hands out of the way, but couldn't, the quickly swelling knuckle on his left hand convincing the doubting umpire that he did indeed deserve first base. Jake Johnson bunted Mendonca to second, Grubb walked, and then Danny Muno hit a grounder to first that appeared to give USD a chance at a double play. Jose Valerio bobbled the ball at first and had to settle for stepping to the bag ahead of Muno, allowing the runners to move up to second and third with two outs.

If there was one offensive mantra the Bulldogs had heard their hitting happy coach repeat over and over again, it was "ballgames are won with two outs and two strikes." It had become a game within a game, tweaking the hitters' mental approach in a way that turned a pressure-packed situation into an opportunity. Opportunity came knocking for Hedstrom, already 2-for-2 in the game, when Solis snuck a slider past him to move the count to a ball and two strikes.

 "1-2 with two down...the Bulldogs trail 1-nothing. The pitch to the plate, hit into right field, BASE HIT! That'll score one run—headed for home Grubb, SAFE at home, and the Bulldogs lead it, 2 to 1." — Bill Woodward

Playing just about fifteen miles from the Irvine home where he grew up, Hedstrom thrilled the throng of family, friends and former teammates who had come to see him play. The Bulldogs had broken through, but they still had a dozen outs to go.

Burke was warming in the bullpen as the sixth inning got underway. Once Sprague found himself in a one out, runner on second situation, Batesole pulled the trigger, calling on Fresno State's all-time saves leader to tackle the longest and most crucial save situation of his career. Eleven outs is a little more than the typical closer can handle. But Burke is not your typical closer. Throughout his four years at Fresno State he had occupied just about every pitching role you could imagine, he had never shied away from a challenge, and rarely, if ever, was he rattled by what unfolded on the diamond. That last quality came in handy right away.

Gelbrich hit Burke's first pitch to Muno, who promptly bounced it past Ahmady again for his second error of the game, and the third for the Bulldogs as a team. Not even showing an inkling of irritation, Burke went back to work, getting the second out on a fly ball to center, and then striking out Kevin Muno to end the inning. If Coach Batesole was calling in his closer early, Rich Hill was going to do the same. After Solis struck Susdorf out, Hill lifted the freshman for 6 foot 5 inch sophomore A.J. Griffin, who had been among the national leaders in saves all season long. Griffin struck out Ahmady and Detwiler to end the sixth. Then, after Burke worked a perfect top of the seventh, Griffin fanned

Mendonca, Ribera and Grubb in succession.

Still trailing 2–1 in the top of the eighth, USD got a one-out single from Ryan Davis. Burke bounced back with a strikeout of Valerio, and worked the count to 2–2 on Gelbrich. The game plan was to throw a breaking ball low and away and see if Gelbrich would chase it.

"Here's Brandon's pitch, low and away, gets away from the catcher, runner goes, the throw to second, GOT HIM!" — Bill Woodward

Seeing the bouncing ball ricocheting off Grubb's chest protector was enough to make Davis break for second, but Grubb's quick reaction, hustle, and yet another strike to second kept the lead intact. "That's Danny Grubb at his best!" shouted Ray O'Canto.

Now it was the other Danny's turn. Griffin had struck out all five Bulldogs he'd faced to that point, and he went ahead 0–2 on Muno, leading off the bottom of the eighth. Determined to become the first Bulldog to put the ball in play against Griffin, Muno chopped one up the middle, hustling to first to beat Hansen's throw. After Hedstrom laid down his school-record 17th sacrifice bunt of the season to move Muno to second, Wetzel gave the Dogs yet another two-strike hit, a double that scored Muno to make it 3–1. San Diego walked Susdorf intentionally to set up a potential double play, but Ahmady threw a wrench into that idea with an infield single to load the bases. Next up was Steve Detwiler:

"Griffin winds, the pitch, [ping!] hit to third. To second for one, relay to first. HIGH! NO GOOD! One run is in,

two runs will score!" — Bill Woodward

A strong, hard slide by a hustling Ahmady had altered Hansen's throw enough to foil the double play, and instead of being out of the inning down only by two, San Diego now trailed 5–1. For Burke, a four-run lead with three outs to go in a pitcher's park against his hometown team was about as good as it could get. Two years earlier, the San Diego native had been on the mound with the tying run on third base and picked off a San Diego runner at first to end the Toreros' season. Burke wanted to send USD packing again, but he was hoping he wouldn't have to cut it so close this time. Gelbrich swung at the first pitch, grounding out to Wetzel at second. A full swing by Sanchez moved the ball all of a few feet in front of home plate, where Grubb grabbed it and threw him out. That left Kevin Muno as the Toreros' last hope to keep their season alive.

"Again, ready to work, Burke. [ping!] Ground ball to first, up with it, over to first, Ahmady, and the Bulldogs are headed to the Super Regionals!" — Bill Woodward

"Wow! That's awesome, the dogpile on the mound, the greatest thing about baseball, man!" — Ray O'Canto

It wasn't quite a dogpile, it was a little more reserved than that, as if the Bulldogs knew they'd have an even bigger reason to celebrate down the road. Hedstrom emerged from that congratulatory confab to find a mob of friends and family ready to congratulate him on his clutch performance.

Fresno State players celebrate their historic win in Long Beach, advancing to the school's first super regional. *Eric Sorenson*

Gavin Hedstrom hugs his mother, Karen, after his 3-for-3 performance against USD in the regional final. *Hedstrom Family*

Fresno State was headed to the Super Regionals thanks to a 3-for-3 game from a guy who had just two hits his freshman season, and only four throughout his sophomore season. When a family friend remarked to Hedstrom's parents that this was an impressive win for such "underdogs," his mother Karen replied, "They're not underdogs anymore. Maybe we should call them the wonderdogs."

Up in the radio booth, Batesole was busy receiving congratulations on overcoming the odds—his Diamond Dogs were now just the second #4 seed (out of a pool of 160 now) to ever advance to the super regional round. True to form, the coach soaked in his milestone moment and promptly directed the credit elsewhere. "It's the culmination of a lot of things," Batesole told the radio audience, "but we said from day one that getting this done and continuing to play weekend after weekend is way too big a job for 25 players and four coaches. It's our alumni, it's our community, it's our administration, it's our Dugout Club, everybody pulling on the same end of the rope. There's no way we do this alone. What a crowd we had here tonight, and that's pretty special when that many people are down here on a Monday, bringing these kids home. It was outstanding."

As Mendonca, the All-Regional third baseman, strapped on a headset, Woodward quipped, "I hesitate to shake your hand, I'm afraid I might hurt it." Mendonca replied, "It's alright, adrenaline's still going. Thank goodness it wasn't my right hand. But it got the left hand pretty good, so it got my mind off my right hand. But now it's on my left hand, now I've got both hands to worry about."

Not that worrying was on the team's agenda. With a date with #3 national seed Arizona State waiting in Tempe, rest wasn't in the plans either. "There will be plenty of time to rest here in July," Mendonca continued.

"The deal now is to leave it all on the field every weekend, and that's what these guys have been doing."

NCAA Regionals Summary

Fresno State 7, Long Beach State 3
Fresno State 6, San Diego 0
San Diego 15, Fresno State 1
Fresno State 5, San Diego 1

All-Regional Team:
RHP Clayton Allison,
3B Tommy Mendonca,
OF Steve Susdorf

Next Stop: NCAA Super Regional vs. Arizona State in Tempe, AZ

A sore-fingered Tom Mendonca was all smiles after the Long Beach Regional. *Dennis Simpson*

NCAA SUPER REGIONALS:
TURNING SUN DEVILS INTO STUNNED DEVILS

Arizona State is a college baseball juggernaut, and has been for while. Signs above the wall in right field at Winkles Field-Packard Stadium at Brock Ballpark represent the five NCAA titles claimed by the Sun Devils, most recently in 1981 when a San Joaquin Valley product, Stan Holmes of Dos Palos, claimed Most Outstanding Player honors in Omaha.

Back then, ASU's home field was simply called Packard Stadium, but when you have the kind of history and tradition that sets you apart from other programs, you might as well celebrate it. Bobby Winkles and Jim Brock both won championships as Sun Devil coaches, so their names are now immortalized, and you'll also find their numbers, as well as that of Barry Bonds, among the sixteen retired jerseys gracing the outfield fence. Sixteen retired numbers? That sounds like a lot... and it is. But again, when you have a rich tradition, why not keep it alive with a constant visual reminder of how great you've been and how great you can be?

Fresno State has retired ten, and it's a safe bet that Mike Batesole's championship trophy will someday secure his #44 a spot next to Bob Bennett's #26 and Pete Beiden's #2. If the Diamond Dogs want to catch the Sun Devils, I'd recommend starting with the great Fibber Hirayama, a true trailblazer, then taking a gander at Dan Gladden, John Hoover, and Jeff Weaver.

That's enough of memory lane-back to 2008. ASU coach Pat Murphy has had to stare at those five NCAA title banners for fourteen seasons. He's come close to hanging another one, but hasn't been able to push the Devils over the hump. This was the year that the stars could align, and the Devils, the #3 national seed in the NCAA field of sixty-four, were tapped by quite a few experts as the team to beat. Why? Take a look at the first six spots in their batting order for their first game against Fresno State:

1. Ryan Sontag (RF): .390 average, 4 HRs (in only 154 at bats), 36 RBI
2. Jason Kipnis (LF): .363 average, 14 HRs, 69 RBI, 24 stolen bases
3. Brett Wallace (3B): .414 average, 21 HRs, 81 RBI, 16 stolen bases
4. Ike Davis (1B): .394 average, 26 doubles, 16 HRs, 73 RBI
5. Petey Paramore (C): .361 average, 7 HRs, 49 RBI
6. Kiel Roling (DH): .344 average, 8 HRs, 50 RBI

The Devils boasted a team batting average of .341, and those first six hitters had combined for 70 of ASU's 83 home runs. There are only nine play-

2-time Pac-10 Player of the Year Brett Wallace high fives fellow All-American Ike Davis. *Paul Connors/AP*

ers on the field at one time, but the Sun Devils had a school-record fifteen players selected in Major League Baseball's amateur draft. Wallace and Davis were both first-round selections, with Wallace going 13th overall to St. Louis, and Davis taken five picks later by the Mets. The 1927 Yankees long ago laid claim to "Murderer's Row," but perhaps this powerful procession of Arizona State sluggers deserved a nickname of its own. Guillotine Gauntlet? Lumberjack Lineup? Super Scary Sextet? Whatever you decided to call them, they were big boys with big bats, and it wasn't as if slugging was the team's only strength.

Fresno State would have to start by facing the Pac-10 Pitcher of the Year, Mike Leake, with his 10–2 record and 3.12 ERA, and there was an even bigger dragon to slay. The Bulldogs would have to find a way to overcome Arizona State's overwhelming home field advantage.

Northern Colorado, Oregon State and Nobody Else (June 7, 2008)

Thirty-eight and three. That's where Arizona State's home record stood heading into Super Regional play. The last fourteen NCAA postseason games in Tempe had all gone the Sun Devils' way, dating back to 2003. They had also won their last fourteen home games in 2008. Only two visiting teams, Northern Colorado and two-time defending NCAA champ Oregon State, had beaten the Devils in Tempe in 2008. The Beavers were the only ones to have bested ASU twice on this diamond, but the Bulldogs would have to join that club if they wanted their season to continue. Of all the Super Regional showdowns, this appeared to be the biggest mis-

match. Arizona State carried the #3 national seed, and the best home field record of any of the eight Super Regional hosts.

We've already established that Fresno State wasn't even supposed to make it this far. Further underscoring their underdog status was the fact that the Bulldogs, though one of just sixteen teams still playing, had only risen to #17 in Baseball America's rankings. "That was probably the funniest thing," said pitcher Clayton Allison. "That cracked me up, and fired us up a little too. We're still playing, and they've got a team that's already out ranked ahead of us."

Batesole did not mince words in our pre-game interview. "The last thing we are is happy to be here," the coach said, in a tone clearly indicating his disdain for that phrase. "If I have one more person tell me that I'm gonna throw up. We came here to win this. We're 18 innings away from getting to Omaha, and we're gonna leave it all on the field every inning."

More than 4,000 vocal Sun Devil fans showed up to watch their team continue its postseason perfection, but it would be Batesole's Bulldogs who got on the board first. A two-out single up the middle by Erik Wetzel brought Steve Susdorf to the plate, and Arizona State's Coach Murphy made a curious decision. Susdorf came in with a .342 average, due in large part to his ability to drive balls to all fields. Murphy aligned his defense as if Susdorf were a dead pull hitter, shifting both the infield and outfield well around to the right side. It was clear even from our perch on the roof of the press box that Susdorf recognized the challenge. It was as if they were daring him to hit the ball to left field. After patiently watching Leake's first three pitches, Susdorf was ready to pull the trigger.

"3–0 pitch, fastball swung on, sliced down the left field line. If that ball's fair, he can run forever. That ball drops fair, it's headed for the corner, Kipnis still chasing it, Wetzel being waved around third by Matt Curtis, he's heading for the plate, the play will be at third base, but Susdorf is in there standing up with an RBI triple! The Bulldogs lead it one to nothing, and how's that for bat control?"

Remember Batesole saying Susdorf never took a swing without a purpose? That swing fulfilled its purpose, and the Devils learned the hard way that the shift wasn't going to work against Susdorf, who had just been selected in the 19th round by the Phillies. The 1–0 lead wouldn't last long, however. In the bottom of the first, a leadoff walk, an error on Alan Ahmady, and a single by Kipnis put runners on the corners with nobody out, and the next two hitters were the first-round draft choices, Wallace and Davis.

Wallace is one of the scariest hitters I've ever seen. Listed at 6 foot 1 inch and 245 pounds, he carries a good chunk of that weight in his monstrous thighs, which at different points in this super regional I described as "tree trunks" and "golf bags." His incredibly quick hands allow him to get the bat around on just about any pitch anywhere near the plate. Facing Wallace for the first time, Justin Wilson, a fifth round selection of the Pirates, battled him to a full count, then won the battle by getting Wallace to hit a ground ball to Wetzel, who started a 4-6-3 double play. Sontag scored from third to tie the game, and now the bases were empty for Davis, the other All-American. Again taking the count full, Wilson froze Davis with a 3–2 fastball at the belt, and the strikeout ended the inning with the score still tied 1–1.

While Leake was busy retiring ten Bulldogs in a row, Wilson wasn't getting a lot of help from his defense, or the diamond. Diametrically different from Long Beach, the stadium in Tempe is a hitter's haven. Not only did the ball carry well in the outfield (particularly to right), the infield grass was cut very short, making it play very fast. After Wilson worked a scoreless second, Greg Bordes led off the third with a ground ball on the right side. Ranging to his right, Wetzel fielded cleanly, but threw low, and despite a great effort by Ahmady, the first baseman could not control the ball in time for the out. That would prove costly, thanks to Sontag, who started the Devils' second trip through the batting order with a bang.

"Left-handed batter swings, hits one high in the air, deep to right field. Detwiler won't even look at it. That one is on the road behind the right field wall. A two-run homer for Ryan Sontag—it's now 3 to 1 Arizona State."

Rural Road, with two lanes in each direction, runs parallel to the right field fence. If you ever find yourself in Tempe while a Sun Devil game is going on, stay off of Rural Road, especially if the wind is blowing out toward right as swiftly as it was that night. Sontag's blast bounced across the road without hitting any cars, and it didn't dent Wilson's focus either. The junior lefty gave up a single to the next hitter, Kipnis, then proceeded to retire six straight. The score would remain 3–1 until the bottom of the fifth. Bordes singled up the middle and, after striking out Sontag, Wilson sur-

rendered successive singles to Kipnis, Wallace, and Davis, scoring Bordes to make it 4–1. Switch-hitting catcher Petey Paramore came up next. A leg injury had rendered Paramore the slowest runner on the field. A firm ground ball off his bat would be a surefire double play, and that's precisely what Wilson needed with the bases loaded. It appeared that's what his 3–2 fastball would produce.

"Wilson, the Bulldog lefty, sets and delivers. Payoff pitch, hit on the ground toward second, a HUGE hop over Wetzel's head! Would've been a double-play ball, but it took a crazy hop, and two runs are gonna score. That is just a really bad break for the Bulldogs. I don't know what that ball hit, but it looked like it hit a trampoline!"

So now, thanks to that wild bounce, instead of being out of the inning with just a three-run deficit to tackle, the Diamond Dogs were now down 6–1. Wetzel had just been chosen by the Colorado Rockies in the 13th round of the draft, and is about as flawless a defensive second baseman as you'll find, but he never had a chance. The ball got within six feet of him and then treated him the way Edwin Moses would a hurdle. OK, I realize quite a few of the 2008 Diamond Dogs weren't even born yet when Moses won the last of his 122 consecutive races in 1987, but he remains the most dominant hurdler of all time, and Wetzel had about as much chance of stopping that ball as one of those hurdles had of derailing Moses. I suppose that analogy is appropriate, because a "track meet" in baseball circles refers to a high-scoring game, and ASU was ready to run away.

Kiel Roling followed with an RBI single to center to make it 7–1, and that was the end of the road for Wilson. One hundred five pitches only carried him through four-and-one-third innings, and while the cluster of Fresno State fans behind the first base dugout gave him a standing ovation as he headed to the dugout, Wilson knew that he had likely just made his last start on the mound in a Bulldog uniform.

On came Justin Miller to face Mike Jones, one of the Sun Devils' best football players who was moonlighting on the baseball squad. Miller's 1–0 slider produced a grounder to short. Danny Muno fed Wetzel for the first out, but Jones and his wide receiver speed beat the relay to first. That kept the inning alive for Raoul Torrez to pull one through the left side of the infield, scoring a limping Paramore to push the lead to 8–1. Miller then struck out Bordes to end the inning, but the damage was done. That "Edwin Moses" ball had cost the Bulldogs four runs and their starting pitcher.

The Devils' lead would remain at seven until the top of the seventh. With two outs, the Dogs caught a break. If you read the official scorer's play-by-play report of the game, you'll see "Mendonca doubled to shortstop." That's a head-scratcher, isn't it?

Here's what happened: Mendonca launched an infield pop up so high that the ASU infielders, not helped much by the stiff wind that continued to blow, all failed to find it as it came screaming down on the grass between the mound and second base. It was in the air so long that Mendonca had time to hustle all the way to second before the Devils could catch him. An infield single by Ryan Overland moved Mendonca to third, Steve Detwiler walked to load the bases, and then a wild pitch brought Mendonca home before Jordan Ribera flied out to right to end the inning.

So the Bulldogs were one run closer, and after Jason Breckley came in and pitched a perfect bottom of the seventh, the Bulldog bats fought back in the eighth, once again in their signature two-out style. After Wetzel reached on Wallace's error, Susdorf looped one about three feet inside the left field line for his 29th double of the season, breaking Derek Feramisco's record. That set the table for Ahmady, who demonstrated again why he was among the national RBI leaders. A double to right center plated Wetzel and Susdorf, and all of a sudden Fresno State was back within four, 8–4.

It was time for Murphy to make a move, and all he had to do was swap his first baseman and his pitcher. Davis, the big first baseman and son of former major league closer Ron Davis, was also a hard-throwing lefty who was tied for the team lead in saves. The southpaw struck out Mendonca to end the threat, so it remained 8–4 going to the bottom of the eighth. Breckley remained on the mound, and with one on and one out faced Sontag, who had hit just four home runs during the regular season but had taken Wilson deep earlier.

> "Breckley checks the runner, comes home, Sontag swings, gets into another one! High and deep to right center field, forget about that one too! That one's across Rural Road, the second two-run homer of the ballgame for Ryan Sontag, who tagged that one!"

That made it 10–4, and the Devils would make it an even dozen with two more runs off of Jake Floethe. All-American Tommy Rafferty's 1-2-3 top of the ninth made it official. Sun Devils 12, Bulldogs 4.

Arizona State was still perfect for the postseason, and the Devils had done what they were supposed to do. Maybe that would make them a little *too* comfortable the next day. Mike Batesole wasn't thinking about ASU, he was focused on the twenty-five guys in his dugout, who once again had their backs to the wall. "They've been able to focus and keep their brains clear, when we've gotten into situations like this," the coach said. "There are a lot of distractions around here, there's a lot of *stuff* going on, and we'll have to do a good job of keeping our brains clear. "

"Stuff" was a veiled reference to a newspaper piece published that morning in the *Fresno Bee*. Columnist Matt James included quotes from pitching coach Mike Mayne, voicing his displeasure about the way Batesole had handled him and the pitchers. Mayne, the father of longtime major league catcher Brent Mayne, was several years removed from a successful junior college coaching career; he had come out of retirement in 2008 to work under Batesole, who had once served as Mayne's assistant at Orange Coast College in Southern California. Tack on "dissension in the ranks" to the list of factors seemingly piling up against Fresno State. Batesole and Mayne would eventually patch things up like a pair of brothers after a childhood fistfight, but at the time the situation certainly held the potential to divide a team that had made it this far on the strength of a spirit of unity, teamwork, and unselfishness.

Another line from Bob Bennett's quote book seemed apropos: "Your attitude toward adversity is related to your ability to overcome it."

Still 18 Innings Away From Omaha (June 8, 2008)

One very small consolation for the road team in a Super Regional series—an infinitesimal consolation when considering ASU's home record—is the chance to bat last and occupy the home dugout for the second game of the series. That meant that as Tempe's triple-digit Sunday afternoon heat simmered toward an evening start, Fresno State got to trade the aluminum bench of the visitors dugout for the soft, crimson-padded bench on the home side. Both dugouts were flanked by misting fans, but for some reason the mist seemed a little cooler on the home side too. Those physical comforts only further highlighted the calm in Batesole's voice as he matter-of-factly described the task at hand.

"We started this series knowing we had to play 18 good innings out of the 27, and we're still in that same spot," the coach said. "It's right here within our grasp. We need to do two things: we need to be ahead in the ninth inning and the eighteenth inning, and if we do that, we get to keep playing."

Doesn't sound like a guy facing elimination, does it? If Batesole set the tone, the players stayed on key. It didn't hurt to have Clayton Allison, the model of quiet confidence, striding to the hill. Coming off the dominating performance against San Diego in Long Beach, Allison carried a streak of eleven consecutive scoreless innings into the do-or-die dance with the Devils.

Starting out by striking out Sontag, the man who had homered twice the previous night, Allison then got Kipnis out on a fly ball to center to bring the dangerous Wallace to the plate. His average up to .418 after a three-hit game the night before, Wallace looked at a first pitch fastball for a strike, then fouled off a changeup, putting Allison ahead in the count 0–2. After Wallace fouled off the next two pitches, Allison broke out the "splitter," and Wallace swung through as the ball dove to the dirt. It was only the 32nd time Wallace had struck out in close to 300 plate appearances, and it sent a clear message: things were going to be different today.

Crafty left-hander Josh Satow set the Bulldogs down in order in the bottom of the first, and then Allison stretched his scoreless innings streak to 13 with a smooth top of the second. After Ahmady led off the bottom of the inning with a walk, I wondered aloud if Batesole would ask Detwiler to bunt the runner over.

"The lefty Satow works out of the stretch, first pitch to Detwiler, not bunting, he swings, lifts one in the air to right, that ball's hit pretty well! Newman back, at the track, it's GONE, over the fence, an opposite field home run for Steve Detwiler, and the Bulldogs lead it two to nothing in the bottom of the second inning. And I guess it's a good thing they didn't make him bunt!"

Batesole had told his hitters that with Satow, a speed-changing lefty on the mound, Fresno State's key to success was to keep the hands back and hit the ball up the middle or the other way. Detwiler's home run followed that game plan and injected even more confidence into the Bulldog dugout. The Dogs had landed the first blow, but like any proud heavyweight would, ASU was about to swing back.

Allison had maneuvered through that six-pack of sluggers, but the bottom of the order would prove prob-lematic. Back-to-back singles by Matt Newman and Raoul Torrez brought up the last hitter in the lineup, junior shortstop Greg Bordes, in a textbook bunting situation. After twice failing to get the bunt down, Bordes was left with a 1–2 count, forced to swing away. It was a blessing in disguise for ASU, as Bordes connected on Alli-son's fastball and drove it deep to right center field for a game-tying two-run triple. After a walk to Sontag, Kipnis scored Bordes with a single to right, giving the Devils a 3–2 lead. If you're paying close enough attention, you know who was due up next. It was Wallace, with plenty of motivation after striking out the first time. Alli-son got ahead in the count 1–2, then threw one to the backstop, moving the runners to second and third. A base hit could bust things open, and the guy at the plate was perhaps the best hitter in the nation. It was one of those pivotal points in the game in which the prominence of the show-down seems to auger up with each pitch. The pitches would keep coming and coming: eight pitches, nine, and then ten. Already fouling off five two-strike pitches, Wallace was waiting for Allison to finally make a mistake. There wasn't anything he could throw that Wallace hadn't already seen. His best bet would be to go with what worked against Wallace the first time, the specialty pitch he first learned from his pitching coach at the College of the Sequoias, Dana Gomez.

"Allison ready again, here comes the 3-2, swing and a miss! He got him with that split-finger as Wallace could not touch that one. A HUGE strikeout for Clayton Allison!"

That was a relief, but the right-hander was still in a pretty precarious position. Intentionally walking Davis to load the bases and set up a poten-tial double play, Allison proceeded to strike out Roling, then got Paramore on a groundout to first to leave the bases loaded. Allison's statline for the game would not end up being one he was necessarily proud of, but getting through those hitters in that danger-ous of a situation might have been the most crucial and impressive three-out sequence of his career.

Sparked again by Torrez and Bor-des at the bottom of the order in the fourth, the Devils would score twice to take a 5–2 lead into the bottom of the fourth, setting the stage for an-other one of the Diamond Dogs' patented two-out rallies. Hit by a pitch, Detwiler was aboard at first with two outs when seldom-used freshman Jake Johnson, a .212 hitter, laced a single that moved Detwiler to third. Danny Grubb stepped up with his .155 average and promptly scored Johnson with a single to right. A sin-gle by Muno not only kept the inning alive, it loaded the bases, and knocked Satow out of the game, with hard-throwing righty Stephen Sauer com-ing in to face Gavin Hedstrom.

Now trailing 5–3, Fresno State had a golden opportunity to tie the game. All it would take was one more of those two-out, two strike hits. Going into the season with a grand total of two starts in his career, how could the third-year Bulldog ever have imagined being at the plate for a moment like this? While Sauer warmed up, Batesole pulled Hed-strom over for a quick powwow. "Speed your bat up," the coach said. "You look slow."

Hedstrom felt a little slow. The fa-tigue of three weeks in a row on the road had started to set in. Sauer's 93-mph fastball could make a lot of bats look slow, and the right-hander used two fastballs and a curveball to put Hedstrom in a 1–2 hole. Hedstrom just missed crushing the curve, and he was hoping to see it again.

🎙 "This stadium full of ASU fans, making plenty of noise. The 1–2 pitch, fastball, swung on, hit in the air left-center field, hit pretty well. Sontag going back. Still racing, on the track, leaps—that ball is gone! It is a GRAND SLAM for Gavin Hedstrom on a 1–2 fastball, and Fresno State has taken a 7 to 5 lead in Tempe!"

In the stands, all a beaming Karen Hedstrom could say was "Wonderdogs!" Her son hadn't homered since that 24–6 game in Las Cruces on April 20. He had gone 48 days, 29 games, and 109 at bats without going deep, which in baseball parlance translated to "he was due." Gavin would later set me straight. It was a breaking ball, not a fastball, that he launched over the wall, slingshotting the Bulldogs from two runs down to two runs ahead. He also admitted he thought about the possibility of a grand slam as he stepped to the plate, before tunnel vision took over. "As soon as I hit, it felt like every one of my home runs," Hedstrom said. "I was watching it go out. Then, when I touched second, I looked at home plate. I had completely forgotten there were three people on base." No one will ever let him forget it again.

Taking over for Allison on the mound, Holden Sprague worked a scoreless fifth before surrendering a run in the sixth. The Dogs' lead was down to 7–6, and ASU had the tying run aboard at first with Wallace coming up. With his season on the line again, Batesole didn't hesitate to bring in his closer. After all, hadn't Brandon

Burke just proven he could handle an eleven-out save situation?

For a moment, it looked like Burke's very first pitch would get him out of the inning. Wallace ripped a one-hopper right at Muno, but the freshman shortstop couldn't handle it, and instead of an inning-ending double play the error gave the Devils two men on for Davis. It was another one of those classic confrontations. Right-handed bullpen ace against left-handed power hitter, and the count would tilt in the hitter's favor, three balls and one strike.

🎙 "The 3–1 to Davis, fastball hit on the ground towards short, another chance for Muno, to second for one, Wetzel on to first, DOUBLE PLAY, and the inning is over!"

Just as Allison's strikeout of Wallace had doused a Devil rally in the third, Burke had battled the best and lived to tell of it—but he still had nine outs to go. Three of those came in short order in the seventh, with Burke fanning Roling, Paramore, and Newman in succession. It remained 7–6 as

Clayton Allison pitching against #3 Arizona State in the Tempe Super Regional.
Ross D. Franklin/AP

they moved to the eighth, when Torrez and Bordes came through again with back-to-back singles. Sontag tried to bunt the runners over, but Ryan Overland, who had replaced Grubb behind the plate, burst out of his crouch to field the short bunt and nail the lead runner at third. It happened so fast that Mendonca thought he might have a shot at Sontag at first, but his throw was off the mark, sailing past Ahmady, so the Devils got what they wanted after all: runners at second and third with one out.

Kipnis could tie the game with a fly ball to the outfield or a well-placed groundout, but instead Burke slipped a 3–2 sinker under his bat for the second out. Walking Wallace intentionally was a textbook move, but of course that brought the other first-round pick, Davis, to the plate with the bases full.

"Infield will play a little deep all the way around, with the power-hitting Davis at the plate. Four thousand Sun Devil fans on their feet. First pitch hit on the ground toward short. Muno to his left, picks it up, flips to Wetzel, they *get* the out at second base, and the side is retired.

How great has Brandon Burke been down the stretch for Fresno State? The Devils, one of the best hitting teams in the country, had second and third with one out, they do not score. The scoreless innings streak continues for Brandon Burke. Make it ten-and-two-thirds now for the senior right-hander. If the Devils are gonna win it, they'll have to do it in the ninth."

But before they got to the ninth, the Bulldog offense made sure to pro-duce a little cushion. Overland led off with a double, and after Muno singled him to third, Hedstrom added to his career game with a run scoring single. Burke took the mound in the ninth with an 8–6 lead, and all of a sudden it seemed like the strike zone started shrinking. Roling walked on five pitches, Paramore on four. Newman bunted the runners over, and now the Devils were a hit away from tying it up. Torrez squibbed one toward first base, where Ahmady stuck his body in front of it and made the play, with the runners staying put. It would all come down to the number nine hitter, Bordes, who, in a lineup full of heavy hitters, happened to be the only Sun Devil the Bulldogs hadn't gotten out that day. Bordes was 3-for-3, just a home run shy of the cycle, but two quick curveballs from Burke put him in the hole, 0–2.

"Burke went three-and-two-thirds innings scoreless to get the save on Monday and get the Dogs to this Super Regional. Trying to do the same exact thing here to get 'em through to Monday. The righty sets, the 0–2, breaking ball, swung on, lifted in the air, left-center field, Hedstrom coming over, he's gonna be there. He makes the catch, and the Fresno State Bulldogs have done it! Brandon Burke for the second straight outing goes three-and-two-thirds innings of scoreless relief. He gets his school-record 12th save of the season. The Dogs get the victory and this series is on to tomorrow."

The dream lived on for the Diamond Dogs, while the stunned Devils tried to wrap their brains around something they'd never experienced. None of the players in Pat Murphy's dugout had ever lost a postseason game at home, and it hadn't happened to ASU at all in five years. Said Detwiler, "I think they thought they could stomp all over us the way they did the other day, but now they know who we are. We're having fun, that's when we play the best."

Muno couldn't help but marvel at how the undrafted Burke had silenced so many superstars. "Making all those first-round draft picks look that bad today," Muno said, "that was incredible."

Batesole was clearly pleased, but not surprised: "Most guys get in those situations and what they want to do is try harder. Burkie's been there and done that, when he was a freshman and sophomore, and sometimes last year, as anybody would. But now he's been through the wars enough times that he's smart enough and can control his body enough to keep trying easier. That's really easy to say, and it's really hard to do, but that's exactly what won this game today, he was able to keep his composure and pitch. I'm really, really proud of him."

From clutch pitches to get the team out of scary situations, to those heroic swings with two outs and two strikes, to making plays in the field with the game on the line, the Bulldogs had measured up to every challenge they faced. It's hard to encapsulate it any better than Bruce Farris did. Farris, a retired sportswriter who had covered Pete Beiden's early teams at Fresno State and still remembers the tear in Beiden's eye when his Bulldogs landed in Omaha in 1959, had come to Tempe in the hopes of witnessing history. With the enthusiasm of a teenager propelling his octogenarian body, each day he climbed all the stairs, then the ladder to the roof of the press box. When I asked the man who had observed every Bulldog squad for the last six decades for his synopsis of the game, Farris had a pretty straightforward response: "That was just the guttiest team I've ever seen. "

Before boarding the bus, Batesole had one more job to do. He had to call the coin flip that would decide which team occupied that cushy home dugout for the third and deciding game. "Tails never fails," he said as the coin spun into the air. It landed on heads. The coach could handle that. The bigger concern was who would be available to pitch. "We pretty much had to empty the tank today to get to tomorrow," Batesole said. "We got there, now we'll see what we've got left."

Is 17 Years Long Enough to Wait? (June 9, 2008)

When National Pitcher of the Year Bobby Jones flustered Florida State to open the 1991 College World Series, Fresno State fans never would have believed that seventeen years would pass without a return trip to Omaha. Fans all over the San Joaquin Valley turned on their radios or switched on their televisions to see if the wait would finally come to an end on that Monday in Tempe. No one would have projected the Bulldogs in this situation two weeks earlier when they limped into the conference tournament off that split at Sacramento State. Batesole had to be busting at the seams with excitement and anticipation, as he sat on the cusp of every college program's dream. You wouldn't know by looking at him. There Batesole was on that unpadded bench in the visitors dugout, shoulders back, arms relaxedly stretched out, right leg crossed over the left. Handing him the stick of red licorice my daughter Avery had sent along for him—she gave me one for each game, and coin-

cidentally I forgot on the first day and remembered the second—I asked the coach how long he had been dreaming of a trip to Omaha.

"It's been important," Batesole said, "but more important has always been these kids growing as men, and getting their degrees done, and doing things right. I don't live and die by that like a lot of coaches do and a lot of players do. I'd really, *really* like to do it, it's high on the priority list, but it's not really very near the top."

We all, naturally, knew he wanted to win, but the coach made it clear his biggest motivation came from a desire to see his players experience something that remarkable. "It's why I coach at this level, because when I played, it was the best three years of my life, and that's always our goal for these kids when they come in, that it will be the best three or four years of their life while they're here—and the experience that they have, they're never gonna forget. Getting them to Omaha, and being able to say that they did that, I'd certainly appreciate that."

He would not be alone. Just a few rows up in the stands, mixed in between school administrators and the players' families, sat couples like Jim and Sharlene Gomes and Herb and Mary Fung, families who had been chasing the Diamond Dogs all over the country for about as long as some of the current players had been alive.

With a 4 p.m. start time, this game would put the players under the dry desert sunshine that had dissipated in time for evening starts the two previous days. That early start on a Monday afternoon also had an impact on the crowd, which weighed in more than a 1000 people thinner than the night before. The Devils never expected to be in this position, and Wallace and Davis, the two offensive stars

who had struggled the night before, decided they'd try to fire up their team by staging a fight as ASU wrapped up infield practice. The "fight" aired repeatedly on ESPN2's telecast, and the Sun Devils landed the first jab of the game, too.

Freshman Matt Newman retired the Bulldogs in order in the top of the first, and in the bottom half ASU got a one-out single from Kipnis, followed by a Wallace walk. Bulldog starter Justin Miller bounced a pitch past Grubb, moving the runners up, and then Davis started the scoring with a soft looper that fell in shallow left, bringing Kipnis home from third. Paramore connected with a 1–2 count, driving Wallace in with a single to right.

Now the Devils led 2–0, and had men on the corners with just one out for Newman. Murphy called for a safety squeeze on the first pitch, but Newman bunted it foul, and that failure to get the run home with a productive out would turn more glaring when Newman, after fouling off three two-strike pitches, hit into a 4-6-3 double play to end the inning.

Now it was up to the offense to carry that momentum to the plate in the top of the second. Susdorf and Ahmady delivered back-to-back singles to begin the frame, but a foul pop up by Detwiler did nothing to move the runners. That brought up Mendonca, who had been steadily improving his success rate against left-handed hurlers, and knew one surefire way to bring those runners home.

"Newman sets and delivers, Tommy swings and hits one in the air, right center field, that ball is hit pretty well. Going back Kipnis, and he won't catch it, it's outta here! The 15th home run of the season for the

Tom Mendonca celebrates his home run, which gave Fresno State a 3-2 lead.
Paul Connors/AP

sophomore Mendonca, and just like that the Bulldogs have the lead. It's 3 to 2 in the top of the second!"

Miller made that one-run advantage stick with a scoreless second inning, and when Murphy switched pitchers to start the third, the Dogs made sure to hang a run on Reyes Dorado. Ahmady scored Hedstrom from third with an infield single that ricocheted off Dorado, so it was a 4–2 lead for the Bulldogs as they moved to the bottom of the inning.

With one out, a Wallace wallop wowed the crowd. Batesole had been referring to the southpaw slugger as "the Bambino," and the laser he launched off Miller was a Ruthian rocket that landed beyond the two southbound lanes of Rural Road, beyond the median, beyond one northbound lane, bouncing in the middle of that farthest lane and onto one of the greens of the Karsten Golf Course. As impressive as that blast

was, it only brought the Devils within one, and Miller rebounded nicely, retiring Davis and Paramore to end the inning.

Fresno State loaded the bases with one out in the fourth, only to have Davis take over on the mound and roll up an inning-ending double play off the bat of Wetzel. Newman led off the bottom of the fourth with the second home run of his career, tying the score at four apiece.

A strikeout, walk, and single later, Miller got the hook, with Batesole summoning Breckley out of the bullpen. The senior picked up out number two when Sontag flied out to left, but then he did the one thing everyone in the ballpark knew he couldn't afford to do. Breckley walked Kipnis to load the bases for Wallace, whose home run ball, depending on the cut of the green on the golf course across the street, may still have been rolling. Murphy could not have drawn it up any better. He had his best hitter, perhaps the most impos-

ing hitter in the country, up with the bases loaded in a tie game. With the count at two balls and a strike, Breckley hoped to fool Wallace with a changeup.

"The pitch to Wallace, lined toward Ahmady. A DIVING catch! He grabs it in foul ground and that'll end the inning. Alan Ahmady laying out to his left in foul territory, has dirt all over his jersey and a big badge of courage on his chest. Pats on the back of his head as he helps save the day here in the fourth."

Saving the day might have been an understatement. That play may just have saved the season. If Ahmady had not caught that ball—and it took a lightning quick reaction, gutsy dive, and perfect coordination to snag it before it hooked into the ground—it would have bounced in foul territory, and left Wallace at the plate with a 2–2 count. We couldn't quite hear the sigh of relief from the roof of the press box, but I'm sure it was audible a little closer to the dugout.

The bullets kept flying, and the Diamond Dogs kept dodging. Sprague took over for Breckley to start the fifth, and after picking up two outs, surrendered a home run to Newman. The freshman may not have lasted long as the starting pitcher, but he now had more home runs in this game than he had in his career coming in.

A 5–4 Devils' lead threatened to grow. A single and two walks loaded the bases for Sontag, now two days removed from *his* two-homer night. Using his changeup to get Sontag out in front, Sprague coaxed a ground ball to Ahmady to leave the bases loaded for the second inning in a row.

Tying the game when Susdorf's single plated Hedstrom in the top of the sixth, the Bulldogs would again have to face that Kipnis-Wallace-Davis triumvirate in the bottom of the inning. Sounded like the perfect challenge for the ever-improving Kris Tomlinson. The southpaw's slider never had a sharper break. Kipnis? Strikeout. Wallace? A rocket to right, but too low to trouble the golfers and caught by Detwiler for the second out. Davis? Fooled by the slider, couldn't check his swing in time. Striking out the All-American to end the frame, Tomlinson lifted his cap as he headed for the dugout, revealing the seldom-seen "mullethawk" look: hair long in back, with temples shaved close by the clippers of Sprague (read on for more on this bizarre bullpen barbering). Tomlinson barely made it across the first base line before being hounded by teammates hurrying out to congratulate him, and that enthu-siasm would carry over to the plate in the top of the seventh.

With two on and one out in this tie game, Grubb was due up. Right-hander Mike Leake, who had started the first game of the series, was now on the mound for ASU. If he followed the precedent set throughout the season, Batesole would have pulled Grubb here so the left-handed Overland could bat against Leake. Grubb had gone 2-for-3 in the game against left-handers, and the coach played a hunch, deciding to stick with him.

 "First pitch fastball, swung on, hit softly on the left side, they won't get two out of this, Leake won't even get one! The third baseman Wallace came in, so there was no one on the bag at third."

Grubb's full swing produced what amounted to the perfectly placed bunt, and by the time the pitcher realized third base was unattended it was too late to get the out at first. With the bases loaded with just one out, the Dogs were primed to break the 5–5 tie—but it would not come easy against Leake, the Devils' ace. When Muno struck out looking, it meant it would take another one of those two-out rallies to take back the lead. Hedstrom, less than twenty-four hours removed from his two-out grand slam, was up with the bags full again, and he would put the Bulldogs in front again...with his hand. That's where Leake's 3–1 pitch hit Hedstrom, scoring Mendonca with the go-ahead run and keeping the inning alive for Wetzel, who was 0-for-3 in the game.

"Bases loaded, two outs, top of seven, Leake sets, and delivers. [ping!] Wetzel swings, lines one down the right field line—FAIR BALL headed for

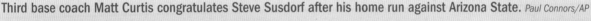

the corner! One run is in, here comes Grubb to the plate. Rounding third, heading for home is Hedstrom, let's see the relay. No, they missed the cutoff man. Three runs are in, a bases-loaded double for Erik Wetzel, and Fresno State leads it 9 to 5!"

It was that clutch bases loaded hit Arizona State had failed to come up with in the fourth and fifth, and they weren't singing "Take Me Out to the Ball Game" yet. Leake still had to face Susdorf, who had singled, doubled, and tripled against the Pac-10 Pitcher of the Year two days earlier.

With the Bulldogs maintaining such a loose and comfortable demeanor, I had the opportunity to engage Susdorf in a lighthearted conversation during pre-game batting practice. Susdorf had been tied for third on the Bulldogs all-time home run list with Beau Mills, his former teammate now playing in the Indians' farm system. "If you need a little extra motivation," I said to Susdorf, half-jokingly, "Beau homered the last two nights in a row. It's about time you passed him." The ever-focused Susdorf was not thinking about that conversation, or his chance at notching a cycle in five at-bats against Leake. He just trusted that smooth, consistent swing, diligently developed by all those hours in the backyard batting cage with his dad, Bill, and fine tuned by four years with Mike Batesole.

🎙 "2-2, swing and a drive, right-center field, that ball is hit very well! Kipnis going back. Kipnis won't catch it, NOBODY'S gonna catch it! A two-run homer for Steve Susdorf, and it is 11 to 5 Fresno State!"

I wish we'd had a microphone on Bill Susdorf, in his seat above the Bulldog dugout. Steve said afterwards, "It felt amazing! I can't even describe it."

A six-run lead felt awfully good, but Arizona State would threaten again in short order. Tomlinson walked Paramore to start the bottom of the seventh, then hit Newman with the first pitch. That brought Sean Bonesteele in from the bullpen. After a passed ball, the sophomore right-hander was staring at a nobody out, runners at second and third situation. Fooling Roling with a 2–2 changeup, Bonesteele produced a clutch strike-out, but the sacrifice fly was still in order for the Devils. That changed when Bonesteele got Torrez to chase a 1–2 breaking ball down and away for the second out. When Bordes grounded out to Muno at short, Bonesteele, who entered that outing with a 6.38 ERA, had successfully extinguished the Sun Devil threat.

"I am so proud of him," Grubb said afterwards. "That is by far the most guts I have ever seen. He just got in there and was hucking strikes."

Bonesteele held the Devils score-less again in the eighth, and it remained an 11–5 lead for the Bulldogs going to the ninth. Heeding Batesole's admonition to play "all 27 outs," the Dogs added an insurance run with what else?—another two-out, two-strike hit, a single by Mendonca that brought Wetzel home. So it would be a seven-run lead, with just three outs separating Fresno State from that long-awaited trip to Omaha.

Bonesteele began the bottom of the ninth by striking out Newman, but proceeded to walk a man and hit a batter, and that was enough for Batesole. Brandon Burke had thrown 55 pitches the night before, but there was no one the coach would rather

have on the mound at the end of the game than the senior from San Diego. On this fun-loving ball club, Burke was the class clown, always cracking jokes and relishing his role as judge of the kangaroo court. This was no laughing matter. This was wrestling an alligator, resisting a rhino, and fending off a shark with blood in the water, all mixed into one. This was the Sun Devils' last stand, and they were prepared to go down swinging.

After a walk loaded the bases, Sontag delivered a run-scoring single to right, cutting the lead to 12–6. Kipnis followed with a single to center, scoring a pair to make it 12–8. When public address announcer Randy Policar introduced Wallace as the next hitter, the Sun Devil fans broke into the chant of "Let's go, Devils!"

Starting the All-American out with a fastball on the outside corner for strike one, Burke came back with a fastball inside, yielding a lazy pop fly to left that Susdorf corralled to take the Devils down to their final out. It wouldn't come off the bat of Davis, who singled to center, scoring Sontag to make it 12–9.

Things just kept getting scarier and scarier. Paramore walked to load the bases, which brought up Matt Newman. Newman's father, Randy, had been the winning pitcher for ASU in the 1981 national championship game. Matt Newman already had two home runs in this game, and now a third deep ball would win it for the Devils and allow him to follow in his father's Omaha footsteps.

Burke's first pitch fastball found the strike zone at the knees; his 0–1 changeup missed high and away. The fearless reliever had now thrown 84 pitches in the last twenty-five hours. He knew he needed at least one more.

"Bases full, two outs, the A-S-U chant going up in Tempe. The 1–1, Newman swings, lines it into left, Susdorf coming on, Steve *makes* the sliding catch, and the Bulldogs have done it! Gloves flying in the air all over this diamond. Ray O'Canto's gonna fall off the roof of this press box! Seventeen years of waiting have come to an end, the Fresno State Diamond Dogs are headed to the College World Series!"

O'Canto, thankfully, did not fall off the roof, if only for the headset cable holding him back. "Wow, Paul, it doesn't get any better than this," he shouted, still jumping up and down. "Wow, what a great, great ballgame. Unbelievable!" He couldn't hide his alumni pride, and the Bulldogs on the bottom of the dogpile couldn't find their breath.

Down on the field, we could see Batesole sharing a bear hug with Athletics Director Thomas Boeh. Matt Curtis had blonde curls bouncing back and forth in front of his eyes, courtesy of his daughter Lauren, now taking a victory lap on daddy's shoulders while little brother Jacob chased alongside. The Bulldog baseball family celebrated the unprecedented upset. Fresno State was the first #4 regional seed to win a super regional and go to Omaha, and up in the booth, Ray and I were busy opining.

"They weren't happy just to be here, they won't be happy just to be in Omaha," I told our listeners. "There is something magical about this team right now, much like Oregon State last

Steve Susdorf makes the sliding catch to send Fresno State to the College World Series. *Paul Connors/AP*

The Diamond Dogs celebrate Fresno State's first trip to the College World Series since 1991. *Paul Connors/AP*

Brandon Burke and Alan Ahmady are going to Omaha! *Paul Connors/AP*

year. They're not going there just to be there, they're going there to win."

Then Ray chimed in: "These guys want to be the national champions. They're gritty, they're determined, they give you 100 percent effort." Fortunately, the listening audience didn't have to take our word for it. Tommy Mendonca was the first to join us.

"We're going there to win the whole thing. We have business to take care of," Mendonca said. "Everybody left everything on this diamond, now we're gonna leave it all in Omaha."

Danny Grubb, fresh off a season-high four hits, could hardly believe it. "It's one of those impossible stories," the catcher said, shaking his head in awe. "It's just surreal. We don't even know how we did it. Every day, we show up to the ballpark, and when we strap it on, we're gonna play as a team no matter what happens. We had struggles, we had problems, everything you could think of went wrong , but we stuck together and we knew that we had a ballclub still, and we knew we could get it done. And now look at us today, we're getting it done." Adding that he had never seen Batesole pace back and forth in the

dugout the way he did in the ninth inning, Grubb confirmed that the usually stoic coach was now grinning ear to ear.

Batesole was about to deliver another uncharacteristic moment. "You've probably never heard me single out one player, it's always 'we' and 'us,'" the coach began, "but what Steve Susdorf has done for this program, wow. He turned down a lot of money twelve months ago, and this is why he came back. He's gonna have his degree in engineering, and he's given his heart to this program, and I don't know if I've ever been any prouder of any player that I've ever coached. He's the heart of this team, and he's more than any other reason, the reason that we're going to Omaha."

Hearing those gratifying words from his coach made for a special moment, but Susdorf was still thinking about that last ball off Newman's bat. "That ball was hit, and there was no chance I was ever gonna be dropping that ball," he said, "because we are going to Omaha, and I can't believe it." He also couldn't believe that he had forfeited his claim on that ball, throwing it up in the air as he raced

to join the dogpile. Where is the ball now? Ask Alan Ahmady.

Batesole reflected back to the day he took the Fresno State job six years earlier, how he talked about what it would take to get to the College World Series, and how much community pride it would produce when it finally happened. That moment was here, and he wanted to share it: "We've got twenty-five players in that dugout busting their butts, and a whole lot of other people, thousands, putting their heart and soul into this program. To make this happen and to bring it back to Fresno is really, really cool."

Before heading back the next morning to Fresno, where they'd be greeted by an impromptu gathering of enthusiastic fans at Beiden Field, most of the Bulldogs lingered at the scene of their victory, celebrating with their families until the bus was ready to leave. Susdorf didn't have that luxury, because his dad had to work the next morning, and after waving goodbye from a distance, had begun the long drive home to Southern California. They would have plenty of time together in Omaha, if things went according to plan.

"We've been the underdog the whole way," said Susdorf, "we're gonna be the underdog again, and we've played great as the underdog. So we're gonna go in there and keep doing what we've been doing, and hopefully we get to that final game."

NCAA Super Regionals Summary

Arizona State 12, Fresno State 4
Fresno State 8, Arizona State 6
Fresno State 12, Arizona State 9

Up next: College World Series, Omaha, Nebraska

THE COLLEGE WORLD SERIES: DIAMOND DOGS OF DESTINY

The Diamond Dogs were back in Fresno for less than twenty-four hours before taking off for the College World Series, but June 11 was not a good day to be flying in to Omaha. Severe thunderstorms blanketed the eastern part of Nebraska that Wednesday night, forcing the plane carrying the team to land instead in Lincoln after encountering some pretty forceful turbulence. Upon landing in Lincoln and boarding a bus for the hour-long ride to the team hotel, the players received some sobering news. Three tornadoes had just touched down in the Omaha area. They would later learn that four teenage Boy Scouts had been killed when the building where they had sought shelter was destroyed by one of the twisters.

Not reaching the team hotel in Omaha until after midnight, the team would awake Thursday morning to the red carpet treatment. Signs everywhere trumpeted the College World Series, known also as "The Greatest Show on Dirt." The Bulldogs would be carted around the city, with police escort when necessary, in a big red bus with "Welcome Fresno State University" plastered on the door.

The next three days would provide a flurry of thrills: autograph sessions, media interviews, the obligatory practices, a riverbank barbecue, and plenty of time to round up

CWS memorabilia to supplement the gift bags the players received when they arrived. By the time word came that Mike Batesole had been named National Coach of the Year by the Na-

tional Collegiate Baseball Writers Association, Batesole and his family were already toting armloads of CWS merchandise.

Players enjoy a riverbank barbecue. *Minorwhite Studios/Fresno State Athletics*

Players board the team bus to head to Rosenblatt Stadium. *Mary Fung*

The Batesole family in Omaha. Left to right: Susie, Korby, Mike, Kody, Kassy, and Kally. *Batesole Family*

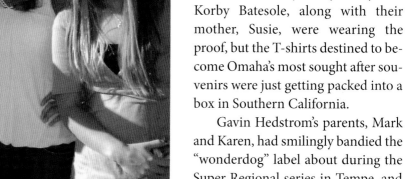

Mark and Kenan Hedstrom wearing their "Underdog to Wonderdog" t-shirts with Gavin in the team hotel. *Hedstrom Family*

"I've had a lot of opportunities to come here for free the last 15 years," said the coach, "and I've turned it down every single time because I didn't want to come here until we earned it, and now we did. I never even bought anything at any of the regionals because even that stuff has 'CWS' on it, so I haven't wanted to even touch it. Now that we're here, I've dumped a lot of money into the city of Omaha." Kassy, Kally, Kody, and Korby Batesole, along with their mother, Susie, were wearing the proof, but the T-shirts destined to become Omaha's most sought after souvenirs were just getting packed into a box in Southern California.

Gavin Hedstrom's parents, Mark and Karen, had smilingly bandied the "wonderdog" label about during the Super Regional series in Tempe, and on the way home to Irvine, Karen turned to Mark and said, "You know, you could sum up their whole season by the fact they went from underdogs to wonderdogs over the course of the postseason." The Hedstroms had been at every game since the start of the WAC Tournament, and Mark admits that he wasn't sure the Dogs would still be playing after Ruston. Now they were on to Omaha, and the couple agreed "Underdogs to Wonderdogs" would be the perfect slogan for a T-shirt. Karen and a friend scrambled to put together the graphics, and Mark put a rush order on five dozen shirts, which he would hand out to friends, fans, and the parents of players, once they made it to Nebraska. Little did he know what that creative, kind-hearted gesture would spawn.

By Friday night the Hedstroms were watching Gavin and his teammates, along with the other seven teams, parade into Rosenblatt Stadium for the opening ceremonies. Hedstrom's grand slam against Arizona State played on the video board in left field. The Dogs had practiced at Rosenblatt earlier in front of about 5,000 fans—more than twice the size of Fresno State's biggest home crowd in 2008—and attendance for the opening ceremonies approached 20,000. When the player with the

Mike Batesole watches the Bulldogs take batting practice before their CWS opener against Rice.
Minorwhite Studios/Fresno State Athletics

highest grade point average from each team went down to accept plaques, Kris Tomlinson was the only one to keep his hat on.

Starting with the last weekend of the regular season in Sacramento, Holden Sprague had mutilated Tomlinson's hairstyle a little further each week, and now it had reached the "skullet" stage, with a patch on top separated from the tail in the back by a close shave all the way around. By the end of Fresno State's two weeks in Omaha, that hairdo (or is it hairdon't?) was a nationwide sensation, even becoming the topic of an extended discussion on ESPN's "Pardon the Interruption." But the Bulldogs didn't want to be a punch line. They didn't come this far, overcoming such ridiculous odds, to play the role of the quixotic little underdog that would "be gone in a couple days," as some players heard fans muttering. They

were ready to ride their fun-loving wave as far as it would take them.

As Sunday's opener against the Rice Owls inched closer, the Diamond Dogs resolved to savor every second of the Omaha experience. "You've heard that expression, 'act like you've been there before?'" said Detwiler. "Well, we decided to do the opposite. We've never been here before, so we're going to act like we've never been here before. We're going to enjoy all of it and just have fun."

Renewing the Rice Rivalry (June 15, 2008)

If Fresno State was trying to go where no Diamond Dog squad had gone before, what better opponent to lead off against than the Rice Owls? In their nine seasons in the WAC, from 1997 to 2005, the Owls won or shared conference titles all nine years, with the Bulldogs finishing as runners-up four

times. There had been some tremendous battles and wild finishes, but twenty-nine times in forty-five meetings the Owls and their veteran skipper, Wayne Graham, had come out on top. Graham, who played briefly for the New York Mets when the legendary Casey Stengel was the manager, led the Owls to their first national championship in 2003, and 2008 marked his seventh trip to Omaha in the last dozen years.

Batesole wasn't all that familiar with Rice's current talent—only a handful of players on either side had seen action when the Owls and Dogs last met in 2005—but he knew Graham's tendencies. He knew the way the Owls' endless array of power pitchers liked to approach the game, and he knew his hitters would have to be aggressive.

The Rice-Fresno State rivalry had given me some of my biggest thrills as a baseball announcer. From left

Steve Susdorf's focus is on display in batting practice at Rosenblatt.
Minorwhite Studios/Fresno State Athletics

Danny Muno after his home run against Rice. *Minorwhite Studios/Fresno State Athletics*

fielder Casey McGehee's perfect throw to Oscar Lopez at second, gunning down Hunter Brown to seal a 1-0 Bulldog victory in 2001, to closer Chad Edwards needing one more out to beat the top-ranked Owls, only to give up a game-winning homer to Enrique Cruz in 2003, to Beau Mills and his walk-off dribbler through the infield off of Joe Savery in 2005, I had the privilege of calling all those captivating conclusions.

There would be no nail-biting ninth inning this time, and I wasn't at the mic for this Sunday showdown either. My grandfather's funeral would take place Monday, and with the Bulldogs guaranteed another game on Tuesday, I would arrive in Omaha Tuesday morning. Bill Woodward had enjoyed his time with the Diamond Dogs in Long Beach and was ready to step in. I was a young high school first baseman when I listened to Woodward announce Fresno State's last College World Series game in 1991, and it put a smile on my face to know that Bill would get to experience the excitement of Omaha again.

With Rice carrying a #6 national seed, not to mention a perfect 5-0 record in the postseason, the Owls would be the home team, and right-hander Ryan Berry would be Graham's main man on the mound. The 6 foot 1 inch 195-pound sophomore came in with an 8-4 record, and had won eleven games the year before when Collegiate Baseball named him National Freshman Pitcher of the Year. Think about the starters Fresno State had faced over the last two weeks: Liebel, Romanski, Leake, et al. Berry wasn't going to do anything those guys hadn't done.

Berry and Bulldog starter Justin Wilson both turned in scoreless first innings, and it might have turned into the same story in the second, but with

Jordan Ribera's mighty swing against Rice produces a 3-run home run for the freshman designated hitter.
Minorwhite Studios/Fresno State Athletics

two on and one out Owls second baseman Jimmy Comerota misplayed a Steve Detwiler grounder, loading the bases for Danny Muno. The freshman shortstop had stopped taking "freshman at bats" a long time ago. His patience and discipline at the plate had made him one of the toughest outs on the team. Working the count full, Muno eventually came through with a single up the middle, giving the Bulldogs a 2-0 lead. Hedstrom followed by lining Berry's 0-2 offering to left for a bases-clearing double that made it 4-0. "We played aggressive," Batesole said later. "The last thing we wanted to do was sit back and let the action come to us."

If Wayne Graham was thinking a four-run second was troublesome, wait until the fourth inning rolled around. Still ahead 4-0, the Bulldogs got singles from Ryan Overland and

Jordan Ribera at the bottom of the order to bring Muno up with one out. The freshman picked a pretty good time to pull out his third home run of the year, launching one down the right field line to score three more and make it 7-0. Muno had now driven in a career-high five runs, and the game wasn't even halfway done.

After Hedstrom walked, Erik Wetzel brought him home with a double, and seeing 8-0 on the board was enough to make Graham go to his bullpen. Freshman lefty Matt Evers came in, hit Steve Susdorf with his 2-1 pitch, then stayed in the game to face Alan Ahmady. Oops! When Ahmady launched a three-run bomb of his own to left, the crowd of 18,108, the largest to ever watch a Fresno State game, was starting to get a pretty good idea about where this game was headed. It was exactly the opposite of

what the "experts" expected: Rice was playing like the team that was out of its element and Fresno State looked like the squad that was in Omaha for the third year in a row.

The Bulldogs' lead was now 11-0, Graham was making a pitching change, and the nearly 1,000 credentialed members of the media were starting to take notice. Apparently the single run Rice picked up in the bottom of the fifth made the Dogs hungry for more. A two-run single by Detwiler preceded a three-run blast to center by Ribera. The freshman DH, who entered the CWS hitting .194, later said that home run against the Owls, which sailed over the 408-foot sign, marked a turning point for him personally. "That really helped me out in terms of confidence," said Ribera, who would end up hitting .353 in Omaha. "My dad kept telling

Junior Justin Miller was Fresno State's starting pitcher against North Carolina. *Minorwhite Studios/Fresno State Athletics*

me that it's not how you start, it's how you finish, and that made me start to believe him."

It was 16-1 at that point, and 17-2 after a Tommy Mendonca homer in the eighth that his parents were thankful they made it in time to see. Ray and Tami Mendonca and Tom's brother T.C. had hopped in an SUV in Turlock, teaming up with a long-haul trucker friend to drive all the way to Omaha. The trip started out swimmingly. They saw antelope, buffalo, and all kinds of wildlife against the backdrop of majestic mountains and rock formations. But about halfway through Wyoming the bat-

tery light came on in the dash. The radio stopped working, then the A/C followed suit. Soon the windows were stuck and the power door locks were dead. None of that deterred them, but when the fuel pump shut down too, it was time to call AAA. One tow truck, two hours, four hundred dollars, and one new alternator later, they were back on the road. They finally arrived in Omaha about three hours before the game began, and each one of those 17 runs made their misadventures a little easier to stomach.

The game's final tally would stop at 17-5, giving the Bulldogs the greatest offensive performance in the Col-

lege World Series since Miami scored 21 against Tennessee in 2001. Not bad for a bunch of "goofballs," as Detwiler would famously call them, who came into the CWS with the lowest team batting average (.297) in the eight-team field. True to form, the Dogs had delivered 11 of their 13 hits on two-strike pitches.

The "neutral" fans in Omaha were starting to jump on the bandwagon, the talking heads in the media were getting a feel for it, and if there was anyone in that Bulldog dugout who didn't really believe the team was capable of winning it all, the blowout win over Rice was pretty compelling evidence. "Fresno did an incredible job of hitting today," said Graham. "It's hard to hit that good in batting practice."

Not to be lost among the slugging superlatives was the pitching performance of Justin Wilson, who held the Owls to two runs in his seven innings, and after the game received a humongous hug from his dad, Jim. It was Sunday, June 15, Father's Day. To a man, every Bulldog dad in Omaha designated that victory as the greatest Father's Day gift ever. Quite a few of those dads were wearing "Underdog to Wonderdog" T-shirts, and now the Hedstroms were all out. Mark Hedstrom made a phone call. Four dozen more shirts were on their way.

Central California and North Carolina Meet in the Middle (June 17, 2008)

Omaha is about 1,600 miles from Fresno, and only 1,200 from Chapel Hill, North Carolina, so it's not quite equidistant, but close enough. West Coast teams have dominated college baseball for decades. Cal's win over Yale in the inaugural NCAA championship game in 1947 was the first of 31 titles in 61 years for schools from California, Arizona, or Oregon. The Golden State alone had been home to 21 of those champions. Over the last quarter-century, money resulting from college football's Bowl Championship Series has led to bigger investments in baseball for schools from conferences like the SEC, Big XII, and ACC, and threatened to chip away at that western supremacy.

The revival of North Carolina's program had been as impressive as any, and Mike Fox was the architect of that resurgence. A second baseman on the 1978 North Carolina team that made it to Omaha, Fox had ended a

17-year CWS drought for the Heels when he guided them there in 2006. UNC would finish runner-up to Oregon State that season, and experience déjà vu in 2007, falling to the Beavers in the final once again.

The #2 national seed in 2008, the Tar Heels had been tabbed by countless experts as the team to beat in Omaha. Over the last three seasons, no program in America had more victories, and the Heels arrived at Rosenblatt that Tuesday evening with a perfect 6-0 record in the postseason. They had put themselves in this pivotal game by becoming just the second team to beat LSU in the Tigers' last twenty-six games, but to do it, they had used their fireballing ace, Alex White. So instead of White and his 97-mph fastball, Fresno State *only* had to face Adam Warren and his 22-1 career record. North Carolina's bullpen wasn't shabby either. The Tar

Heels boasted the lowest team ERA in the country, 2.84.

Compounding the situation for the Dogs was the fact that Clayton Allison was experiencing pain in his throwing arm and could not take the mound. "We're probably gonna have to throw five or six guys," Batesole said in our pre-game interview. "We're gonna have to give them different looks and different matchups."

Batesole would begin with Justin Miller on the bump, but wouldn't hesitate to try anything. "It changes everything if you win this game," he said. "All of a sudden somebody has to beat *you* twice, and that's a big, big difference." The winner of this game would be one win away from a spot in the best-of-three championship series, while the loser would need to rattle off three straight wins to accomplish the same.

Assistant coach Matt Curtis discusses North Carolina hitters with senior catcher Ryan Overland. *Minorwhite Studios/Fresno State Athletics*

The Bulldogs would be the home team this time, so the first task would be dealing with a pair of .400 hitters in the first inning. First baseman Dustin Ackley, a .408 hitter, went after Miller's 2-0 fastball and grounded out to Muno at short. Kyle Shelton subsequently singled, which brought up Tim Fedroff and his .401 average.

"The pitch to Fedroff. [ping!] Lined right to Ahmady, who gloves it and will *walk* back to first base for the double play. That ball was hit a *ton*, but right into Alan Ahmady's backhand glove."

And so the "at 'em balls" began. Perhaps we can chalk it up to the level of competition, but I can't remember a series where so many times balls were hit extremely hard, but right at

'em in the field. Adam Warren would hold the Dogs scoreless in the first (it didn't help when Muno got picked off), and Miller retired the side in order in the second. In the bottom of the inning, Overland would come up with two outs and the bases empty, and after Warren fooled him so badly on a 2-1 changeup that the senior catcher lost his footing, Bulldog fans weren't expecting what came next.

"2-2 swung on [ping!], that ball's hit well to left center field! Going back on it, Shelton, to the track, he won't catch it, it's gone! An opposite field home run for the senior Ryan Overland, and Fresno State is on the board!"

Overland's first home run since April 27 came with—say it with me

now—two outs and two strikes. In the stands, a pair of schoolteachers from California's Central Coast embraced in elation. That was why Dale and Jean Overland traveled all the way from Atascadero. "If there's one guy who deserved to experience that, it was Ryan Overland," says Allison. "His baseball IQ is incredible. He never got much attention, but he was a real leader on our team."

Overland got plenty of attention from his teammates as he circled the bases, and Miller made sure that 1-0 lead would last at least another inning. Carolina's bats would come alive in the fourth with Tim Fedroff's triple to center scoring Kyle Shelton to tie the game, and a double by Kyle Seager bringing Fedroff in to put UNC ahead. Chad Flack's RBI single made it 3-1 going to the bottom of the fourth. Some 23,314 fans, another Bulldog record, waited to see how Fresno State would respond. With Susdorf batting first, they wouldn't have to wait long, unless you consider four pitches a long time.

"1-2 breaking ball, swung on, hit in the air, hit well to right field! Fedroff going back, Fedroff looking up, that ball is gone! A home run for Steve Susdorf, and the Bulldogs are back within one!"

That would certainly earn another dog paw sticker for Susdorf's helmet—not that there was much surface area left—but the Bulldogs would still trail 3-2 after four, and in the fifth Miller gave up a single to Ackley before hitting Shelton with a pitch. Fedroff had fired two bullets already, and Batesole wasn't about to let Miller face him a third time, not with two men on.

In came Tomlinson, his ERA still perfect for the postseason. A ground ball to Ahmady at first gave the Dogs their first out, but moved the runners to second and third in the process. Intentionally walking Tim Federowicz to load the bases, Tomlinson then went after the left-handed bat of Seager, the Heels' RBI leader. After spotting a 1-1 curveball for a strike on the outside corner, Tomlinson fired another curve down and away, and Seager waved at it and missed for strike three. Chad Flack, a big right-handed batter and UNC's career hit leader was up next, so Jason Breckley came out of the bullpen to face him. Tomlinson had done his job, and now he just had to trust Breckley to do his. When Breckley got Flack to pop his 1-1 fastball lazily in the air to right, that trust was reinforced. Batesole was making all the right moves. It's easy to focus on offense when you try to identify momentum shifts, but sometimes momentum changes more when something *doesn't* happen.

The Tar Heels had the bases loaded with one out and did not score. Now it was time for the Bulldog offense to take that spark and run with it. Muno led off the bottom of the fifth with a single, and Hedstrom followed suit. Wetzel's bunt was placed so perfectly down the third base line that he beat Warren's throw to first, so now the bases were loaded with nobody out.

Fox brought in left-hander Brian Moran to face Susdorf, and the move paid off. The All-American hit a

Alan Ahmady congratulates Steve Susdorf after his home run against North Carolina.
Minorwhite Studios/Fresno State Athletics

Fresno State's starting infield, left to right: Danny Muno, Erik Wetzel, Alan Ahmady, Tom Mendonca. Is Mendonca taking a bow after all his show-stopping plays at third base? *Minorwhite Studios/Fresno State Athletics*

ground ball to third, and Flack threw home to force Muno, but the Heels couldn't turn two, and the bases were still full for Ahmady. Moran is a tall, lanky lefty who likes to drop his arm angle down, almost to a sidearm release point. If Fox had ever seen Ahmady bat against that style of pitcher, he probably would have made another move.

"Ahmady 0 for 2 in this ball game, but on the season, 87 runs batted in. The 1-0, swung on, lined into center field, a base hit! Scoring easily from third is Hedstrom, right behind him, Wetzel, he'll score standing up. The Bulldogs have the lead as Alan Ahmady comes through one more time. 4-3 Dogs in the bottom of the fifth!"

Moran bounced back to strike Mendonca out, stayed on the mound long enough for Danny Grubb to be announced as the pinch-hitter, then left in favor of righty Rob Wooten, who stranded runners at second and third when Grubb lined out to short. Holden Sprague took over on the mound and maintained that one-run lead with a scoreless sixth, striking out Ackley to end the inning.

Fresno State would load the bases with no one out in the bottom of the inning, only to have Wooten get Hedstrom, Wetzel, and Susdorf out without allowing a run. Just like those wild games against Arizona State, only with an exponentially larger audience, the intensity seemed to increase with every pitch, every out. No one made more big plays on

college baseball's biggest stage than Fresno State's third baseman.

"The 1-0 [ping!] hit hard on the ground, a one-hop stop by Mendonca near the bag at third, he throws across the diamond in time. Another sparkling play by the sophomore from Turlock, taking potential extra bases away from Federowicz, robbing him down the third base line."

Leading off the top of the eighth, Seager hit a 400-foot blast down the right field line. It would have tied the game...but it was about three feet foul. After breathing a sigh of relief, Sprague got Seager to line out to Susdorf in left for the first out. With a man on first and two outs, Seth

64

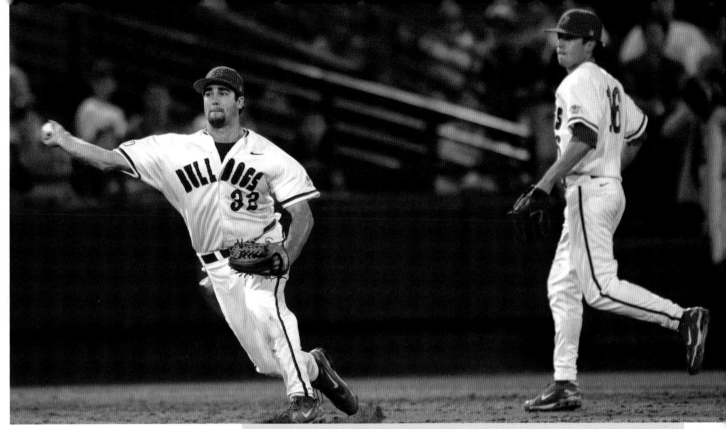

Tom Mendonca fires another bullet to first base. *Minorwhite Studios/Fresno State Athletics*

Williams dropped one in front of Hedstrom in center and Gavin threw all the way to third, trying to gun down Flack. Flack was safe, and when the throw went through to third, Williams broke for second. Mendonca's throw to Wetzel appeared to beat Williams to the bag, but umpire Mike Conlin called him safe. Batesole came out to argue, and when that failed, with the tying run at third and the go-ahead run at second, the coach decided it was time for Brandon Burke. The closer came in to face pinch-hitter Garrett Gore, who, after taking a ball, was ready to swing.

🎙 "Swings at this one, hits a one hopper on the left side, Mendonca off one big hop, fields, fires in a hurry, IN TIME to first base! Right when they need a rocket, Mendonca unleashes it!"

If Mendonca's throw had gotten to Ahmady a split-second later, the game would have been tied. "Huge, huge!" the first baseman said later.

Teammates including Jake Floethe and Blake Amador congratulate Danny Muno after his run gave Fresno State a 5-3 lead. *Minorwhite Studios/Fresno State Athletics*

Steve Detwiler pumps his fist after catching the final out of Fresno State's 5-3 victory over #2 North Carolina. *Minorwhite Studios/Fresno State Athletics*

"He's got a cannon for an arm, and I'm willing to break my hand if I have to. Man, he can throw the ball!"

That close call was all the reminder the offense would need. It was time for an insurance run, and the Dogs went to a reliable formula. Muno, whose on-base percentage throughout the College World Series was a remarkable .500, started the bottom of the eighth with a single to right. Hedstrom tacked another sac bunt onto his school-record, and then Wetzel brought Muno in with a single to left to produce a 5-3 lead for the Bulldogs.

With the speedy Ackley hitting one softly on the left side to start the ninth, it took another hustling effort and strong throw from Mendonca to produce out number one in the ninth. "Tom's definitely the best third baseman defensively, by far," said Burke afterward, "that I've played with in my entire life."

Burke's strikeout of Kyle Shelton brought the Heels within one out of their first loss of the postseason, but Fedroff singled to center, bringing Federowicz to the plate as the tying run. How dangerous was Federowicz? Well, the next time out against LSU, Federowicz would break a 3-3 tie with a ninth inning grand slam. That wasn't what Burke had in mind when he eyed the rally caps in the Tar Heel dugout and prepared for his 2-2 pitch.

"Brandon Burke shakes off the first sign from Danny Grubb. Trying to keep the Dogs perfect in Omaha. The 2-2 fastball, swung on, lifted in the air to right. Detwiler coming in, toward the line, HE MAKES THE CATCH, and Fresno State has done it again! The Bulldogs knock off the #2 national seed, it is FRESNO STATE in the driver's seat of this four-team bracket."

The 5-3 victory marked the first time since 1959 that Fresno State had won multiple games in Omaha. Bulldog mania wasn't just sweeping the San Joaquin Valley, this had become a major national story. Mark Hedstrom needed to order more T-shirts. And the players were smiling ear-to-ear. "It's a great, great feeling," said Ahmady. "We are playing so well right now, and our pitching is just doing a phenomenal job."

Batesole pointed to the pitching, too, praising his veteran relievers. "They've been doing things right, on and off the field, and today was a great display of that when you see Tomlinson and Breckley and Burke coming in and doing their piece, really unselfishly. And that's what they decided about six weeks ago, is that this is how it's gonna be. It would be really easy for them to think that they have to start and they have to be the stars, but they've accepted their role, and been outstanding at it, and once again, it was them that brought it home."

With a little help from that tough as nails third baseman. Had those dislocated fingers stopped bothering Mendonca yet? "No, they're hurting," the sophomore said. "I haven't even had a specialist look at them. We've been on the road for six weeks, so I'm just playing through it." And playing incredibly well. Before Mendonca left our radio booth, I had to ask the question: How could a team that had to win the WAC Tournament just to get into the NCAA field find itself a win away from playing for the national championship? Tom didn't hesitate. "Trust, trust, trust," he said. "When pitching, defense and offense come together, you're not going to lose too many ball games."

The Waiting Game

The Bulldogs knew they wouldn't be playing again until Friday, but a combination of the weather and the TV-dictated schedule ended up pushing that back until Saturday. A few parents had flown back home, but the families and fans who stayed in Omaha ended up with three gameless days. The Henry Doorly Zoo, with its Desert Dome altering the skyline beyond Rosenblatt's right field wall, was a popular attraction. Some parents made the buffet lunches at the casinos along the Missouri River their daily staple. Mike and Susie Batesole shared morning walks for coffee. Longtime booster Mary Fung had the staff at the team hotel wrapped around her finger, and those Hilton Garden Inn folks hadn't even sampled her legendary baking. Wide-eyed James Gomes, a 10-year-old from Visalia, flashed a telling smile every time he got a player's autograph. McKay France, 12, from Clovis, was the envy of every Little Leaguer. He was in Omaha as the Bulldogs' bat boy.

Kenan Hedstrom, Gavin's 10-year-old brother, was back home in California now, but he had received a raucous cheer from the Bulldog players when he learned he'd made his All-Star team in Irvine. The boyish enthusiasm wasn't reserved for the 12-and-under crowd. Coach Batesole repeatedly referred to his team as acting like "a bunch of sixth-graders at recess," and the evidence was everywhere.

Fresno TV reporter George Takata tracked down a boxed set of Disney books and got several players to act out scripted roles, repeatedly knocking the "Cinderella" book to the floor. If you saw a Bulldog fall to the ground, he must have been hit by an invisible "death ray," part of the "gog-

Bulldog batboy McKay France.

James Gomes with his mighty mitt.
Gomes Family

Noah Mayne, grandson of pitching coach Mike Mayne, hangs out in the dugout with injured pitcher Gene Escat. *Minorwhite Studios/Fresno State Athletics*

gles" game the players had picked up from a few Louisiana Tech players before leaving Ruston.

Nobody masterminded more mischief than Holden Sprague, and I'm not just talking about what he did to Tomlinson's hair. On a two-hour radio special we aired from the team hotel, we learned the whole story behind the fast one Sprague pulled on ESPN analyst Barry Larkin. Sprague's dad, Don, is a financial advisor. His mom, Lesley, is a kindergarten teacher. For Holden's freshman season, Fresno State's media guide transposed those professions, listing Don as the kindergarten teacher. Don's reaction? He'd rather be an astronaut. That exchange came to mind for Sprague when filling out the annual questionnaire for the 2008 media guide. He decided to put down "astronaut" for his father's occupation,

and got a pretty hearty chuckle when that tidbit actually ended up in print.

Filling out a fresh survey in Omaha for ESPN's research team, he repeated the trick, and when a North Carolina batter launched a "rocket" off of Sprague, Larkin, the former All-Star Reds' shortstop, saw an opportune moment to share with the national TV audience what he believed to be true: Sprague's father was an astronaut. If the surplus store around the corner from the team hotel had been stocked up on NASA jumpsuits, the other Bulldog parents would have paid a premium just to have Don autograph them. Walking past the crowd of reporters encircling his son after that win over the Tar Heels, Don shouted, "I have a space shuttle to catch."

He'd have to settle for watching the conclusion of the Diamond Dogs' meteoric rise. That night I sent an e-

mail to an ESPN researcher I'd been trading notes with, just to make sure the announcers were in on the joke the next time Sprague pitched. I quickly received a response: "Holden 1, ESPN 0."

That radio show in the hotel lobby provided a good opportunity to hear the players and coaches reflect on the incredible journey to this point, and send thanks to all the family and friends back home who had helped them get here. We fielded calls from Sprague's uncle, cousin, and grandmother, Gloria, who proved that smile I saw in the top row at Beiden Field every time I walked up to the press box could even come across on radio.

Burke told us how all four pitching coaches he had worked under—Tim Montez, Bobby Jones, Ted Silva, and Mike Mayne—had contributed to different elements of his stretch-run success. Justin Wilson explained the bracelet he wears when not pitching, honoring the memory of his high school friend, Anthony Butterfield, who had been killed two years earlier while serving with the 1st Marine Division in Iraq.

The Bulldog Baseball family was showing its true colors, and growing by the day. Omaha residents wanted to board the bandwagon too. Jim Hall, a tireless 49-year-old with fourteen siblings, was the perfect example. The underdog theme had made him a Fresno fan, despite the fact that North Carolina was the squad next to his name on the little piece of cardboard that tracked the CWS pool at Orsi's Italian Bakery.

Four dozen more "Underdog to Wonderdog" shirts disappeared about as soon as the shipment arrived. By this time, the shirts had received plenty of ESPN exposure, and drawn a good measure of additional media

Junior RHP Holden Sprague had a little fun at the expense of ESPN's Barry Larkin.
Minorwhite Studios/Fresno State Athletics

attention too. Mark Hedstrom says he was relieved when Fresno State officials approached him with a desire to copyright the slogan. He quickly agreed, on the condition that the royalties from any merchandise employing the "Underdogs to Wonderdogs" phrase would be passed on to the baseball program. The Hedstroms had been giving the shirts away, but with the marketing rights now secure, the university had its own shirts for sale in Fresno within hours. You can tell the officially licensed shirts from the ones the Hedstroms printed by the green "V" (for Valley) on a chain around the Bulldog's neck. In Karen Hedstrom's haste to finish the initial design, she had inadvertently inserted a green V-less logo the school no longer uses.

When the aforementioned Federowicz grand slam on Friday

Bulldog dads Mark Hedstrom, Jim Wilson, and Don Sprague are wearing Hedstrom's original shirts. *Wilson Family*

Steve Susdorf, assistant coach Pat Waer, and Danny Muno wait out the rain delay from the Bulldogs' dugout. *Minorwhite Studios/Fresno State Athletics*

Gavin Hedstrom slides around UNC catcher Tim Federowicz to score the game's first run. *Minorwhite Studios/Fresno State Athletics*

lifted North Carolina past LSU (who had already eliminated Rice), the Bulldogs finally knew the identity of their opponent the next day. With Allison's shoulder still tender, Batesole would be forced to keep the senior on the bench again.

Flack Attack, the Tar Heels Are Back! (June 21, 2008)

Mother nature put on quite a show between games that Saturday in Omaha. Arriving several hours early, I watched Georgia eliminate Stanford, 10-8, then had a pretty spectacular view of the thunderstorms from my press box perch at Rosenblatt. Lightning darted through the sky in the distance, thunder rumbling close behind. Rain moved in quickly and pelted the field, but the grounds crew lived up to its reputation, paving the way for a first pitch that was only delayed forty-eight minutes.

While right-hander Matt Harvey started for the Tar Heels, Wilson would get the call for the Bulldogs. Batesole would have loved to save his southpaw for the championship series against Georgia, but the Dogs had to *get* to that championship series first. Fresno State would be the visiting team this time.

Muno got things started off with a walk before being forced at second when Hedstrom reached on a fielder's choice. A two-strike single by Wetzel moved Hedstrom to second, bringing up the Bulldog's all-time RBI leader.

"One ball, two strikes on Susdorf, two on, one out, top of the first, no score. Steve swings, hits it hard on the ground, right side, through into right field! Matt Curtis will wave Hedstrom around third. Here comes the throw from Fedroff in right, Hedstrom is SAFE AT HOME PLATE, going right around the catcher Federowicz, a very close play. It is 1-to-nothing Fresno State."

With men on the corners now and just one out, the Diamond Dogs appeared to be primed for a big inning. Guessing the 2-1 pitch to Ahmady might be an off speed offering, Susdorf broke for second base when Harvey stepped toward home. It was a 93-mph fastball, and Federowicz gunned Susdorf down at second for the second out. Ahmady subsequently flied out to right, a swing that would have scored Wetzel if the Dogs hadn't gambled with the steal attempt. Wilson would hold the 1-0 lead with a bottom of the first featuring strikeouts of Fedroff and Seager. In the second, a pair of walks got Wilson into trouble, but after a well-timed mound visit from Curtis, Wilson got Ryan Graepel to hit into a 4-6-3 double play to end the inning. It was a nice double play, and the Fresno-leaning crowd erupted when Ahmady caught Muno's throw at first—but it wasn't the double play of the day. It wasn't #1 on the list of the top ten diamond dazzlers (major leagues included) on ESPN's "Baseball

Tonight." That would come in the bottom of the third. Singles by Ackley and Fedroff had Tar Heels at first and second with one out for Federowicz, fresh off his grand slam the night before.

"The 2-1, swung on, popped up first base side, foul ground. Ahmady hustling, slides and MAKES THE CATCH! Tagging at second is Ackley, here comes Alan's throw, Mendonca tags him, a collision, and he is OUT! A double play to end the inning and Ackley is shaken up!"

With fresh dirt all over his gray jersey, Ahmady had sprung to his feet, pivoting to his inside shoulder toward home plate, and fired a bullet to his bookend corner. "I was hoping the guy was tagging," Mendonca said afterwards. "I mean, Ahmady has probably the greatest arm on our team, and I don't know if that guy knew it or what." And did that collision bring back memories of his days as a safety for the Turlock High Bulldog gridders? "Yeah, but usually *I* had the full head of steam," Mendonca joked.

Collisions between his bat and a pitched ball were more to Mendonca's liking, and he'd produce another memorable one of those in the next half-inning. Ahmady's two-out single ended a string of nine straight batters retired for Matt Harvey, bringing up the other half of the double play that had thrilled the crowd just moments before. Harvey had not allowed a single home run all season, but Mendonca was looking for a fastball.

"Now Mendonca, left-handed batter against the righty Harvey, swings at the first pitch and HAMMERS IT! High and deep to right field and

Tom Mendonca holds on to the ball after colliding with North Carolina's Dustin Ackley, completing a double play started by Alan Ahmady.
Minorwhite Studios/Fresno State Athletics

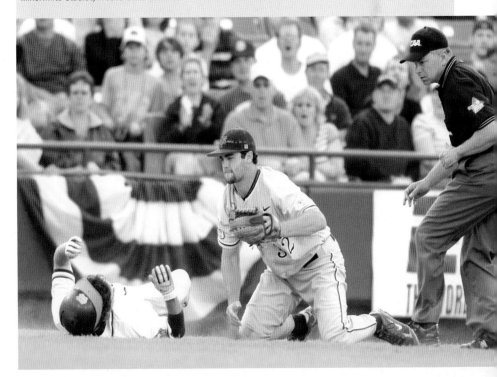

that ball is gone! A two-run homer for Tom Mendonca, his 17th of the season, and Fresno State's lead is three to nothing!"

North Carolina would finally get to Wilson in the bottom of the fourth with a one-out double by Flack, followed by a Garrett Gore single, set-ting the stage for an RBI single by Seth Williams. Facing Ackley—now a .413 hitter for the year—with the bases loaded and one out, Wilson got ahead in the count 1-2 before drawing a ground ball to Muno, whose only play was to Wetzel at second for out number two. That scored Gore and left men on the corners for Kyle Shelton, who Wilson promptly struck out swinging to preserve a one-run lead, 3-2. Again not sure if this outing would be his last as a Bulldog, Wilson left with one out in the sixth after throwing 112 pitches.

Sprague took over on the mound and kept the Dogs on top through six. Credit Mike Fox with a key decision

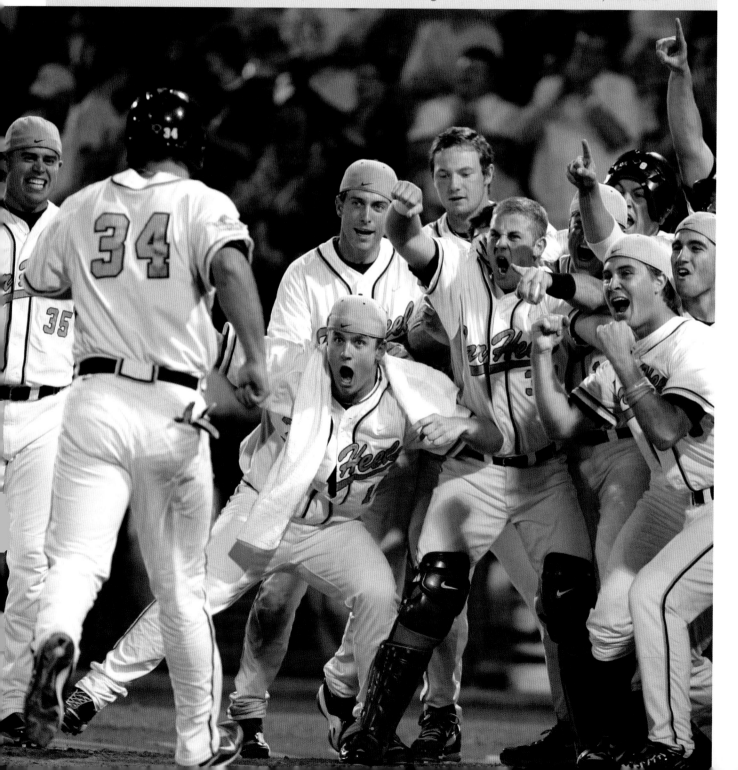

North Carolina's Chad Flack is greeted at home plate after his home run gave the Tar Heels a 4-3 lead. *AP / Dave Weaver*

in the top of the seventh. After a Detwiler double, a walk, and a passed ball had Bulldogs at second and third with just one out, Fox had Muno walked intentionally to load the bases, then went to the bullpen for Alex White.

Arguably the most intimidating pitcher in the College World Series, White had thrown 29 pitches the night before against LSU, working the final two innings of that victory to improve to 12-3 on the season. With his overpowering fastball, complemented by a wicked splitter, he was almost unhittable when his control was on and he got ahead in counts.

The super sophomore blew three fastballs by Hedstrom: 93 mph, 94, and then 95 for strike three. Wetzel fared no better, striking out to leave the bases loaded, as a pumped-up White strutted off the mound toward the Carolina dugout.

Following Fox's lead, Batesole made all the right bullpen moves in the bottom of the seventh. Tomlinson entered and struck out Fedroff, then Miller came in and got Federowicz swinging to strand the tying run at second. White retired the side in order in the top of the eighth, but Miller walked to the mound in the bottom of that inning knowing that the Bulldogs were 34-1 on the year when carrying a lead into the eighth. Seager led off with a rocket to right center which, despite a great diving effort by Detwiler, bounced in for a double.

Every coach in the country could tell you what was coming next. With the season on the line for Carolina, Flack would surely be bunting the potential tying run over to third. He tried to put the first pitch in play, but bunted it foul down the third base line. Squaring around on each of the next three pitches, Flack pulled his bat back each time as Miller missed the

Erik Wetzel and Steve Detwiler are disappointed after a 4-3 loss to North Carolina. *Minorwhite Studios/Fresno State Athletics*

strike zone. Now, with the count at 3-1, Fox played a hunch. He had seen the Heels' hit king come through time and time again, and he decided it no longer made sense to take the bat out of his hands. Giving Flack the green light to swing, Fox watched as Flack fouled a fastball straight back. There was no question the 6 foot 3 inch 224-pounder would be swinging on the 3-2, and the Bulldogs decided their best bet at getting him out was for Miller to fire a slider.

"Payoff pitch, swung on and CRUSHED down the left field line, high and deep into the dark Omaha night! A two-run homer for Chad Flack, who has plenty of those postseason heroics."

The entire UNC roster spilled out of the dugout to greet Flack, whom Fox later called the "clutchest" player he'd ever coached, as he circled the bases. Batesole said afterwards that the pitch Flack hit was not a mistake. "He made a good pitch," the coach said. "It was a 3-2 slider, which is what he does really well. Give Flack credit for hitting a good pitch."

And give Miller credit for bouncing back to retire the next three hitters in order to keep Fresno State within one as the game moved to the ninth. There was one problem—White was still on the mound. The flamethrower got Overland to ground out before striking out Detwiler and Trent Soares to end the game. In picking up his third win of the College World Series and his 13th of the season, White had faced eight batters and retired all eight, five of them via the strikeout. But he did have to throw 34 pitches, giving him 63 over the last two nights, and time would tell if that would become a factor the next day.

The 4-3 victory kept the Heels' season alive and moved the Bulldogs into that oh-so-familiar position. Elimination would be staring them in the face for the fourth time in their last eight games. In the post-game news conference, Fresno Bee reporter B.J. Anteola asked, "Do you feel it's a little demoralizing to have had the lead for most of this game and then lose it down the stretch?"

Susdorf dismissed that like he would a batting practice fastball. "It's just a little unfortunate," the senior said, "but we did it against San Diego. We've just got to shake it off and clear our minds, and move on to tomorrow."

Wetzel wanted a piece of that one too. "I don't think we have anything to be demoralized about," he said, "because that's a really good baseball team in the other dugout. Sometimes that happens." It was exactly what Batesole would want them to say, and the beauty of it was, it wasn't a forced facade, it was completely sincere.

Wilson was more than sincere. His comments smacked of dogged determination: "We're never gonna back down from anyone, that's our mentality. If we get backed into a corner, we're gonna come out fighting. We're kind of in a corner now, and we've got to go from here." But could they finally go with Allison on the mound? It had now been two full weeks since he last pitched at Arizona State.

"We'll try to get him loose tomorrow before we start," Batesole told the media. "If he feels good, he'll start. If he doesn't, we'll go to Plan B." What was Plan B? "I don't know," the coach deadpanned, deep down knowing that Allison's heart would outweigh the hurt.

Georgia Is Waitin', It's Time for Clayton (June 22, 2008)

While all of Batesole's comments throughout the week pointed to a reluctance to count on Allison's arm, Allison himself had been consistently clear: he would be ready to pitch. He had wanted to pitch the day before, but knew if the Bulldogs had won without him, he could take the mound in the best-of-three championship series. There was no more

time for "ifs." Fresno State's fourth elimination game of the postseason made it put up or shut up time for the senior right-hander. His parents, Buddy and Sharla, had, like so many other parents, made financial sacrifices to extend their stay in Omaha. The Dogs had been there for ten days now, and the Allisons had braved lightning and rain to cheer on the team, but they still hadn't seen their son pitch.

It wasn't something he thought about every day, but there was an experience in Allison's past that kept driving him to succeed. As a senior at Golden West High School in Visalia, on a team that included Beau Mills, Ryan Blair, and Chris Schwinden—all playing now professionally, not to mention his Bulldog teammate Tomlinson—Allison had learned a painful but valuable lesson. Caught drinking beer, Allison was kicked off the team and had to watch from a distance with his dog as the Trailblazers went on to a thrilling victory over Centennial of Bakersfield for the 2004 CIF Central Section title. The incident also cost him the chance to prove himself to Division I recruiters, and he ended up enrolling at Visalia's College of the Sequoias to play for former Bulldog Jody Allen. Hard work and solid coaching would make a D-I pitcher out of Allison, always driven by that missed opportunity in high school.

"At the time it was a terrible thing," Allison says now. "But for me, in the big picture, it was one of the best things that ever happened." Determined to be part of the trophy celebration this time, Allison says his arm felt great as he took the mound for the most important baseball game Fresno State had ever played.

Already assured of matching the 1959 team's third-place finish, the Dogs were counting on Allison to

Buddy and Sharla Allison excited to see their son pitch.
Fung Family

take them further than that, to put them in the CWS championship series. "He's been waiting a long time for this, and he's earned it," Batesole said in the dugout before the game, displaying the same kind of calm that had characterized the magical run to this point. "He's nowhere near 100 percent, he hasn't thrown a breaking ball in two weeks, and he's a guy who lives on his sharpness, but he's gonna leave it all out there, and there's a very good chance it will be good enough."

The wet conditions of the previous day had given way to clear skies and sunshine, and with the thermometer reading 83, it was 20 degrees warmer than the day before. The coach speculated that those conditions would lead to more offense, and that the team that walked the fewest hitters and played the cleanest defense would come out on top.

Allison had never thrown a more anticipated pitch, but Dustin Ackley was ready for it. The left-handed batter ripped it beyond the reach of Susdorf

Senior RHP Clayton Allison finally got to take the mound in Fresno State's fifth CWS game of 2008.
Minorwhite Studios/Fresno State Athletics

in left for a leadoff double. Electing not to bunt Ackley over, Fox let Gore swing away, and Mendonca held Ackley at second while making the play on Gore's soft grounder. Ackley would tag and move to third on Fedroff's fly ball out, and then a walk to Flack put men on the corners. Falling behind 3-0 in

A calm and composed Mike Batesole sits in the dugout at Rosenblatt Stadium.
Minorwhite Studios/Fresno State Athletics

Steve Susdorf scores on Tom Mendonca's 2-run single. This evasive slide left Susdorf with a 3-inch abrasion on his arm.
Minorwhite Studios/Fresno State Athletics

the count against the dangerous left-handed bat of Seager, Allison fired a fastball that Seager bounced to Wetzel at second, a routine play that ended the Tar Heel threat. So far so good for the "gamer" from Visalia.

Five days after becoming just the second college team to ever hang a loss on Adam Warren, the Dogs had to face the UNC right-hander again, and he came prepared, striking out Wetzel and Susdorf back-to-back to strand Muno at second in the first. Carrying the confidence from thwarting the Heel threat in the first, Allison worked a perfect second, helped by yet another clutch stop at third by Mendonca, who snagged a one-hop shot off Shelton's bat.

Warren walked three in the second, and even though the Bulldog rally was squelched when Brian Moran got Ribera to ground out and leave the bases loaded, Fresno State had accomplished one of Batesole's keys to the game: force the starting

pitcher out early. Mendonca started a 5-4-3 double play to help Allison through a scoreless third, and then Wetzel and Susdorf stepped things up as the lineup came around for the second time. Wetzel singled, Susdorf doubled, and the Heels walked Ahmady intentionally to load the bases with one out for Mendonca.

Concentrating intently as he camped out in the front of the batter's box against the sidearming lefty Moran, Mendonca ripped a 1-2 slider just foul down the right field line. That got the southpaw's attention, and Moran missed with the next pitch; however, Federowicz snapped a throw over to first to catch Ahmady sleeping, the third time a Bulldog baserunner had been picked off in Omaha. All that meant for Mendonca was that he now had a chance to deliver the kind of hit his coach prized the most, the two-out, two-strike variety. After fouling off a pair of 3-2 fastballs:

"3-2 to Mendonca. [ping!] Swung on, lined to left field, past the shortstop Graepel! One run is in, here comes Susdorf to the plate, Shelton's throw is NOT IN TIME! Susdorf scores, it's 2-to-nothing, and what a job by Tommy Mendonca!"

All season long, Mendonca had struggled to hit breaking balls, especially from left-handers, as he set an NCAA record with 99 strikeouts. This eight-pitch special was one of his most impressive at bats of the season, as he had the discipline to keep his hands back and drive the ball to the opposite field. That's the kind of at bat that makes the poker-faced Batesole crack a smile in the dugout.

But how long could Allison last on the mound? The top of the fourth made fans wonder. Giving up a pair of singles, Allison then walked two in a row to put the Heels on the board.

Down 2-1, Carolina could capture the lead with a base hit from senior Seth Williams, or tie it with a simple sacrifice fly. Displaying the tenacity that the Dodgers cited when they drafted him in the 29th round earlier in June, Allison persevered through the pain and froze Williams with a 1-2 split-finger on the inside corner for the crucial second out. Graepel's grounder to Muno at short would cap Allison's latest escape act.

Going ahead 3-1 in the bottom of the fourth, when an error moved Ribera to second and Muno's single brought him home, the Diamond Dogs made it 4-1 in the fifth when Ahmady walked and Mendonca drove him in with a double to right center off of Rob Wooten.

Buoyed by the offensive support, and the presence of his parents in the stands—he had long ago learned to recognize the tenor of his father's voice as he griped about an umpire's strike zone—Allison was determined to finish strong. The extent of his medical treatment that week (six ice sessions a day, anti-inflammatory agents, and even muscle stimulation with electrodes) would not be revealed until after the game, but it was

clear to the 15,125 at Rosenblatt that the biggest factor fueling Allison's fastball was his heart. That insatiable desire to put his teammates in the championship series drove him to an impressive sixth. He struck out Seager swinging to start the inning, and then with Shelton at third and two out, he got ahead 0-2 on Williams before missing on three consecutive pitches. He had squeezed 89 pitches out of that sore right arm, but he knew he had enough for one more.

"Allison into the windup, payoff pitch to Williams, SWING and a miss! Got him with the changeup, and how about Clayton Allison? The Bulldog fans, including his folks down the third base line, on their feet cheering for the senior right-hander."

Allison insisted afterwards that while his arm felt tired at times, he never felt pain. His teammates weren't necessarily buying that. "It was just an awesome performance," Burke said of his fellow senior, "one of the most gutsiest things I've ever seen on a baseball field."

Clayton Allison was dominant from his first pitch to his 90th.
Minorwhite Studios/Fresno State Athletics

Alan Ahmady dives in safely to score all the way from first on Tom Mendonca's double.
Minorwhite Studios/Fresno State Athletics (left); Eric Sorenson (right)

Erik Wetzel ranges to his left as well as any second baseman in the country. *Minorwhite Studios/Fresno State Athletics*

Alex White wasn't short on guts either. The Heels' sophomore ace had come on with one out in the fifth and rolled up a double play off Muno's bat. That meant that over the last two games, White had faced nine Bulldog hitters and produced ten outs. I can't say I've ever seen a pitcher do that before. After the loss the night before, Wetzel said he'd been hoping for another chance against White. "If everyone got another look at him, we might have done something with it."

He didn't get that opportunity the night before, but he would get it in the sixth inning this time around, and he would deliver a one out single to set the stage for Susdorf. That decision to return for his senior year was looking better every minute.

That morning, Susdorf's sheepish grin had worked overtime in an Omaha Methodist church, with the congregation oohing and ahhing about having "one of those Bulldogs from Fresno" sitting in a pew with his parents. Turns out the pastor had a degree from North Carolina, but was *still* rooting for the "Wonderdogs."

Susdorf had become the first Bulldog to ever hit 30 doubles in a season back in the third inning, and he delivered another two-bagger this time against White, placing one less than a foot inside the left field line, just in front of the wall, moving Wetzel to third. Ahmady and Mendonca would record an RBI apiece in the inning, White proved to be human after all, and the Bulldogs took a 6-1 lead to the seventh, where Holden Sprague

took over for Allison. The Heels hit some balls hard, but they were once again "at 'em balls," one at Detwiler in right, and one to Muno's backhand side that almost pulled the freshman's glove right off his hand. When Sprague handed that 6-1 lead over to Burke to start the eighth, the pitcher changed but the clutch defense didn't. The first hitter, Kyle Seager, battled Burke to a full count.

"Payoff pitch to Seager, fastball, pulled on the ground right side. Wetzel to his left, picks it up, wheels around, throws to Burke covering, THEY GOT THE OUT! What a play by the Diamond Dogs! Wetzel going into shallow right field, pirouetting and throwing to a covering Burke.

BRANDON BURKE
FRESNO STATE

"If you look at the way we started, where we are now is just inconceivable." — Brandon Burke on going to the CWS Championship Series. *Minorwhite Studios/Fresno State Athletics*

They timed it perfectly—like a quarterback bootlegging and throwing to the tight end across the middle."

You didn't have to see the face of Mike Fox to know what the Tar Heels' skipper was thinking, and in the post-game news conference he verbalized it. "They made every play defensively against us, really all three games," Fox said. "They made some plays that were just terrific." And they would save the best for last. After a one-out single by Ackley in the ninth, Garrett Gore stepped up to face the Bulldog closer.

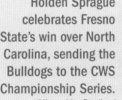

"Burke's first pitch to Gore, right-handed batter, pulled hard, a backhanded stop by Mendonca, to second for one, Wetzel on to first, IT'S A DOUBLE PLAY! The Bulldogs have won it, and what a way to do it! Fresno State will play Georgia for the national championship, after

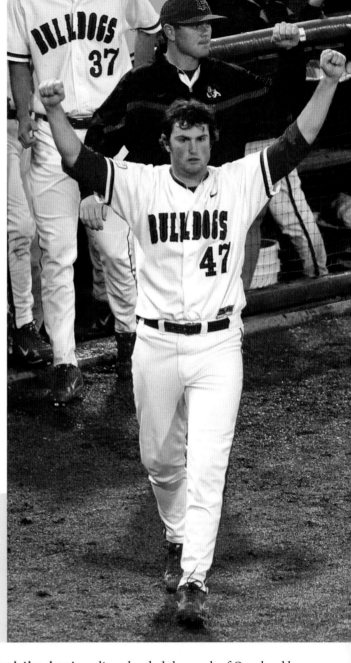

Holden Sprague celebrates Fresno State's win over North Carolina, sending the Bulldogs to the CWS Championship Series. *Minorwhite Studios/ Fresno State Athletics*

Tom Mendonca started the best double play of the night!"

"Burke was screaming like crazy, I don't even remember what he was saying," Wetzel said afterwards, "but I'm sure it wasn't 'we're going to the championship series.'"

Here's how Burke himself summed it up after calming down a little: "If you look at the way we started, where we are now is just inconceivable."

As usual, not one of the Bulldogs at the news conference would talk about his own efforts, choosing instead to point out what others did. Al-

lison lauded the work of Overland behind the plate. Mendonca praised all three pitchers for having such great command and composure. Burke testified to how much easier it was to throw strikes with a defense like that to back you up. Are they really all that humble and unselfish? I'd have to say that for the most part, yes, they really are. But one factor that helped them develop that habit is the longstanding team rule enforced vigorously by kangaroo court judges Allison and Burke: any mention of "I" or "me" carries a non-negotiable fine of $1.

Asked if his Bulldogs were still the underdogs, Batesole answered af-

Mike Batesole being interviewed by ESPN's Kyle Peterson after beating North Carolina to reach the CWS championship series. Fresno State fans still remember Peterson as the Stanford ace who ended the Bulldogs' season in the 1997 regional final. *Eric Sorenson*

College World Series Summary
Fresno State 17, Rice 5
Fresno State 5, North Carolina 3
North Carolina 4, Fresno State 3
Fresno State 6, North Carolina 1

Up Next: CWS Championship Series vs. Georgia

firmatively: "If you look at the two clubs on paper, you have to think that." But if the Bulldogs had knocked off the #3 national seed Arizona State, #6 Rice, and now #2 North Carolina, not to mention San Diego and Long Beach State, why couldn't they tackle a Georgia squad that came in as the #8 national seed?

"We stopped caring about who we were playing a long time ago," said Wetzel, "so we're just gonna go out there and play baseball."

And if anyone in the Bulldog dugout had any questions about the way to approach the championship series, Batesole found the perfect example in the smiling 6 foot 5 inch guy with hair on his chin and a huge bag of ice on his arm. "What Allison did today was really, really special," the coach said. "That was a mental win. It didn't have much to do with what he had physically. That was a mental battle, and he won it."

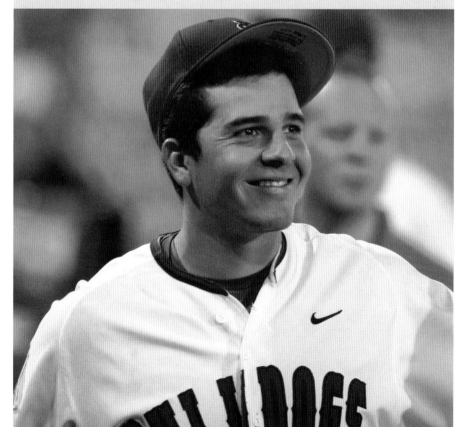

Alan Ahmady is all smiles after eliminating North Carolina. *Minorwhite Studios/Fresno State Athletics*

80

THE CWS CHAMPIONSHIP SERIES: THE ULTIMATE STAGE

"It doesn't get any better than Omaha." College baseball players say that every year about "The Greatest Show on Dirt." But as incredible as the last eleven days in eastern Nebraska had been, the College World Series was about to kick it up a notch. The commencement of the best-of-three championship series would bring out the big guns, or at least the big money and the fast planes.

Billionaire investor Warren Buffett, "the Oracle of Omaha," made his way to Rosenblatt and sat in the booth right next to us. His look of wonderment was just as real as ours when three F-16 fighter jets screamed overhead, timing their flyover perfectly with the conclusion of the Star-Spangled Banner. Sitting next to Buffett in that booth? Major League Baseball's all-time strikeout king, Hall of Fame fireballer Nolan Ryan. If it was a hot ticket when Fresno State football coach Pat Hill and North Carolina basketball coach Roy Williams wouldn't miss it, now the CWS was really sizzling.

There's a First Time for Everything (June 23, 2008)

Georgia and Fresno State had never before faced off on a baseball diamond. There is one player with the distinction of playing for both bunches of Bulldogs. Sean Ruthven,

son of Bulldog legend Dick Ruthven, spent his freshman season pitching for Bob Bennett before transferring back home to his native Georgia to play for David Perno's "Dawgs." Not only had the programs never butted heads, there wasn't a single common opponent on their 2008 schedules.

The mismatch idea made an easy storyline for the majority of the media. Underdog versus favored dog, mid-major conference (WAC) versus BCS conference (SEC), #8 national seed against the lowest-seeded team to ever play for a national championship in *any* sport. Those are all

Steve Susdorf robs Georgia's Matt Cerione with this catch against the left field wall. *Minorwhite Studios/Fresno State Athletics*

valid considerations. But to aluminum bat aficionados, the ones who understand the intricacies and idiosyncrasies of the sport, it was another measuring stick, another classic confrontation between the two concentrations of power in college baseball: the West and the South. Remember that statistic about West Coast teams winning 31 out of the 61 NCAA titles? Another 21 of those came from the South, and diehards are constantly arguing about which region plays a better brand of baseball.

If WAC champ Fresno State, which finished 17–17 against other teams from California while going 30–14 against everyone else, were to knock off Georgia, the regular season champion of the highly regarded Southeastern Conference, it would be perhaps the greatest proof yet of West Coast supremacy. For fans glued to televisions and radios all over the San Joaquin Valley, it was a chance for their oft-overlooked, denigrated, and ignored region to step out of the shadows of Los Angeles and San Francisco

and display its greatness for the nation to see.

But for those "sixth-graders at recess" in the Bulldog dugout, it was just another game. "They haven't taken anything too seriously," Mike Batesole said beforehand, "and I think it's helped them." Batesole wasn't going to mess with what brought the Bulldogs to this point, and if they weren't worried, why should he be? It was the "we over me" mentality that had produced this unprecedented charge to the brink of a championship, and if the Dogs were to keep on marching to the trophy, as Sherman did to the sea (where was that again?), they would have to do it with a consolidated effort on the mound.

None of the individual workhorses were left. "Scheppers is out, Allison won't be able to come back," the coach said. "Wilson? If anything, we might be able to get something out of him Wednesday, maybe six outs or so, so you're looking at a lot of guys who are going to have focus on their piece."

So while Georgia, with a day off leading in, sent a rested 8-game winner to the mound in Trevor Holder, Batesole was left hoping Sean Bonesteele could make it one time through the order and then hand the ball to someone else. You could expect the same scenario tomorrow, too, the coach added.

Danny Muno led off the game with a walk and made it to third before Holder struck Steve Susdorf out to end the inning. Now it was Bonesteele's turn. The 6 foot 5 inch sophomore right-hander battled tendonitis for a good chunk of the year, and wasn't able to make his season debut until March 30. He had a grand total of five college starts under his belt, all in midweek non-conference affairs. When Phil and Jeannine Bonesteele

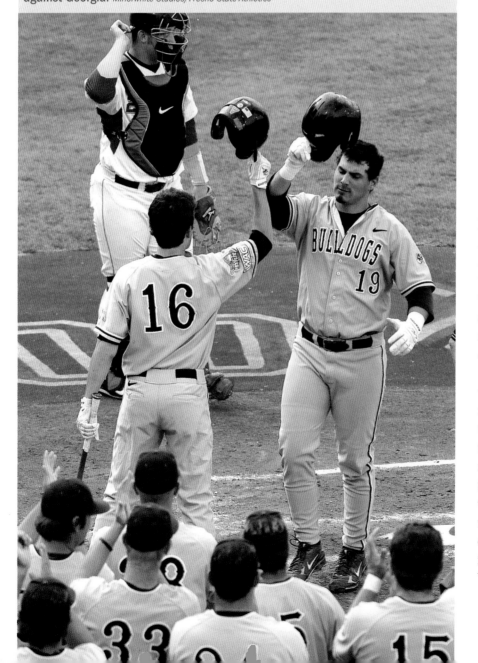

Danny Muno is the first to congratulate Jordan Ribera after circling the bases against Georgia. *Minorwhite Studios/Fresno State Athletics*

envisioned the 2008 season, they could have never imagined their son would be starting the first game of the CWS championship series. But there he was, and Ryan Peisel was ready for him.

The Georgia third baseman was hitting .500 in Omaha, and apparently wasn't content with that as he ripped Bonesteele's first pitch over Tommy Mendonca's head and into left field, then hustled to beat Susdorf's throw to second. Bonesteele bounced back, getting Matt Olson out on a liner to left, then retiring All-American shortstop Gordon Beckham on a pop up to Erik Wetzel.

Rich Poythress, an imposing presence at 6 foot 4 inches and 235 pounds, was up next, and he came up with a clutch two-out single, plating Peisel to put Georgia on the board. That would be the only run Bonesteele allowed, thanks to a Bulldog defense that picked up where it left off the night before. Matt Cerione led off the bottom of the second with a slicing fly ball to deep left field, which Susdorf read well and got to just in time, leaping softly into the wall to make the catch. Susdorf's play drew plenty of applause, but would be upstaged two pitches later with Joey Lewis at the plate to face Bonesteele.

🎙 "Here comes the 1–0, changeup, swung on, hit on the ground left side, a diving stop by Mendonca. He pops to his feet, throws to first, EASY out—5–3 for out number two. I'll tell you what, Ray, if the Bulldogs win the championship, there's your player of the tournament. Mendonca has been SO impressive defensively at third base. That's what everyone around the ballpark has been talking about the last few days."

Hall of Fame pitcher Nolan Ryan smiles as he watches Fresno State and Georgia. To Ryan's left, in the blue shirt, is billionaire investor Warren Buffett. *Jim Leedham*

"Absolutely. THE best defensive third baseman in America." — Ray O'Canto

Perno, the Georgia coach, later referred to Mendonca as "the best defensive third baseman I've seen in a long time." He'd be seeing plenty more of him. Bonesteele retired Lyle Allen on a groundout to Muno to make it a 1–2–3 inning, so it remained a 1–0 lead for Georgia after two innings.

🎙 "Jordan Ribera will lead off the third against Trevor Holder. Left-handed batter swings at the first pitch, hits it well. High in the air, deep to left field. Going back Allen, he won't get there! It's ten rows deep into the seats, and this ballgame is tied. The freshman, Jordan Ribera, unleashing on that first pitch fastball, and towering it high and deep into the left field seats! One apiece now in the top of the third."

Employing that confidence boost he said he got from a home run against Rice, Ribera was helping to transform the bottom of the Bulldog batting order from liability to strength. Bonesteele knew how to make sure it remained tied 1–1 as Georgia came up in the bottom of the third. His secret? Throw strikes and let the defense keep cranking up the "Wow!" factor.

🎙 "Bonesteele winds, first pitch, changeup [ping!], lined into the glove of a leaping Mendonca! Diving toward the third base line, he makes *another* highlight reel play. Where will it end for the sophomore from Turlock? It looked like he had springs in his feet as he pounced toward that third base line and gloved that slicing liner. I don't know if it would have been a fair ball, but either way that was a great play and out number one."

"In-cred-i-ble is all you can say. You know you made a great play when you get Nolan Ryan in the booth clapping for you. That was an absolutely outstanding defensive play." — Ray O'Canto

Steve Susdorf makes a sliding catch to rob Georgia's Matt Olson of a base hit. *Minorwhite Studios/Fresno State Athletics*

Georgia left fielder Lyle Allen reaches over the fence to take a home run away from Steve Susdorf. *Ted Kirk/AP*

Indeed, in the next booth over, Ryan and Warren Buffett were applauding another dazzling defensive display by Mendonca, who would end up earning an invitation to spend the summer traveling the world with Team USA, based solely on his play in Omaha.

Not to be outdone, Steve Susdorf snagged a line drive off Peisel's bat, and then waited to see what Olson would do:

"Two outs, bases empty, tied at one, bottom three. Bonesteele into the windup, his 0–1 pitch, fastball, swung on. That one's lined into shallow left, Susdorf coming on, he slides, and *he makes another catch*! These Bulldogs have been un-believable on defense for the last twelve innings!"

One play like that after another made it abundantly clear why these Diamond Dogs had such unwavering trust in each other. The game was flying along at an impressive pace, with the hitters on both sides aggressively swinging early in counts. Susdorf was ready to try that approach on for size in the fourth.

"Steve Susdorf to lead off the inning, left-handed batter swings at the first pitch, lifts it in the air to left field, hit fairly well. Allen back, onto the track, at the fence, leaps—did he catch it? YES, HE DID, taking a home run away from Steve Susdorf, a great play by the left fielder Allen, and he acted like it was no big deal."

It was definitely a big deal to Holder, who proceeded to set down Ahmady and Mendonca in order. Freshman Jake Floethe took the baton from Bonesteele, and quickly got past Georgia's two power threats, Beckham and Poythress. But a single by lumbering catcher Bryce Massanari and a walk to Cerione gave Joey Lewis a chance to give Georgia the lead back.

"Here comes the 2–1. [ping!] Fastball ripped on the right side, through into right field. That should score a run. Massanari wheeling around third, here comes Detwiler's throw to the plate, he might have him! The tag NOT IN TIME. Overland just got it a split second too late."

Another one of those plays that reinforces baseball's "game of inches" adage, Bryce Massanari's hustle spoiled another near-perfect throw from Detwiler, who counted "Rocket" among his nicknames, but preferred the "Rhino" moniker bestowed by Batesole as a reference to the sophomore's penchant for fearlessly ramming his body into outfield walls.

With Allen's left-handed bat up next, Batesole called in his lone lefty in the bullpen, and Kris Tomlinson (who now had a Fresno State logo carved into the top of that "skullet") again rose to the occasion, needing just one pitch to roll up a ground ball that stranded men on the corners. Now trailing 2–1, the Dogs hoped the bottom of their order could chip away at Holder in the fifth.

Ryan Overland, who set the plate discipline bar high for his teammates

Kris Tomlinson had a Fresno State emblem carved into his "skullet" before he carved one into the Georgia Bulldogs' memory.
Eric Sorenson (below); Tomlinson Family (right)

375

Georgia's Bryce Massanari gets his hand on home plate a split second before Ryan Overland applies the tag. *Eric Sorenson*

all season, worked a leadoff walk, bringing up Detwiler. The Rhino was injured (that torn tendon wouldn't be operated on until after the season), and a little mad after just missing the out at home plate, and now his coach was asking him to bunt Overland to second. Bunting at Holder's first pitch, Detwiler fouled it straight back. Georgia expected to see Detwiler squaring around again on the next pitch.

"Here comes the 0-1, Detwiler swinging away—swings and hits one high in the air, *deep* to left field, they'll have to watch that bounce just in front of the scoreboard! WAY beyond the left field wall, a two-run homer for Steve Detwiler, and Fresno State has its first lead of the game. It is 3 to 2 Bulldogs in the top of the fifth, and again, good thing he didn't get the bunt down."

"He absolutely crushed that ball. Perfect balanced swing, and that ball got out of here in a hurry. It got small very fast." — Ray O'Canto

Detwiler, the seventh different Bulldog to go deep in Omaha, had given Fresno State its first lead of the game. After bouncing his way through the sea of appreciative teammates, Detwiler instinctively reached inside his shirt to clutch the St.

Christopher charm hanging on a chain around his neck. In Roman Catholicism, St. Christopher is the patron saint of travelers, invoked for protection from dangerous obstacles and acts of nature. The reckless abandon with which Detwiler played the game made that pendant a very fitting choice.

Tomlinson made the one-run lead stick with a 1–2–3 fifth inning, highlighted by a hair-raising development that would foreshadow a more light-hearted moment to come. Fooled badly by Tomlinson's 0–1 breaking ball, Olson lost hold of the bat, which went flying toward the first base dugout, narrowly missing Allison and Floethe along the railing.

In the top of the sixth, a one-out triple by Susdorf went to waste when Mendonca and Overland failed to bring him home. Taking over for Tomlinson in the bottom of the inning, Breckley put two outs in the books before Cerione's soft single up the middle plated Poythress with the tying run. It would take another notable defensive effort to end the inning. Charging to field a weak ground ball off the bat of Lewis, Wetzel actually had to curl around umpire Frank Sylvester to get a throw off to Ahmady in time.

After Holder and Breckley traded scoreless seventh innings to keep the score tied at 3–3, Perno brought in left-handed reliever Alex McRee to start the eighth. While Coach Curtis had been studying the tendencies of Georgia's hitters the night before, Batesole had been examining video of Georgia's pitchers. McRee in particular, he'd noticed, had a definite pattern

Ryan Overland congratulates Steve Detwiler on his home run against Georgia.
Minorwhite Studios/Fresno State Athletics

against left-handed batters: he had a hard time throwing off-speed pitches for strikes, and his fastball generally stayed up in the zone and on the inside half of the plate and in. That scouting report, if accurate, would narrow things down for lefties like Susdorf and Mendonca, allowing them to wait for an elevated fastball and drive it.

The hard-throwing southpaw walked Wetzel on five pitches, then Susdorf jumped all over his first-pitch fastball, driving it into right center field for a double that brought Wetzel home with the go-ahead run. Susdorf found success swinging at the first pitch, and Ahmady was hoping to do the same.

🎙 "Now Ahmady swings, rips one hard, right at Beckham. He catches it, dives toward Susdorf, and GOT HIM! A double play!"

Watching it unfold live, I was sure Susdorf had scrambled back to second before Beckham put the tag on him, but the photographic evidence is hard to deny. Without the luxury of that freeze frame, Bulldog fans weren't even bothered by Sylvester's call after what they saw the next hitter do.

🎙 "Here's the 1–2. Swing and a drive, left center field and deep. They won't even chase it. WAY out of the ballpark, a solo home run for Tom Mendonca, and Fresno State leads it 5 to 3."

Batesole's diligent and detailed analysis of the video on McRee had a direct impact on those big moments, and it underscored the mutual trust that had been forged down the stretch of the season. By easing off the reins

Fresno State players duck as Matt Olson's bat comes flying into the dugout.
Eric Sorenson

and trusting his players to be leaders, the coach ended up saying more with less. When something was important enough for Batesole to mention, the players paid extra attention, with a trust in his advice that matched his trust in them.

The Bulldogs would chase McRee, and Detwiler would welcome Justin Earls with a double to right center to make it a 6–3 lead; and that three-run cushion is what Fresno State would lug into the bottom of the eighth. Georgia had already staged a couple of clutch comebacks in Omaha. Opening against #1 seed Miami, the Dawgs trailed 4–3 going to the ninth and were down to their final out before putting together a four-run rally to win 7–4. Against Stanford, it was a 3–2 deficit with two outs in the seventh when Beckham singled to start a two-run outburst and produce a 4–3 victory. Still un-

Erik Wetzel dodges umpire Frank Sylvester to retire Georgia's Joey Lewis at first.
Eric Sorenson

Georgia shortstop Gordon Beckham doubles off Steve Susdorf after catching Alan Ahmady's line drive. *Eric Francis/AP*

beaten in the College World Series, Georgia would need its most impressive comeback effort yet to keep it that way.

Matt Olson led off with a single off of Breckley. The next hitter was Beckham, the #8 overall pick in the major league draft who ranked second in the nation with 26 home runs, but hadn't gone deep yet in Omaha. When his teammates teased him about that, he told them he would hit one when the team needed it the most. Batesole turned to the guy who may have had the biggest hand in getting Fresno State to this point. Offense hogs headlines, but the bullpen had been the difference, and no one had been better than Brandon Burke. Burke hadn't hung a loss on his record since April 26, and had allowed just one home run all season, in 72 innings pitched. The senior came in and quickly fired a changeup for a strike. Beckham choked up, sliding his hands a half-inch higher on the handle of the bat, and resolved to be ready when Burke fired a fastball.

"The 0-1, Beckham swings and drills one, high and deep to left field, the ballpark will not hold that one. A two-run shot, and Georgia is within one in the bottom of the eighth."

With one out and Poythress on first, Georgia struck again. Sometimes it pays to have a baserunner with broad shoulders and a sizable back.

"Runner goes. A swing, and a slicer down the left field line. Fair ball, scooting toward the corner. Poythress heading around third, they're gonna send him on home. Susdorf gets it in to Muno, Muno's throw to the plate, Overland has the ball HIT THE RUNNER IN THE BACK! Muno threw the relay right on the money, but Poythress' big build had that ball hit him square in the 33 on his back. He scores the tying run and Cerione gets all the way to third on the play."

With Cerione at third and still just one out, the Diamond Dogs were forced to bring the infield in, hoping to gun down the runner at home on a sharply hit ground ball. Joey Lewis, a 6 foot 4 inch 220-pound sophomore, battled Burke to a full count.

"Payoff pitch. [ping!] Swung on, hit back past Burke, past Wetzel, OFF THE BAG at second base, ricocheting into left field, the run scores easily, and now Lewis digging for second, he'll get there safely. What a break for Georgia!"

Not only were those Dawgs in the other dugout now ahead 7–6, that 90-degree turn the ball took when it caromed off of second base allowed Lewis to reach scoring position, and there was still only one out. Burke needed to nip the rally in the bud if he wanted to give the offense a shot in the ninth. After retiring Allen on a fly ball to Susdorf in left, Burke got David Thoms to pop out to Muno to end the inning.

The Bulldogs had the top of the order coming up in the top of the ninth, but Muno, Hedstrom, and Wetzel would have to face the most dominating reliever in the country, Joshua Fields. A first-round selection of the Seattle Mariners, the right-hander had converted all 17 of his save situations in 2008. In those 17 appearances, he had allowed just one run and three hits, and for the season, opposing batters were hitting just .137

against him. Fields' first pitch to Muno clocked in at 96 mph. The next one? 97. But velocity doesn't always come with accuracy, and Fields fell behind in the count, three balls and a strike. Muno figured he'd see a pretty good pitch, and he did, bringing the bat around and ripping one down the right field line, but a nice running catch by Olson produced out number one. Reaching 98 on the radar gun against Hedstrom, Fields picked up his 63rd strikeout in just 37 innings on the year.

As Susdorf waited in the on-deck circle for his chance to face the All-American, Wetzel tried to keep the game alive. After taking a strike, and then a ball, Wetzel felt he had timed Fields' fastball, and was ready to swing away:

🎙️ "Here's the 1–1 to Wetzel, swung on and popped up, that should do it. Right side, Thoms, the second baseman, will watch Poythress, the first baseman, take it. And Georgia has won the ballgame. A four-run bottom of the eighth inning to come from behind and beat Fresno State. Game one goes to the Dawgs of Georgia, 7 to 6."

It was eerily reminiscent of the second game against North Carolina, but this time, the Bulldogs didn't have Allison waiting in the wings. Batesole speculated he'd have to use at least a half-dozen pitchers again the next day, and hope they could muster more than the one strikeout against Georgia's hitters they got this time around. Fresno State had gone an uncharacteristic 0-for-7 with runners in scoring position, and that would have to change.

But how much did these Diamond Dogs have left? Had the un-precedented string of upsets finally run its course? Had the "little Bulldog engine that could" run out of steam, like those basketball Cinderellas from Valparaiso, George Mason, and Davidson? Had surrendering that three-run lead in the eighth taken all the wind out of the Dogs' sails, or the fun out of their loose and light-hearted dugout? Asking those kind of questions of Batesole, Mendonca, and Detwiler in the post-game news conference was akin to the 6-year-old asking his dad if Captain Hook is *really* going to kill Peter Pan.

"We've been in this situation in Regionals and Super Regionals and we made it here. Last night? Same position. You can't be angry about every little thing, it's baseball, you're gonna fail. Be loose, be calm, be easy."

— Mendonca

"We're fine, I think we could go out and play another nine right now. We feel good."

— Batesole

"We're gonna come back and do whatever we need to do to win tomorrow, we're gonna come back and have another dogfight."

— Detwiler

Still 18 Innings Away from the Championship (June 24, 2008)

That soggy Saturday against North Carolina paled in comparison to this torrential Tuesday. Heavy, consistent rains throughout the day had everyone around the team hotel wondering if the field would even be playable. Some were even talking about how a rainout might benefit the beleaguered Bulldog pitching staff.

"We're fine, I think we could go out and play another nine right now. We feel good." — Mike Batesole after the 7–6 loss to Georgia.
Minorwhite Studios/Fresno State Athletics

After calling my wife to wish her a happy anniversary—I had sent a poem and flowers and other goodies, too, and trusted my key would still work when I got home—I figured I might as well get to the ballpark early and see for myself what the grounds crew was up against. As I sat in our booth, going through all the preparations for a game I wasn't sure would take place, the heavens unleashed extended waves of pounding rain, rattling off the tarp with a decibel level that rivaled the occasional bursts of thunder. The long lines of lightning ripping above the downtown Omaha skyline beyond left field were much more impressive, and more frequent, than what we'd experienced days earlier.

Establishing our radio connection early, I popped on a headset, cranking up the volume to listen to Fresno's top-rated talk show above the sound of those steady showers that continued to fall. I had seen the Diamond Dogs' incredible run unfold in front of my eyes, and I had seen the highlights airing nationally, but listening to host Ray Appleton, his callers from up and down the state, and the special guests he brought aboard, helped me widen out the lens and get a real taste of how significant this was for the people of the San Joaquin Valley.

Legendary basketball coach Jerry Tarkanian, a Fresno State graduate who won the 1990 NCAA basketball championship with UNLV, called it the most amazing thing he had ever witnessed. "I've never met the baseball coach before," he said, "but when I get up to Fresno, I want to shake his hand. They've made me a baseball fan. I can hardly wait to see the game tonight." Gus Zernial, an All-Star slugger in the majors who later called Fresno State games on the radio, talked about how impressed he was with the team's demeanor, and predicted that the players on this team would be "household names" in Central California for decades to come.

Jim Patterson, who had spent eight years as the mayor of Fresno, commented on how the team's tough and scrappy nature was a reflection of the values and virtues of the people of the San Joaquin Valley. "It transcends sports," Patterson said. "It talks to us about who we are, what our region is like, what we have in our future. We are a place that matters. Whether we win or lose, we've already won." His point was valid—there would be innumerable ancillary benefits of what the Diamond Dogs had done, whether they prevailed or not.

But passing those sentiments on to the guys dancing through puddles toward the third base dugout would not be advisable. The team arrived about two hours before the scheduled start time, right about the time that the rain started to slow down, and a shred of clear sky became visible in the distance.

There were some pretty enormous puddles to reckon with, but the legendary Rosenblatt grounds crew came through again. The game would get underway just twenty-six minutes late this time, and what Fresno State's players did to pass the time is another testament to that "bunch of goofballs" moniker: they found themselves thoroughly entertained by the childhood game of "telephone" in the dugout.

"We're gonna have to score a lot of runs," Batesole said in our pregame visit, "because this is going to be a higher scoring game than yesterday." A bit of an understatement, but very prescient, as was this nugget: "They've been slugged in the mouth plenty of times. They know how to get up off the mat and keep swinging. They're gonna finish this thing, they're gonna fight it out to the end, there's no doubt about it." Mirroring his mantra from the Super Regional in Tempe, Batesole reminded the players that they were in the same position they'd been in before the heartbreaking loss, "still 18 innings away from the championship."

The grounds crew readies Rosenblatt Stadium for Game 2 of the CWS Championship Series. *Eric Sorenson*

Georgia's Dawgs were only nine innings away from holding the trophy, and they didn't wait until the eighth inning to erupt this time. Surrendering singles to Peisel and Beckham, Fresno starter Justin Miller quickly faced a first and third situation with just one out. Miller worked ahead of Poythress, 0–2, then wheeled to first and appeared to have Beckham picked off, only to have Sylvester call him safe.

Poythress poked the next pitch into right field, scoring Peisel, moving Beckham to third—and with Detwiler's throw chasing Beckham to third, Poythress was able to advance to second. Picking up the second out on a Massanari pop up, Miller then walked Cerione intentionally to get the righty-righty matchup against Lewis. The move backfired, as Lewis brought two runs home with a single to center; and when Miller hit Allen with a pitch, the bases were loaded again. Already trailing 3–0, with the red-hot Peisel in the on-deck circle, Miller knew finding a way to get #9 hitter David Thoms out was imperative. The lanky junior used his fastball to get ahead in the count 1–2, then got Thoms swinging on a slider to leave the bases full.

A three-run first did not appear to have rattled Fresno State, but what about a blown call? Would that do the trick? In the bottom of the first, Muno led off with a walk, bringing Hedstrom to the plate:

Mike Batesole arguing a call with umpire Jim Garman.
Minorwhite Studios/Fresno State Athletics

"1–2 to Hedstrom, breaking ball hit on the ground in the hole at short, Beckham will go to second base, they get the out there, or did they? He is out at second base, the ball came loose from the second baseman Thoms, and here comes Mike Batesole to argue that call."

Batesole had a beef. With the luxury of a television monitor in our booth, we could clearly see that Thoms never caught the ball. He was hoping to turn two, and had tried to use the back of his glove to control it and quickly fire to first. Umpire Tony Walsh let Batesole plead his case, but the call stood, and the next hitter, Wetzel, grounded into an inning-ending double play.

Peisel's leadoff single in the second was his 10th hit in just 20 Omaha at bats, and he promptly stole second, then moved to third on Olson's fly ball to center. Beckham walked, then watched Poythress score Peisel with a sacrifice fly to make it 4–0. Georgia was trying to run away with it, and Beckham would continue that aggressive theme with Massanari at the plate.

Erik Wetzel tags Gordon Beckham out at second base, after a perfect throw from Ryan Overland.
Minorwhite Studios/Fresno State Athletics

It was just the third time all season the speedy Beckham had been thrown out, and as the Diamond Dogs congratulated Overland on his way back to the dugout, they hoped that play would spark some offense. Georgia starter Nick Montgomery dismissed that idea, allowing just a Mendonca single in his scoreless second. In the top of the third, Georgia upped the lead to 5–0, when a two-out line drive by Thoms glanced off the glove of a leaping Muno, sneaking through into left field to bring in a run.

Every little detail was tilting in Georgia's favor, and Batesole was ready to change pitchers. In came Holden Sprague, who, thanks to the work of his bullpen buddies, had been able to rest up the day before. Unfazed when Georgia caught yet another break on a pop up that Overland dropped, Sprague stranded two more Georgia runners when he got Peisel swinging on a 3–2 changeup. Peisel had already been up three times, and Steve Detwiler was just stepping up to the plate for the first time. He led off the third with a single, stole second, watched Muno walk again, and then moved to third on Hedstrom's single to left. Detwiler scored when Montgomery uncorked a wild pitch. Wetzel walked to load 'em up again in front of Susdorf, who singled to right, scoring two runs to cut Georgia's lead to 5–3.

Sensing the momentum starting to shift, Perno pulled the plug on Montgomery's outing, calling in another right-hander, Stephen Dodson, from the bullpen to face the lefty Mendonca. "You can bet," Ray O'Canto told our listeners, "they're gonna pitch him really fine, knowing that Overland's on-deck. They're not gonna give him anything that he can hammer."

The thunder three hours earlier had nothing on the reaction of the crowd when Mendonca's majestic blast sailed out. I'll correct myself though—technically not *all* the Bulldog fans were on their feet. Georgia Bulldog fans were probably slumping down in their seats at that moment, especially if you could peer into the future and tell them their team would never again go ahead on the scoreboard in the 2008 College World Series.

But they would tie it, and they'd do that quickly. Beckham followed Olson's leadoff double with an RBI single that upped his average to .409 and knotted things up at 6–6. The bottom of the Bulldog batting order came through again in the bottom of the fourth, with singles by Detwiler and Ribera giving Muno a chance to get the lead back for Fresno State.

"Dodson, the tall right-hander, sets and delivers—the 1-1 to Muno, swung on and driven in the air right center field, that's gonna be extra bases! Scoring easily is Detwiler, Ribera on his way to third, will be waved home by Matt Curtis. Muno's gonna try for a triple! Thoms will eat the ball, scoring is Ribera, Muno a two-run triple, and it's 8 to 6 Fresno State!"

Two batters later, Muno would make it a 9–6 lead, scoring when Wetzel's liner was too hot for Beckham to handle, going in and out of the shortstop's glove. The run chased Dodson, with lefty Will Harvil coming in to face Susdorf. That matchup worked for David Perno when Susdorf went down looking, but then Ahmady doubled, moving Wetzel to third. Perno had already seen two of his pitchers serve up gopher balls for Mendonca, and he didn't want Harvil to become the third. Mendonca was intentionally walked so the southpaw could face Overland's left-handed bat with the bases loaded.

"1-1 to Overland, swung on, lifted in the air, shallow left field. Going out, Beckham, still racing out. Coming in and WATCHING IT FALL IS ALLEN! It's down for a hit! Two runs score, it's 11–6 Bulldogs, and I don't know what the left fielder Allen was thinking there!"

As an announcer, you never want to embarrass a player, regardless of

Tom Mendonca is mobbed by his teammates after giving Fresno State a 6-5 lead over Georgia with his 3-run blast. *Dave Weaver/AP*

which team you're calling the game for, but you're obligated to describe and explain what's unfolding. With Beckham flying far out into left, Allen very leisurely started coming in, and

what should have been a fairly routine catch for the left fielder turned into two more Fresno State runs. Asked about the play after the game, Beckham called Allen one of the best left

Jordan Ribera hustles home on Danny Muno's 2-run triple.
Minorwhite Studios/Fresno State Athletics

fielders he'd ever played with, then added in a frustrated tone, "I thought he would be there."

Overland received a rousing ovation from the Fresno faithful as fellow senior Blake Amador went in to run for him. With Mendonca already at third, Amador's presence made it a special moment for Turlock. The Central California city of 70,000 people now had two native sons on the bases at the same time in the College World Series.

After four innings—less than halfway through the game—it was already 11–6 Fresno State, and after Sprague secured a scoreless top of the fifth, the Bulldog bats came alive again. A Ribera walk, a Muno single, and a Hedstrom double made it 12–6. Then an RBI groundout by Wetzel increased the lead to 13–6. Harvil may

have struck Susdorf out the first time, but that wasn't about to happen again.

"The 1–1 to Steve Susdorf—swung on, ripped! High and deep to right field. Olson going back, the ballpark WILL NOT HOLD IT! Steve Susdorf has done it one more time, a two-run homer, it is 15 to 6 Fresno State. His grandfather was a B-24 bomber pilot in World War II, and he knows how to drop some bombs too. 15 to 6 Fresno State in the bottom of the fifth."

The first time Susdorf looked up at the scoreboard this postseason and saw 15 runs, it was in Long Beach, and the 15 runs belonged to San Diego. That was the day he'd buried his grandfather, Willis Miller. If the

Bulldogs had been playing anywhere but in Southern California, he wouldn't have been able to make the funeral. "I was really thankful it worked out that way," Susdorf said. "He was a great man who really did a lot with his life." Miller flew thirty combat missions during World War II with the 392nd Bomb Group in Europe, earning the Distinguished Flying Cross. He drew on some of those experiences in producing the critically-acclaimed film *Beautiful Dreamer,* a World War II love story starring James Denton. Susdorf's bomb on that Tuesday night in Omaha would definitely have made grandpa proud, and this time seeing 15 runs on the scoreboard felt like a beautiful dream indeed.

With a nine-run lead, Fresno fans felt even bolder about holding up signs reading "Real 'Dawgs are from California," the latest in a series of signs handed out at the team hotel by Chris Pacheco, a former Fresno State football player whose company printed up the signs.

Sprague kept that big lead intact through the sixth inning before Georgia cut it to 15–10 with a four-run seventh. Jake Hower, who had not pitched since the last weekend of the regular season almost six weeks earlier, came in and got the Bulldogs out of the inning. Two walks and a hit batsman loaded the bases for Ahmady in the bottom of the seventh, and his 2-run single to right produced a gridiron-esque score of 17–10. Fresno State, which arrived in Omaha ranked 102nd in the nation in scoring (runs per game), had now become the first team to ever score 16 runs or more twice in the same College World Series.

Danny Grubb's sacrifice fly made it 18–10, and Hower would keep it that way with a scoreless top eighth,

Erik Wetzel congratulates Steve Susdorf after his 39th career home run, tying Lance Shebelut for second in school history behind Giuseppe Chiaramonte.
Minorwhite Studios/Fresno State Athletics

Jim Wilson (left) and Chris Pacheco hold up signs in the stands at Rosenblatt Stadium. It was Pacheco's prerogative to hold that sign however he wanted. His company printed up hundreds of signs to distribute to Bulldog fans in Omaha.
Minorwhite Studios/Fresno State Athletics

Boosters Mary and Herb Fung. Herb is wearing a T-shirt he got at Rosenblatt when Fresno State played in the 1991 CWS. *Fung Family*

Senior RHP Jake Hower is congratulated by fellow pitchers after tossing 3 scoreless innings for his first career save. *Eric Sorenson*

helped out by some more dazzling Diamond Dog defense when Cerione came to the plate:

"The 0–1 is swung on and hit high in the air, deep to right field. Detwiler going back, on the track, reaches up, makes the catch, crashes into the wall, and holds onto the baseball. Steve Detwiler, the rhino in right field, puts a dent in that NCAA sign in the right-center field gap, and that is out number one. His hat's on backwards after that collision. Straighten it out, Steve!"

No wonder he wears that St. Christopher charm around his neck!

Detwiler could now compare Rosenblatt's right-field wall to ones at Louisiana Tech ("that didn't hurt") and Long Beach State ("That one was brick, I was dizzy for about an inning."). He called Omaha's a "soft wall," and when asked what was hurting more, the wall or his shoulder, Detwiler deadpanned, "I think the wall, I heard it talking to me."

An interesting side note on the "warning track power" Cerione displayed there: rumblings from the Georgia dugout included the theory that the balls hit to the track in Omaha were attributable to the bats they were forced to use because of the school's all-sports contract with Nike. Peisel actually told the media what

scared him most about Fresno State was "they swung Easton bats and we didn't." Blaming it on *what* the Bulldogs were swinging doesn't do justice to *how* they were swinging, but that quote would make for a pretty good commercial for the company producing Fresno State's bats.

Wetzel put his Easton to work in the bottom of the eighth, scoring Muno with a single that made Fresno State 10-for-17 at that point with runners in scoring position. That's a far cry from the 0-for-7 the night before. As the game moved to the ninth, all Bulldog eyes were on Hower. The always-smiling senior had been there in Ruston and Long Beach and Tempe, never getting a chance to make a memory of his own on the mound. Now he was three outs away from putting his team in the ultimate game, and by pitching the final three innings could earn the first save of his career.

Peisel's Nike bat couldn't touch a 1–2 fastball, giving Hower his third strikeout of the night. Olson came up next and hit a grounder to Ahmady, with Hower hustling to first to receive the throw for the out. After Beckham reached on a Muno error to extend the game, Hower squared off with Poythress, the big first baseman.

"The 2–1 pitch, fastball, swung on, popped in the air right side, Erik Wetzel backing up onto the outfield grass. He's there, he makes the catch, and your Fresno State Bulldogs will be playing for a national championship tomorrow! What a performance by Mike Batesole and his bunch of determined Dogs!"

Teammates hurried to congratulate Hower, who says he should have been nervous, but instead was "so calm that I may as well have been pitching in an intrasquad game." Going a month-and-a-half without pitching was worth the wait. "I just loved being out there just soaking it in," Hower said. "I finally got my chance to help the team." He was the latest in a growing list of unlikely heroes, an underdog who became a wonderdog when the team was once again faced with elimination.

Coach Perno tried to inject a little levity into the post-game news conference: "We had a tough time defending the post pattern across the middle. Killing us. They missed a late extra point and we tried to hang in there."

Susdorf told the media there was "no panic" in the dugout when the Diamond Dogs fell behind 5–0, and both he and Detwiler pointed to Mendonca's home run as the pivotal moment. "I got lucky," Mendonca said, but Susdorf quickly cut him off.

"I wouldn't call it luck because it's happened 18 or 19 times this year," said Steve. Nineteen, to be exact, including four times in Omaha, which tied a CWS record. That deep ball duo was joined at the podium by Muno and Wetzel, and the players were asked if they could have pictured themselves in this situation when they entered the WAC Tournament. Wetzel responded with a bit of a chuckle, recalling that at that point the Bulldogs were coming off a weekend that saw them lose twice to Sacramento State.

Mendonca jumped in there. "We started playing as a team at that point," he said of the trip to Ruston. "When a team starts playing like a team—not taking selfish at bats, not pitching to get a strikeout, not trying to make a web gem—you're gonna win a lot of ball games."

Batesole couldn't have made the point any better, but he did get the last word in, or last three words, to be exact. "Good job, Danny," he said, as he and the four players rose to leave. The microphone in front of Muno had been unnecessary. The freshman made it through the entire news conference without uttering a single word. Is there a kangaroo court fine for that?

All Eyes on Omaha: Bracing for the Big One

The "Underdog to Wonderdog" story was more than a cute slogan on a T-shirt. It was a feel-good sensation captivating the attention of people all over the country, baseball fans and non-fans alike. Fresnans who had never paid attention to the Diamond Dogs were wearing their red and clearing their calendars. All over the country, people with no connection to Fresno or the team tuned in, simply to find out if one of the biggest longshots in sports history could really finish the job.

While many of the players' parents were still in Omaha, some had been forced to return home because of other commitments. Holden Sprague's mother, Lesley, didn't tell any of her friends she was back from Omaha, preferring to nervously watch it all play out from the solitude of her Fresno living room. Danny Grubb's father, Gary, did the same in Orange County, using his DVR to replay each pitch a time or two. Steve Detwiler's parents had already made two round trips from the Bay Area to Omaha, and now they were back in Marin County, heading to the local saloon to watch the final game of the college baseball season.

Longtime boosters Jim and Sharlene Gomes had been in Omaha until

business sent them to Lake Tahoe. There they found conference-goers from places like Tennessee, Minnesota, and Iowa cheering along with them with every thrilling moment of those first two games against Georgia. Most of those folks couldn't believe the couple had been at Rosenblatt and left. Driving from Tahoe, they would make it home to Lemoore in Kings County roughly an hour before the final game began. No matter where they were, Sharlene Gomes says, "It was amazing, it was magical, it was a journey we would cherish, wherever we watched, cheered, and cried."

Clovis baseball fan Tom Wright was in Williams, Arizona, near the Grand Canyon, and was pleasantly surprised to pick up KMJ's signal on his AM radio. His brother Russ, of Atascadero, had taken his wife Judi to a bluegrass concert at a San Luis Obispo restaurant. The performer finally gave up when it became clear the sound system could not compete with the parade of roars emanating from the crowd glued to the game on the TV at the bar.

Pat Ogle, executive director of the Bulldog Foundation—the booster group that funds scholarships for student athletes—was following the games from Carmel. With a stunning Pacific Ocean vista right behind the TV, the Ogles matched ESPN's video with our radio calls. Wearing a Fresno State hat whenever he golfed that week, Pat received countless comments about the Bulldogs, highlighted by the gentleman in the pro shop who had to share how proud he was of his grandson, Tommy Mendonca.

No one had more fans in more places than Mendonca, but his uncle Lenny has to take the cake. Lenny and his wife Christine were celebrating their 25th anniversary with a two-week trip to Italy, bringing their two daughters along for the ride. The time difference between Omaha and Rome meant they'd have to stay up until 1 a.m. just to hear the first pitch, which they did religiously, tapping into the internet feed of our radio broadcast from across the Atlantic. Putting in a good word for the Diamond Dogs at the Vatican on June 24th, they stayed up until the wee hours of the morning to hear the last of those 19 runs cross home plate.

The next day, the day of the final game, was also the day of their anniversary. After visiting an ancient precursor to Rosenblatt, the Coliseum, as well as the Forum, they had one more stop to make. "We all went to the Trevi Fountain," Lenny said, "and threw a euro over our shoulders. I wished that Tom would be named MVP." He would need plenty of strong Italian cappuccino if he was going to stay up long enough to find out if that wish came true.

Georgia had won the coin flip, so just as they had been for the deciding game in Tempe, the Diamond Dogs would be the visiting team. They had worn their gray uniforms and lost to Georgia, then scored 19 while wearing white, but Georgia would be wearing white. As the starting pitcher, Wilson had the honor of choosing which uniforms they'd don for the final game. Brandon Burke was quick to lobby Wilson for red. "I liked the red jerseys, and we never got to wear 'em," said Burke, who was willing to pull out all the stops. "Dude, you look so much better in red," he told Wilson. "It's a slimming color." Wilson gave his blessing, and everyone in the clubhouse seemed to like the idea.

As they made their way to the stadium one last time, it would have been easy to feel a little overwhelmed by the emotion of it all, the magnitude of their previously unthinkable real-

ity hitting home. Every game they had ever played, all those backyard swings with their dads, every minute spent mastering the mechanical minutiae of pitching, hitting, and fielding—it had all prepared them for this one and only shot at baseball immortality. They would be representing a lot more than twenty-five players and four coaches in the dugout. They'd be stepping out onto that diamond as the personification of a program, a university, a community, the Valley that green "V" on their helmets represented, and of underdogs everywhere who had latched onto their remarkable story.

A quick scan of the stands that day revealed key figures from great Bulldog teams who never made it quite this far. Lock eyes with Lance Shebelut, whose school-record 32 home runs in 1988 had carried the Dogs to a #1 national ranking before going 0–2 in Omaha. Look further and find Bobby Jones and his family of five. Jones had tossed a one-hitter to outduel good friend and fellow Bulldog Mark Gardner to send the Mets to the 2000 World Series. The 1991 Fresno State squad he starred on had gone 1–2 in Omaha, and he was counting on these young men to finish the job, especially since he had coached many of them, including starting pitcher Wilson, two years prior.

Pete Beiden's 1959 squad, which lost a coin flip to Arizona for a spot in the title game and finished third at the CWS after a loss to Oklahoma State, had been represented at Rosenblatt by outfielder Merv Carter and Augie Garrido, who had since gone on to claim four NCAA championships as a coach. Gardner, now the San Francisco Giants' bullpen coach, had played on the 1984 Bulldog squad which won a then-school record 54

games but didn't make it to Omaha. He was in Cleveland with the Giants, who, he told Ray Appleton's radio audience that day, were all rooting for Fresno State.

Listening and watching back in Central California were figures like Bob Bennett, who succeeded his mentor Beiden and went on to coach the Dogs for 34 years; and Fibber Hirayama, the diminutive dynamo of the 1951 team which finished 36–4, but could not reach Omaha under the then-invitation only format, seeing its hope of battling USC for one of those eight invites go unfulfilled.

Six decades of unfinished business and unrealized dreams were riding on their shoulders. None of that was even on the radar screen for the guys in the red shirts. "Just another game," said Detwiler. "If we play it like a national championship game and we get all tense, we're not gonna be our goofy selves out there." In case you weren't paying close enough attention, "goofy," for this team, was good.

The Ultimate Do-or-Die Stage (June 25, 2008)

Given all the talk of "magic" and "divine intervention" that had accompanied Fresno State's unprecedented journey to the brink of a national championship, it's not surprising that the Diamond Dogs began their final game of the season by kneeling in prayer. So who would it be, giving voice to their most heartfelt plea of the year? Susdorf, the guy who wrote "Luke 9:26" on his glove as a junior as a reminder of who he was ultimately playing for? Ahmady, whose mother proclaimed her faith so freely and fervently? Grubb, the kid from Orange Lutheran High, a school that lists "For His Glory" as its theme for the year? No, no, and not him either.

Jordan Ribera (#19) leads Fresno State's prayer before the CWS championship game. *Minorwhite Studios/Fresno State Athletics*

It would be freshman Jordan Ribera, who had been Fresno State's pregame prayer leader all season long. The son of a Fresno pastor, Ribera is a natural leader who starred at linebacker for three years in one of the best high school football programs in California. In fact, Bulldog football coach Pat Hill invited Ribera to join his team as a walk-on, believing he'd earn his way onto the field. Ribera loved football, and says he still does. But when he broke his wrist in Fresno's famed City-County All-Star Game, he took it as a sign from God that baseball, not football, would be the right athletic path to pursue. The last six weeks had certainly cemented that feeling in his mind.

When the Bulldogs took off those red caps and bowed their heads, Ribera's words would reflect back in thanks as much as they projected forward in anticipation. "Help us remember who gave us the ability to even be athletes," he prayed, "and how blessed we are to play this game called baseball and represent Fresno. Let us honor you in victory and defeat. Thank you for bringing our team so close this year, and for helping us through struggling times. Give us the strength to play one more game. And most importantly, Lord, help us to go out there and have fun, and represent you every chance we get. Amen."

If Batesole looked thinner as he walked out to exchange lineups with Perno, perhaps his only half-kidding comment in our pre-game interview provided the explanation. "I haven't slept much, and I haven't been able to eat much for about two months now," the coach said. "We've kind of been in that mode of knock it out or go home for a lot of weeks now."

It had now been forty-one days since they opened that final regular season series in Sacramento, and they'd been living out of their big Easton duffel bags ever since. Georgia on the other hand, after an early exit from the SEC tournament in Alabama, had been home for the Regional and Super Regional rounds and didn't have to leave Athens until heading to Omaha. The lineup Batesole delivered from home plate served as another reflection that trust existed, not just from teammate to teammate, but from coach to player as well.

Since cementing Wetzel, Susdorf, and Ahmady as the 3–4–5 hitters in Hawaii in March, Batesole had been very consistent with his batting order. When facing a right-handed starter, Mendonca would bat sixth, Overland seventh, and Detwiler eighth. But whenever a lefty was on the hill, Detwiler would be the sixth man up, with Mendonca behind him. Mendonca had been an equal-opportunity destroyer in Omaha, pounding pitches regardless of which hand delivered them. His most impressive blast had come off Georgia's top lefty reliever, McRee.

With southpaw Nathan Moreau making the start for Georgia, I was curious to see if Batesole would let the red-hot Mendonca bat sixth. When I asked him about it in the dugout before the game, the coach said, "I thought about it, but I decided we've got to stick with what got us here." Batesole had to practice what he was preaching. If he expected the players to trust each other unconditionally, he would have to demonstrate his trust and belief in them.

Another reflection of Batesole's priorities came in his handling of Justin Wilson. Thirty seconds with Wilson is enough to give you a taste of his competitiveness, his will to win. Packing his 6 foot 3 inch frame with 210 pounds, he's a little thicker than the prototypical pitcher, and he's a little tougher too. Spend a little longer and you'll catch a glimpse of his softer side: the genuine look in his eye when he says "thank you," the patience and sincerity he displays around young autograph seekers, that bracelet around his wrist, honoring his fallen friend. Combine the unshakable drive that helped him lead Buchanan High School to its first CIF Central Section title (wearing red jerseys, coincidentally), with that big heart that had him wanting to win the championship for his teammates and his family as much as for himself, and you end up with a guy who didn't want to take "no" for an answer.

Accustomed to pitching on six days rest, the standard for a college starter, Wilson had asked Batesole to

let him take the mound the night before, which would have been just *two* days rest. The season was on the line, there was no guarantee of another game, but the coach wouldn't budge. Wilson's health and imminent pro career were too important to risk for a game, no matter how significant that game might be.

"We tried to do things right," the coach said in our pre-game interview, "and maybe it's gonna end up right for us because of that. We're hoping to get three innings out of him, maybe four. He's still going on short rest even today, but he'll gut it up and give us everything he has."

Wilson wasn't thinking about how many innings he'd last, how many pitches he'd throw, or how many days it had been since he pitched. "All I knew," said Wilson, "was that it was my last college start regardless. I wasn't gonna hold anything back. I just wanted to blow it out and compete."

Before he could do that, he had to watch his Georgia counterpart, Moreau, work a scoreless top of the first, allowing just a single to Hedstrom. If Wilson was looking to set a tone with the first batter he faced, he accomplished it with the way he pitched to Peisel, who stepped up still hitting .458 for the CWS. Firing fastball after fastball, Wilson saw the count go to 2–2 on the Georgia lead-off man.

 "The wind by Wilson, the 2–2 pitch, fastball, CALLED STRIKE THREE on the inside corner! Perfect location at 90 miles an hour."

Not to pick on Peisel, but those Nike bats really can't help you when you leave them on your shoulder. Wilson would allow a two-out single

to Beckham, but then end the inning on a Poythress pop up. Poythress, the hefty first baseman, almost robbed Susdorf a few moments later, leaping and getting a glove on a rocket line drive that bounced out of the webbing and allowed Susdorf to reach first. After Ahmady flied out to left, up came Detwiler, his average for the College World Series at .231, and that tendon in his left hand still waiting for the surgery that would have already taken place if the Bulldogs hadn't kept extending their season.

As long as he made contact, the hand was OK, but when he swung and missed at Moreau's 2–1 offering, the pain in his thumb was written all over his face. The next pitch came inside and Detwiler turned his hips in, hoping to get hit and take his base. He didn't lean in quite enough, so the count went full, and the battle intensified. The sophomore fouled off two 3–2 pitches before Moreau finally gave him what he wanted:

"He'll come home with another 3-2, Detwiler swings, hits it in the air down the right field line. This ball's hit well! Olson going back, at the track, at the fence, he leaps, HE CAN'T CATCH IT! It's over the fence, a home run for Steve Detwiler, and Fresno State has a 2-nothing lead in the top of the second inning! How's *that* for opposite field power?"

The Paper Mill Creek Saloon in Forest Knolls, California got pretty loud right about then, and 18,932 at Rosenblatt weren't exactly quiet. Georgia's "Junkyard Dogs" threatened to take a bite out of that 2–0 lead in the second. Massanari reached on Muno's error, then Cerione singled him to second. In what would typi-

THE CWS CHAMPIONSHIP SERIES: THE ULTIMATE STAGE

cally be a bunting situation (2 on, 0 out), Perno elected to let Joey Lewis swing away, which only heightened Wilson's focus. The pitcher had been called "Wild Thing" more times than he could count, thanks to struggles with his control over the years. There would be no wildness on this hot and humid Heartland evening. Not here, not now.

With pinpoint precision, making the ball go exactly where he wanted it to, Wilson struck out Lewis on three pitches, capping it off with a late-breaking curveball that made the hitter look silly. Lyle Allen, a lefty, looked even sillier when Wilson did the same to him for the second out.

Miles Starr proved a little scrappier, fouling off five two-strike pitches before hitting a one-hopper to Muno that should have ended the inning. But the freshman shortstop, all of a sudden appearing tentative after playing so flawlessly for weeks, committed his second error of the inning, throwing high to Wetzel at second to load the bases. The dangerous Peisel was coming up with a chance to tie it or give Georgia the lead.

"Here's the 1–0. [ping!] Swung on, driven in the air, right center field, that ball's hit well! Hedstrom going back, Hedstrom approaching the track, reaches up on the track and makes a running catch to end the inning."

No more Nike/Peisel references, I promise, but how about Hedstrom? He had experienced a couple adventures in the outfield earlier in the week, but in this game, in this bases loaded situation, he had the perfect read, got the perfect jump, and made the perfect play, keeping that 2–0 lead intact. His 10-year-old brother

Steve Detwiler hits an opposite field home run just beyond the reach of Georgia right fielder Matt Olson. *Minorwhite Studios/Fresno State Athletics*

Kenan, back again from Southern California, smiled ear to ear.

Moreau retired the Bulldogs in order in the third. Wilson recorded another zero of his own, ending the frame with his fourth strikeout when he got Massanari swinging. In the fourth, Fresno State had Susdorf at first with two outs when Moreau's first pitch to Detwiler bounced away from the catcher Lewis. Susdorf broke for second, then watched the catcher's throw sail into center field. What did Detwiler see? Another run 90 feet and one swing away.

"Moreau sets and delivers. [ping!] Detwiler swings and hits this one well, left center field, that ball's hit well! Cerione going back, onto the track, he dives, it's bouncing off the track and off the wall! Susdorf

scores easily with two outs, Detwiler stops at second base, claps his hands a couple times—he's *always* pumped up, and he's given the Diamond Dogs a 3-nothing lead."

I guess trusting Detwiler to handle that No. 6 spot in the order was a pretty wise decision. As for Wilson, remember the coach had said he expected the left-hander to last three innings, maybe four? But Justin was just picking up steam. Cerione led off the inning, checking his swing on a 1–2 fastball he thought was outside. Home plate umpire David Wiley called it strike three, and Cerione proceeded to launch an extended excoriation of Wiley which, if this weren't the national championship game, might have produced an ejection.

The next batter, Lewis, hit a fly ball off the wall in center that Hedstrom felt he should have caught. Feeling the wall with his right hand, he just missed the ball with his glove, and Lewis ended up on third with a triple. Now a sac fly could get Georgia on the board, but Wilson would have none of that. He struck out Allen for the second time, then that pinpoint control experienced a hiccup. The first pitch to Starr was so high it almost sailed to the backstop, but Grubb exploded out of his crouch, leaping in the air to catch it and prevent Lewis from scoring. Wilson fired two strikes to get ahead 1–2, then used a fastball to brush Starr off the plate and set up what happened next.

"Here's the 2–2 to Starr, CALLED STRIKE THREE! Froze him with a fastball at 92 miles an hour on the inside corner. Justin Wilson nothing short of spectacular through the first four innings."

So at the point where Batesole expected his lefty to be running out of gas, Wilson picked up his seventh strikeout with a pitch that marked his highest velocity of the night. After Moreau made quick work of the Dogs in the top of the fifth, Wilson walked out for what would looked like a pivotal inning. Not only was it the halfway point of the game, Georgia had the top of its order coming up,

and if Wilson could keep the 3–0 lead intact here, the pressure would start to mount on the guys in white.

Peisel grounded out to Mendonca at third. Ahead 0–2 on Olson, Wilson slipped on his follow through and came up rubbing his left hand as if he'd hurt it. Batesole started out of the dugout, but Wilson quickly waved him off and got back on the mound, moments later making Olson his eighth strikeout victim of the night. That brought up Beckham, who had gone 1-for-2 so far and actually seen his CWS average go *down* to .524. Continuing to employ the best command of his career, Wilson avoided giving Beckham anything good to hit, with the count

Steve Detwiler follows the path of his second home run in the championship game. *Eric Sorenson*

going full before a pop up to right ended the inning.

Perno lifted the lefty Moreau for right-hander Dean Weaver to start the sixth, and the reliever responded with two quick outs. Fresno State just couldn't let the final game of the year go by without one more two-out rally. It started with Susdorf breaking one more record. Missing a home run by about three feet when his drive bounced off the left field wall, Susdorf cruised into second with the 70th double of his career, eclipsing Joe Xavier's school record. He also extended his own single-season record for two-baggers to 33.

Ahmady was up next, fully aware that he needed one RBI to match Florida State's Buster Posey for the national lead, two to tie Lance Shebelut's Bulldog record. It wasn't time to start getting selfish now. After falling behind 0–2, Ahmady patiently drew a walk, bringing up the guy who would later say, "It was a good time to have a good day."

"Here's the pitch to Detwiler, swung on and CRUSHED! HIIIIGH and DEEEEP to left field, the stands barely hold that one, a mammoth home run off the bat of Steve Detwiler! A three-run blast, his second homer of the game, and Fresno State's lead has just doubled—it's six to nothing in the top of the sixth inning! What is flowing through the veins of the sophomore from San Rafael? He's headbutting his teammates as he tries to get back to the dugout. They won't get out of his way. He is fired up and for good reason. He has driven in all six Fresno State runs in this game."

This celebration was the "Tiger Woods" times ten. But maybe it was a

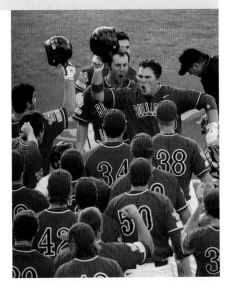

An energized Steve Detwiler celebrates with teammates after his second home run of the game. The celebration was so intense, he lost a pendant off the chain around his neck. *Minorwhite Studios/Fresno State Athletics*

Justin Wilson threw 129 pitches in 8 innings, striking out 9 while allowing just 1 run. *Andrew Dean*

Justin Wilson's family cheering section for his final college game included his sister, Jil, and her sign calling him her hero. *Wilson Family*

little too intense. When Detwiler reached for that St. Christopher charm, it was nowhere to be found. It must have come off somewhere between home plate and the dugout, he figured, and he continued to look for it until it was time to take the field.

How long could Wilson go? Two quick outs in the bottom of the sixth brought up Cerione, who had drawn the ire of Bulldog fans with his unsportsmanlike display after striking out. Two days earlier, Olson had created a scare in the Fresno dugout when his bat went flying there, bouncing off the railing.

Cerione had similar aim here, getting it past the railing and off the bench, and sending Justin Miller diving out of the way. Jake Floethe picked up the bat and tossed it back to Cerione, who had walked over that way. The next time Cerione swung the bat (even though he held onto it this time), all the Bulldogs jokingly flinched, ducking behind the dugout

railing. "*That's* what we're doing in a national championship series? *That's* how loose we are?" Batesole reflected. "There's nothing that's not real about that."

And Wilson was in a real zone. When Mendonca made another nice play at third and threw Cerione out at first, Wilson had retired eight in a row and sent the Bulldogs to the seventh with a 6–0 lead. If the reaction to Cerione's bat-chucking didn't demonstrate the kind of rapport that existed in the Bulldog dugout, what Wilson did in the bottom of the seventh hammered it home. He had gotten the first two outs with just four pitches, and it looked like it would be a five-pitch inning when Starr swung at the first pitch and hit it right at Muno. The freshman took his eye off the ball for a split second and it scooted right under his glove, right between his legs, and into left field.

How did Wilson react to his shortstop's third error of the game?

We watched him step off the mound, walk toward Muno, mutter something quickly, then walk back to the mound with a wry smile on his face. Muno wore a bit of a smirk as well. So what did Wilson say? Both players confirm it was a remark normally reserved for a proctologist's office. In that case, it would be protected by doctor/patient privilege, which "Dr. Wilson" would like to claim in this instance, too. "It made me laugh," says Muno, who wasn't strung quite as tight after their brief exchange.

Wilson wasn't the only one to give Muno a hard time. "He comes in the dugout and they're checking his eyes and they're calling him a spy, 'tell the mole to go sit down by the water cooler' kind of stuff," said Batesole. "This is a national championship game, and instead of guys getting tight and getting on each other, this is the same exact stuff you do out on the playground. The purest form of playing is what they were doing."

After walking Peisel, Wilson stranded two more Georgia Dawgs when he got Olson to fly out to center. Detwiler still hadn't found that St. Christopher pendant, and it was starting to bother him. He would be due up fourth in the eighth, and as a comfort measure, he undid his belt and shook out his pants a little to get rid of any irritating dirt. Falling to the dugout floor was that metallic charm—it had apparently been stuck in his pants since his home run in the sixth.

He delivered a single in the eighth, finishing the night 4-for-4. Fresno State did not score in the eighth, but Georgia did. Beckham led off with his 28th home run of the year, tying him for the national lead. Wilson responded by pulling a pair of pop ups out of Poythress and Massanari, bringing Cerione up with two outs. By this point, it was fair to say Cerione was the least popular player in the Fresno State dugout. Wilson, who Batesole had said would pitch three or four innings, had now fired 124 pitches. He knew this call-arguing, bat-losing lefty would be the last hitter he faced as a Fresno State pitcher. When Cerione fouled off a 2–1 fastball, Wilson knew he had him right where he wanted him.

"Here's the 2–2 to Cerione, fastball, CALLED STRIKE THREE! Listen to this place go nuts! [crowd roars] Fresno State players out of the dugout to congratulate Justin Wilson on his ninth strikeout of the ballgame. He goes *eight* innings."

Not surprisingly, Wilson ranks that last pitch of his college career as his most memorable moment on the mound. Wilson had enjoyed a very successful Bulldog career, but had the

southpaw's pitch location ever been that outstanding? The only one who can answer that with some degree of certainty is Danny Grubb. "Never," the catcher said with a smile. "He had an out of body experience."

The Bulldogs didn't score in the top of the ninth, but Batesole found a way to give a pair of freshmen a piece of the championship game action. Nick Hom, limited by a hand injury to just 27 at bats all year, came up and delivered a solid single. Fellow frosh Trent Soares went in to run for him, stealing second on McRee's 2–1 breaking ball, then moving to third on Grubb's groundout to first. After McRee struck out Muno, Perno called Fields out of the bullpen to face Hedstrom. The National Stopper of the Year had been reduced to an afterthought. Fields got Hedstrom to ground out to end the inning. In the biggest game of the year, Georgia's most dominating weapon threw all of three pitches.

Since Clayton Allison had played such a huge role in getting the Diamond Dogs to the championship se-

ries, Batesole wanted him to be a part of it. The senior took over on the mound, but quickly gave up a single and a walk, and exited to a standing ovation from the Fresno State cheering section as Burke came in to face David Thoms. Burke had been on the mound in Ruston when the Bulldogs won the WAC tournament. Same story in Long Beach when they wrapped up the Regional, and of course, the Super Regional in Tempe. He had closed out the win over North Carolina to earn the date with Georgia, and now, in the senior's college finale, he needed three outs to deliver a national championship. In the stands, cancer survivor Debbie Burke cheered as the youngest of her four children stepped onto the mound. Standing next to her? Her husband Mike. Battling prostate cancer, Mike was skipping out on chemotherapy in San Diego to be in Omaha.

Brandon Burke said seeing his parents endure what they have has changed his perspective on everything in life: "Every day I get to play baseball, I don't take any of that for

Mike and Debbie Burke watch their son, Brandon Burke, pitch in the ninth inning of the championship game against Georgia. *Fung Family*

Steve Detwiler celebrates the final out, then sticks the ball in his pocket.
Getty Images / Kevin C. Cox

Whether all that good-natured ribbing had anything to do with it or not, when it mattered the most, Muno looked comfortable and confident at short as he started that 6–4–3 double play. Lewis had advanced to third, and Burke worked out of the windup against Peisel. A 2–2 fastball looked so much like a game-ending strike that it sounded like the entire stadium gasped when home plate umpire David Wiley called it ball three. Peisel ended up walking to put men on the corners, and the thought immediately entered my mind: how perfect would it be to watch Burke seal the national championship with one more manifestation of his one-of-a-kind pickoff move?

When I saw Ahmady settle in well behind the bag at first, I realized it wasn't going to happen that way, and I'm glad. The ensuing pitch could not have found a more fitting destination.

granted, and I don't take any time I get to spend with my parents for granted." He added that he's learned to tell the difference between things he can control, and things he can't. "That's why I was so fine in clutch situations, when some guys have their hearts beating out of their chest," said Burke. "My mom always says worrying is like a rocking chair, it gives you

something to do, but it's not gonna get you anywhere, so I stopped worrying a long time ago." That even applied to his blown save two nights earlier against Georgia. "I wasn't bent out of shape about it," Burke remembered. "I knew if I got another chance, it wasn't gonna happen again." That second chance had now arrived.

Steve Detwiler holding the ball from the final out, after having surgery to repair the torn tendon in his left hand. *Marin Independent Journal*

Ray O'Canto enthused:

"Get dirty, baby, get dirty, get dirty, get dirty! Whooo!"

Then I added:

"Oh my goodness. From where they were to where they are now. The entire Central Valley's going nuts, and listen to 'em in Omaha! [crowd roars] The unbelieva-Bulldogs write one more chapter in this incredible story. Senior Steve Susdorf pumping his arms on the field. Brandon Burke wheeling his jersey around his head, screaming in excitement. They are finally lettin' it all out. They had such a cool, a calm, a peace about 'em, for their entire stay here in Omaha, and now they have reason to celebrate, and celebrate all night."

After celebrating the final out, Brandon Burke would soon find himself at the bottom of a dogpile. *Minorwhite Studios/Fresno State Athletics*

A joyous dogpile. *Minorwhite Studios/Fresno State Athletics*

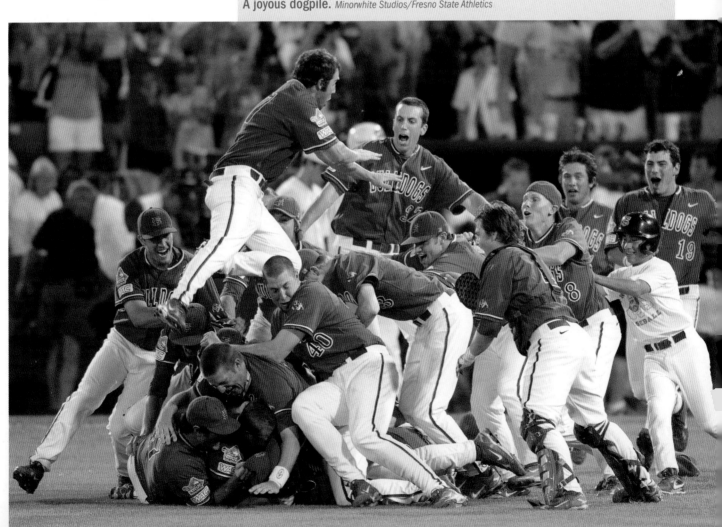

The NCAA Champion Fresno State Bulldogs pose with the trophy. *Eric Sorenson*

Having seen Susdorf make the clinching catch in Tempe and then throw the ball up into the air, Detwiler knew exactly what to do with this one. A split second after squeezing that final out, he was depositing the ball in his back pocket for safekeeping, and that image of a multitasking Detwiler screaming in celebration and storing the ball away at the same time remains one of the signature scenes of this unprecedented accomplishment.

If you were watching ESPN's telecast that night, the next thing you saw was Mike Batesole in the dugout, down on one knee, with his head bowed. "The very first thing that I wanted to do," Batesole said, "was to thank the Good Lord for allowing me to be the head baseball coach at Fresno State for another day. That's exactly what went through my mind. The second thing was, 'where's my assistant coaches?' I had to find them and give them a big hug."

He averaged about two hugs a minute for the rest of the night, but none meant quite as much as the one he shared once his wife, Susie, made it down to the field. "I am his biggest fan," said Susie, "and I had no doubt that he'd be knocking on the door of a national championship someday. I never imagined it happening the way it did." Who could have? Who in his right mind would have predicted that Fresno State, a team that through 64 games had just two wins over ranked teams, would storm through a gauntlet of 14 games, all against teams ranked in the top 15, and win the 10 that mattered most? But there the Wonderdogs were, hoisting the championship trophy.

In sports bars all over the San Joaquin Valley, in living rooms and automobiles concentrated there and scattered across the country, and even in one hotel room in Rome, where it was now a little after five in the morning, the euphoria was as genuine as it was on that field. This was a victory, yes, for underdogs everywhere, but more than anything, it was a victory the players wanted to share with their families, to bask in the championship glow with the people who had been there every time there was no happy ending.

Kenan Hedstrom beat all the parents down to the field, thanks to his big brother's thoughtfulness. As soon as he emerged from the dogpile, Gavin motioned for Kenan to come to the fence, then lifted the 10-year-old over so he could join in the celebration. By the time Hedstrom's' parents made it down in their now ubiquitous T-shirts, Mark was as proud of Gavin for that act of brotherly love as for that grand slam in Tempe.

"This is way better than chemo" was the thought running through Mike Burke's mind as he celebrated with his son on the field. All the surgeries on Debbie's leg had made stairs a challenge for her, so she stayed in the stands, waiting only a few minutes before Brandon raced up to join her in an emotional embrace.

An emotional Dave Wetzel hugged his hard-working son, con-

Justin Wilson shows off the trophy for the fans in the stands.
Minorwhite Studios/Fresno State Athletics

vinced that high above the celebratory scene that graces this book's cover, Erik's late mother Cathy had a finger pointed right back at him, with a smile even wider than his.

The Tomlinson family photos are perhaps the most unforgettable. As if his now world-famous "skullet" wasn't conspicuous enough, Kris emerged from the dogpile with a substantial shiner under his right eye.

The only other left-handed pitcher on the team was part of a quartet of Bulldogs joining Batesole

in the media room. Expected to last four innings, tops, Wilson had turned in the longest outing for any pitcher in the 2008 College World Series. The coach said he could see it all coming. "It was over when I saw the look in his eye in the first inning," said Batesole. "There was no doubt in my mind that it was over. It didn't really matter who we were playing or who was in the other dugout, it was gonna get done. I knew when I saw that look in his eye that he was going to do everything

The Wonderdogs are surrounded by photographers as they pose with the trophy. *Jim Leedham*

Erik Wetzel with his late mother, Cathy, in the 2006 season. Cathy succumbed to cancer just months after that season ended. *Wetzel Family*

Erik Wetzel points heavenward from atop the dogpile. *AP*

he had to bring it home, and that's exactly what happened."

One reporter asked Detwiler to explain his magical night, employing a label that the sophomore objected to. "I wouldn't say it's a one-man wrecking crew," responded Detwiler. "Everyone took good at bats. As a team we're always paying attention and trying to pick up patterns. I got lucky and capitalized on a few of them."

The pitchers weren't going to let him get away with that. "You can't say you got lucky," Wilson interjected. Burke, sitting next to Detwiler, grabbed a printout of the box score to use as Exhibit A, pointed to Detwiler's line and said, incredulously, "We only scored six runs, and you knocked 'em all in." Laughter exploded throughout the room as Detwiler reluctantly conceded with a sheepish grin.

Burke recalled seeing a quote in Arizona State's dugout during the Super Regionals. "It said 'It's amazing what a group of guys can accomplish when no one cares who gets the credit,'" Burke related. "That sums up our team this year," he added.

Calling the Bulldog victory a "great thing for college baseball," Susdorf told the gathering of reporters that it proved you don't have to have a first-round draft pick to win it all. "We're all committed to the team. No one was about themselves. It just goes to show you, you don't need that amazing player to win a national championship, it's just everyone working together."

Hearing those comments from his seniors made Batesole beam even brighter. The coach talked about the leadership of his eight seniors, on and off the field, and the simple message their accomplishment sent to the rest of college baseball: "You don't have to just go for three years and sign, and think about yourself. You can take care of your teammates, you can have your degree when you leave, *and* get a ring." Six weeks earlier, they didn't know if they'd even be in the NCAA Tournament. Now they could reflect on wiping out six top 15 teams, including the best hitting squad (Arizona State), and statistically the best pitching staff (North Carolina) in the nation.

What they accomplished is absolutely staggering. Mind-numbingly magnificent. Or, as Burke said, inconceivable. There was no magic elixir, no shortcut, no secret advantage that could create an asterisk in the annals of baseball history. The crowning characteristic of this championship? It was pure. The secret that transformed underdogs into wonderdogs was really no secret at all. They did it by sincerely seeking the same values and virtues we all can access if we find the discipline and desire to do so. It took trust. It took heart. It took perseverance and cooperation. It took dedication and belief, courage and sacrifice. In the end, it took our breath away.

Easily lost in all the post-game comments is perhaps the truest reflection of the unique distinction this team will hold among all the teams Batesole has coached. "The only thing I'm not feeling that great about right now, " Batesole said, "is that we don't get to play again next weekend."

Kris Tomlinson poses with his mother, Nancy. Under the shadow of Tomlinson's cap, you can make out a black eye sustained in the dogpile. *Eric Sorenson*

Tom Mendonca accepts his College World Series Most Outstanding Player trophy from College World Series president Jack Diesing, Jr. *Eric Sorenson*

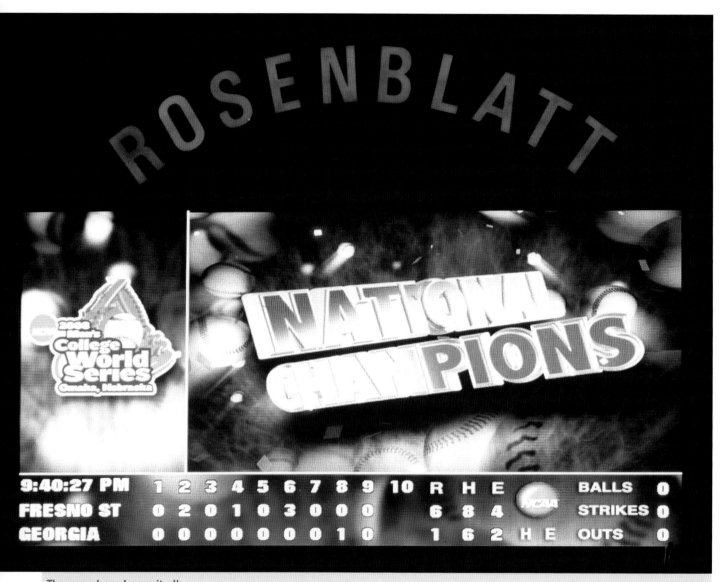

The scoreboard says it all. *Minorwhite Studios/Fresno State Athletics*

College World Series Championship Series Summary

Georgia 7, Fresno State 6
Fresno State 19, Georgia 10
Fresno State 6, Georgia 1

All-Tournament Team:
LHP Justin Wilson,
OF Steve Susdorf,
OF Steve Detwiler,
2B Erik Wetzel,
3B Tom Mendonca (Most Outstanding Player)

THE CHAMPIONS COME HOME

The hugs and high fives continued into the wee hours of the morning at the Hilton Garden Inn, where the staff had welcomed the champions back with congratulatory cake. I felt as drained as I knew the players were, and I had an early flight to catch, so I retired to my room while the crowd in the lobby was still pretty thick. Coming back down to catch a ride to the airport at about 5:30 a.m., I found Brandon Burke and the *Fresno Bee*'s Matt James still soaking in the dregs of a party befitting such an unimaginably glorious ending. I guess it wasn't hyperbole when I said they had reason to celebrate "all night."

Omaha's Eppley Airfield was a sea of red that morning. Fans, media, players' family members, they all greeted each other with a smile, a shake of the head, and one variation or another of "I can't believe that really happened." Copies of the *Omaha World-Herald* with its full-color photo spreads were stuffed into carry-on luggage already bursting at the seams with souvenirs. Long security checkpoint lines, confiscated toiletries, and $4 cups of coffee suddenly weren't so bothersome. The rare amalgamation of extreme exhaustion and sheer exhilaration radiated off of every Fresno face, from school president Dr. John Welty and his wife Sharon, to Jil Wilson, whose pride in her brother Justin was now shared by thousands.

I'd been asked to emcee a celebration at Beiden Field that night, so as my knees dug into the airline seat in front of me, I scribbled in my journal, toying with a little rhyme about the team. I wasn't sure if I would read it or not, but by the time I got those priceless "welcome home" hugs from my daughters, I had squeezed in references to all the players and coaches.

The team's charter was about to touch down around the corner, but the public had been encouraged to skip the landing and welcome the champions that evening at the ballpark. Inman Perkins couldn't wait that long. Perkins, who had been leading cheers at Beiden field for more than thirty years, was

Steve Detwiler, Steve Susdorf, and Nick Hom on top of a fire engine.
Howard Watkins/watkinsphotoarchive.com

Fans line the parade route on Fresno State's campus. *Howard Watkins/watkinsphotoarchive.com*

Justin Wilson, Justin Miller, and Trent Soares ride a fire engine in the victory parade. *Howard Watkins/watkinsphotoarchive.com*

Pete Beiden's statue glimmering in the sun. It is believed to be the only statue of a college baseball coach anywhere in the world. *Jordan Fox*

PETE BEIDEN

"Pete was one of the greatest fundamentalists to ever coach the game of baseball."

Bob Bennett

among a throng at least 200 strong, holding up commemorative copies of the *Fresno Bee* and cheering as the plane touched down and then taxied under a celebratory water arch provided by the Fresno Fire Department. Once the door opened, Steve Susdorf emerged holding the trophy, and the cheers intensified.

That warm welcome was like the first little toothpicked hors d'oeuvre at a gourmet feast—it was just a tiny taste of what the rest of the day would bring. A few hours later, players gathered on campus, climbing on anything with wheels—fire engines, golf carts, a wooden-benched Bulldog trolley—to cruise along a parade route lined with screaming fans.

The parade concluded at the same place where this journey had begun ten months earlier in long practices under blistering triple-digit temperatures. Making their way past the glimmering statue on their way to

the field, it seemed as if the look of satisfaction sculpted onto Pete Beiden's bronze countenance had been designed with this very occasion in mind.

The seats in the stadium had been full long before the parade began, and fans were filing onto the outfield grass to get a glimpse of the Wonderdogs as each player received a rousing introduction from public address announcer Mark Thomas. Thomas had uttered all those names countless times at that ballpark, but never to such a deafening response, and he had definitely never observed "the wave" make it a full 360 degrees around the diamond.

KMJ carried all the festivities live on the radio, while local TV stations did the same. The scoreboard flashed "2008 National Champions" and displayed the line score from the championship game. Among the many homemade signs in the stands was one requesting Detwiler's hand in marriage; another asked if Mendonca was single.

Batesole was the last to be introduced, pumping his fist in the air as the crowd chanted "Fresno State, Fresno State!" After fighting through some momentary microphone feedback to introduce the dignitaries behind me, I got the program underway, segueing into my little rhyme, which is printed here:

How does an underdog become a Wonderdog?
the little boy asked his dad
His curiosity piqued by Omaha's T-shirt fad
That's a really good question, the father replied
It happens when you put the team above your selfish pride
Don't focus on the numbers or a future pro career
Relax and have fun, and above all, have no fear
Trust those other guys in red to step up when they're needed
Point no fingers, place no blame, make sure every effort's feted
If you ever feel like you just don't have the heart
Look at Batesole's Bulldogs, how each one did his part
Justin Wilson on three days rest, firing all those strikes
129 pitches later, all Georgia could say was "yikes!"
Steve Detwiler, the Rhino, bouncing off outfield walls
And cornering the market on one-thumbed home-run balls
How about Gavin Hedstrom, who barely played last year?
His grand slam left those ASU fans crying in their beer
Behind the plate the tandem of Overland and Grubb
With timely swings and all the little things that stabilize a club
At first, Alan Ahmady, whose dazzling defensive display
Might have been Omaha's most electrifying play
Speaking of defense, have you seen a better glove?
Than the one at third those cameras took so many pictures of
Fingers dislocated or not, Tommy Mendonca can pick it
The bombs he hit at Rosenblatt worth the price of any ticket
Also in on the home run fun, freshmen Ribera and Muno
A movie about this team could top *Indiana Jones* or *Juno*
Who would play Steve Susdorf? Don't you say Will Clark
Not even "the Thrill" could match the senior's constant spark
He passed on going pro to get his degree in engineering
And wouldn't you know his graduation present is a national championship ring
The list goes on and on, from the incomparable Erik Wetzel
To Jason Breckley and his changeup rendering the hitter a twisted pretzel
The indefatigable Holden Sprague many a batter would befuddle
And he even convinced ESPN that his dad flew the space shuttle

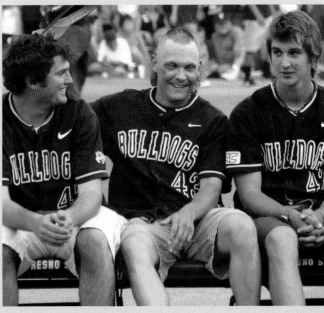

School records for saves were there for Brandon Burke to break
And he found two more suckers for his famous third-to-first fake
Johnson and Soares, Amador and Hom, all made their contributions
Now everyone knows about the champion Dogs, from Florida to the Aleutians
They know what Clayton Allison did to push 'em past UNC
He was even more dominant against Hawaii and USD
His Blazer buddy Kris Tomlinson had Omaha's scariest hair
But he faced the nation's best lefties and said "hit it if you dare"
Sean Bonesteele and Jake Floethe both had their moments at Rosenblatt
An injury kept us from seeing big righty Gene Escat
Justin Miller was quite the thriller with his fastball-slider power
And what could top career save #1 for the smiley-faced Jake Hower
Coach Batesole says it's all the players but he doth protest too much
From Batesole to Curtis, Waer to Mayne, each added a special touch
An entire dugout unified behind a common cause
Never jealous of a teammate because he had more helmet paws
It's that selfless choice of we over me that made this team so great
Wanna know what it takes to be a Wonderdog? Just look at Fresno State!

Interrupted numerous times by applause for the characters mentioned, the "poem" was well received, and I moved on to introduce school president Dr. John Welty, who began by turning toward the team and exclaiming, "Welcome home, Wonderdogs!" Welty brought up the theme of the school's marketing campaign, "Fresno State, powering the new California," and said these Bulldogs had provided a lesson on how to do that.

"If we remember what this team demonstrated these last few weeks," Welty said, "this part of California, and Fresno State, can accomplish anything in the future."

Next up was Fresno mayor Alan Autry, who came to the microphone amid chants of "Bubba, Bubba," referencing the character he played on the TV series "In the Heat of the Night." Autry nipped that in the bud when he shook his head and said, "No...Bull-

dogs!" Calling them "role models" for his 11-year-old son, Austin, Autry wanted the players to understand what their improbable title meant to people there and everywhere. "You won the championship for the underdogs all over this world," the mayor said before declaring it "Fresno State baseball day" in the city of Fresno. He then presented Batesole with a plaque bearing the key to the city, which Batesole hoisted in the air for all the cheering fans to see.

Autry wasn't done just yet. Before telling the crowd that he was lobbying for a Wonderdogs visit to the White House, he read a letter from California Governor Arnold Schwarzenegger. "This will go down in history as one of the greatest underdog stories of all time," the governor wrote. "Your teamwork and your heart have inspired your school, your city, and the entire Golden State."

Injecting more enthusiasm was Fresno State's student body president, Mackee Mason, crescendoing to this final yell: "We are THE Bulldogs, we are THE pride of the Valley, we are THE 2008 College World Series National Champions!"

Now it was time to hear from the team, and with Batesole leading off, I needed a little help from my daughter, Avery. The highlight of the Bulldog baseball experience for Avery has long been the big tub of red licorice in the Beiden Field press box. She routinely joins me in setting up our radio equipment, and never leaves without stopping by to greet the coach. At some point along the way, Batesole noticed her licorice and said, "Where's mine?" Ever since, she's made sure to bring one stick down for her "licorice buddy," who even taught her how to turn it into a straw and drink Gatorade through it. Autry gave the coach the key to the

Mike Batesole shows the fans the key to the city he received from Fresno mayor Alan Autry. *Howard Watkins/watkinsphotoarchive.com*

city, the fans gave him a standing ovation, but there was nothing Avery wanted to give him more than a little box of Red Vines.

As Batesole approached the mic, he motioned for the Diamond Dogs' two most vocal fans to join him. Don "Sugarbear" Kostrub performed "Wetzel While You Work" and "That's Ahmady," two little tunes the faithful fans had heard at almost every home game. Inman Perkins, who started leading cheers at Beiden Field in 1977, had his biggest group of teammates yet for his legendary Bulldog spell-outs.

Batesole recalled the day he was hired, how he sat in the Beiden Field dugout, watching the sun set while he thought about how the Bulldogs could make it to Omaha. The last six weeks had been the fulfillment of everything he imagined six years earlier. "What they've done is they've shown the country how to do things right," the coach told the crowd. "You can go to class and get your degree, and walk out of here with a diploma *and* a national championship ring. That's what these twenty-five guys did. I couldn't be more proud of what

they did. I couldn't be more proud of how they did it, and I couldn't be more proud of who they did it for—and that's you, the Fresno community. Thank you!"

One by one, Wilson, Wetzel, Mendonca, and Susdorf came to the podium to address the fans and answer a few questions. "It's all about family," said Wilson, "and I've got twenty-five brothers right here." Wetzel said he loved the community and loved all the "awesome" fans, "and I love these guys right here," he said, motioning to his teammates. "This has been the most amazing experience of my life, and I've thanked God ever since we won it, because it's amazing."

Susdorf sensed a divine influence, too. "First of all I'd like to thank God for everything He's done with this team," the graduating senior began, later finishing with his advice for the Bulldogs who would return in 2009. "Play your heart out," he said. "The only way this thing got done was by everyone playing together, and everybody knows that. Stay together, take everything inning by inning, and win another national title!"

Mike Batesole thanks 4-year-old Avery Loeffler for the box of red licorice.
Howard Watkins/watkinsphotoarchive.com

The team photo closed the festivities on the diamond, and the players were then escorted to autograph tables, with the line snaking all the way around the Beiden Field concourse. The emotions were still fresh, and the Wonderdogs would be riding the wave for weeks to come.

Invitations flooded in from everywhere. City councils, Boards of

Vocal fan Don "Sugarbear" Kostrub hugs Alan Ahmady after singing his "That's Ahmady" song. *Howard Watkins/watkinsphotoarchive.com*

Inman Perkins leads the huge Beiden Field crowd in a Bulldog spellout.
Howard Watkins/watkinsphotoarchive.com

"Stay together, take everything inning by inning, and win another national title!" — Steve Susdorf, to players returning in 2009.
Howard Watkins/watkinsphotoarchive.com

Players line up to sign autographs while the line snakes around the stadium.
Howard Watkins/watkinsphotoarchive.com

Supervisors, a beauty pageant, a photo op here, interviews there. They couldn't accommodate every request, but they sure tried. A Fresno post office issued a special postmark. Fresno State's award-winning viticulture department even made plans for a special wine commemorating the championship.

Batesole got a surprise phone call from Hall of Fame manager Sparky Anderson. "The stuff he saw in our club, it was like he was in the dugout with us," Batesole said. "His big thing was how the kids carried themselves like champions. Their body language. He understood that, and he saw through that how unselfish they were

and how they picked each other up all the time. That was a really special phone call."

Another call came from the state capitol, and soon Jason Breckley was accompanying Batesole and school administrators to Sacramento, where the California Legislature honored the team.

Breckley recalls one member of the Assembly telling him that the College World Series had even taken center stage during contentious budget negotiations. "We're supposed to be hammering out a budget," the legislator told him, "but we couldn't take our eyes off the game." Governor Schwarzenegger was out of town, but the Fresno State contingent did get to visit his office, where the actor proudly displays the sword from his film role as *Conan the Barbarian*.

Washington, D.C. took notice too. Eventually, the White House invitation would come, with a visit scheduled for November, after this book went to print. Before President Bush

The 2008 NCAA Champion Fresno State Bulldogs.
Howard Watkins/watkinsphotoarchive.com

could congratulate the Bulldogs, Congress already had. Introduced by Rep. Devin Nunes, along with fellow Fresno-area congressmen Jim Costa, George Radanovich, and Dennis Cardoza, not to mention twenty-six others, House Resolution 1327 recognized the Bulldogs' unforgettable season in superlative detail, and drew forty minutes of "debate" on the house floor, televised live by C-SPAN. Rep. Michael Castle (R-Delaware) said, "I watched some of these games on television and you see a Georgia vs. a Fresno State and your immediate thought is, 'Georgia must be dominant in this situation as they are a very dominant athletic team in this country.' But, indeed, Fresno State fought to win two out of three of those games and they deserve a tremendous amount of credit, particularly considering the year they had gone through."

While his alma mater had his name on its marquee, Mendonca was

Mike Batesole and Jason Breckley joke around with the *Conan the Barbarian* sword from Governor Arnold Schwarzenegger's office. *Christian Kozska*

helping the USA collegiate team to a perfect international record, capped off by a 4-for-4 performance in a thrilling 12-inning 1–0 win over Japan for the World Championship in the Czech Republic. The only downside of

the world tour was that it meant the CWS Most Outstanding Player missed out on the ESPY Awards.

Nominated in the Best Upset category, the Diamond Dogs were up against the Super Bowl champion

Speaker of the Assembly Karen Bass, Betsy Mosher, Assemblyman Juan Arambula, Mike Batesole, Jason Breckley, Thomas Boeh, and Assembly Minority Leader Mike Villines at a ceremony honoring the Wonderdogs at the state capitol. *Christian Kozska*

Steve Susdorf, Robert Detwiler, Justin Wilson, and Mike Batesole make their way into the ESPY Awards. Matt Leinart (blue shirt) and Lisa Leslie (red dress) are visible in the background. *Fresno State Media Relations*

Susie and Mike Batesole light up the red carpet at the ESPY Awards. *Fresno State Media Relations*

New York Giants. With ESPN deciding the winners via a nationwide popular vote, outpolling a team from the Big Apple would have been an even *bigger* upset than what they had already pulled off. The Giants took home the ESPY, but unlike the College World Series, this was one case where the Diamond Dogs *were* "happy just to be there."

Mike and Susie Batesole soaked in the sunshine on the red carpet outside the Nokia Theatre. Susdorf, Wilson, and Detwiler were the players invited, and their dates were their dads. "My dad was a little nervous,

he's a low key guy," said Susdorf, "but he had a blast. It was awesome."

The Bulldogs sat right behind the NBA champion Boston Celtics, including star Paul Pierce, whose older brother Steve Hosey was a standout on Fresno State's 1988 squad. Packers' quarterback Aaron Rodgers made a point of coming over to tell the players he had watched every game. "You guys are an inspiration," Detwiler remembered hearing Rodgers say. Batesole received compliments from Kansas basketball coach Bill Self, and reveled in a chance to visit with sportscaster Chris Berman. Robert

Detwiler had watched his son's greatest game from a distance, but now he was sharing this spectacular moment with him, and the longtime 49er fan even got to meet Jerry Rice.

"This whole experience was surreal," said Batesole. "Being in such company and nominated for an ESPY award is truly a tribute to a bunch of hard-working kids." Susdorf had taken a brief leave from the Williamsport Crosscutters to attend the ESPYs, so he was quickly headed back to the Phillies' NY-Penn League affiliate. Wilson would eventually sign with the Pirates, while Wetzel, Allison, and Miller began their professional careers, too.

The undrafted Burke received a free agent offer from the Arizona Diamondbacks—I guess mowing through all those All-Americans in the postseason got someone's attention—but he wasn't sure he'd take them up on it. He was already compiling material for his first stand-up comedian gig in San Diego. Pitching coach Mike Mayne took care of that. "He told me I was gonna go play or basically he was gonna kill me," said Burke with a laugh. "He's the reason I'm still playing baseball, he had such an influence on me. He was only there

Left to right: Steve Susdorf, Steve Detwiler, Justin Wilson, Jim Wilson, Mike Batesole, and Susie Batesole at the ESPY Awards. *Fresno State Media Relations*

a couple months, and he knew everyone's sister's names. He really cared. He's one of my best buddies and I'd take a bullet for him."

What Burke would be forced to take was a lot of ribbing from his minor league teammates. The baseball publications floating around clubhouses were littered with reminders of what the Bulldogs had accomplished. "We get all these magazines with Burke's face all over 'em," said Allison, who two months and a day after the championship game picked up his first professional win for the Dodgers' AA team in Jacksonville. "Stuff like that makes it really sink in." The write-ups on the CWS weren't the only things that caught the Bulldogs' eyes. This full-page ad in *Baseball America* quickly ended up hanging in many a locker.

Kyle Horn, vice president of marketing for Easton sports, had once coached Steve Susdorf's older brother, Billy. When he bumped into Bill and Katie Susdorf in Omaha, he told them, "If they win this thing, your son's going to be in our ad." A little over a month later, Horn was in Williamsport, presenting Susdorf with a framed print of the ad.

"What the Bulldogs did in Omaha reaches far beyond winning a championship," said Horn. "It speaks louder than any sponsor could ever dream of—and the components that make up what was 'said' are the true end-result benefits of what sports are all about. Hard work, perseverance, dedication—we've heard them all. But to personify that with a determined sense of teamwork and a true competitive spirit, speaks not only to the team. It speaks to the coaching staff, the athletic department, the administration, the city of Fresno , the San Joaquin Valley, the college baseball community, the world of amateur ath-

letics. Ultimately, it speaks to success. It speaks to exactly the type of college baseball program with which Easton Sports is proud to be partnered."

Horn had one more thing to say on behalf of Easton, and if given the

chance, all the people represented on the back of that helmet would echo his words. "To the Fresno State Bulldogs baseball team: we're proud to be on your team."

This advertisement was published in *Baseball America* and other publications.
Easton-Bell Sports

YOU MADE HISTORY, FRESNO STATE.
CONGRATULATIONS FROM OUR TEAM TO YOURS.

2008 COLLEGE WORLD SERIES® CHAMPIONS

REFLECTIONS ON A SEASON TO REMEMBER

For decades into the future, anyone who witnessed the transformation of those twenty-five young men from underdogs to Wonderdogs will continue to marvel at the sheer improbability of it. No matter what odds you want to place on this title's likelihood, those odds are just numbers, tangible quantifiers of the way things are *supposed* to play out. Those odds are worth about as much as the final RPI calculations, conducted after the conclusion of the College World Series.

You'll recall that Fresno State ranked 89th in the RPI heading into the Regionals. The *USA Today* coaches' poll saw the Bulldogs go from receiving *zero* votes in the last regular season poll, to #1 in the postseason poll. The RPI computer couldn't figure it out the way those coaches did. Using all the tangible representations of Fresno State's season, the numbers on paper which, when inserted into the RPI formula, produce

the NCAA's approved ranking, the computer spit out Long Beach State at #25, San Diego #24, Georgia #14, Arizona State #5, Rice #4, North Carolina #2, and Fresno State at...#46. Yep, one spot *behind* that UC Davis squad the Bulldogs opened the season against.

That #46 ranking leads me to two conclusions: the NCAA can find a better method of evaluating teams for postseason berths; and, clearly, Fresno State's first championship was won on the strength of its *intangibles*. When someone comes up with a computer that can quantify qualities like trust, guts, and heart, it's hard to imagine any of college baseball's other 295 teams surpassing the Wonderdogs.

I've tried to capture this historic season as accurately as possible, and doing so has been a tremendous privilege. To arrive at a true understanding of the magnitude of this accomplishment, I felt it was important to seek input from others who

felt its impact. In this chapter, you'll find more than three dozen contributions from people around the country. From Fresno State administrators, opposing coaches, local and national media, Bulldog alumni and former major league All-Stars, among others, these sentiments reinforce the significance of what this "bunch of goofballs" did.

Not only is this a story that people in Fresno and the San Joaquin Valley can take pride in commemorating for decades to come, it is a story that resonates with anyone who has ever been overlooked, discounted, or underestimated. What better way to lead off this heavy-hitting lineup than to hear from someone who can vouch for this story's ability to inspire, a young man who demonstrates that those twenty-five players in red weren't the only ones who had their dreams come true.

◆ ◆ ◆

June 20, 2008 was my 15th birthday. I have been watching the College World Series games since 2002—when I was battling cancer and had to *watch* baseball instead of playing it. Every year I saw all the great teams in it—Stanford, Rice, Fullerton, North Carolina, Oregon State, Georgia—and I always wondered if Fresno State, our hometown team and my Dad's alma mater, would ever make it. I asked my Mom and she said "never say never!"

When they got down to the final game of the playoffs I asked my Dad "if they make it to the final series will you take me for my birthday present?" He said, "Yes!!!"

On June 23rd we boarded the flight to Omaha for the best trip of my life. It even surpassed my Make-A-Wish trip to see the Yankees play in the World Series in 2003 (don't tell Derek Jeter I said that). We took my best friend Will along and the three of us were in baseball heaven! From having Coach Batesole's daughter paint our faces and chests with "Go Dogs," to screaming at the top of our lungs with Mrs. Welty in the stands, to hanging out with the team and Ray O'Canto at the hotel, to the ultimate thrill of the final game when the final out was made by Detwiler, was just indescribable!

I remember thinking, "Wow, it doesn't get any better than this!" This is the BEST birthday present I will ever, ever, ever get! Will and I felt like the luckiest "representatives" ever of the Fresno community and so privileged to be there. The way the whole team played was such an inspiration to us. It changed us forever. Anything in life is possible, if you work hard and you have the dream.

— *Hunter Jameson, Bulldogs' fan*

Will Brenner and Hunter Jameson pose with national champion Danny Muno. *Jameson Family*

Hunter Jameson (left) and Will Brenner outside Rosenblatt Stadium. *Jameson Family*

◆ ◆ ◆

In the years ahead, much will be written and said regarding this amazing baseball team. I'll leave the game's experts to analyze the dynamics on the field that led to their extraordinary accomplishment. Rather, I would like to acknowledge these men for the manner in which they performed off the field throughout the NCAA Championship run.

This team put into action the very characteristics of which Coach Batesole often speaks. They embraced the ultimate team approach and consistently displayed extraordinary poise, dignity and modesty throughout the tournament, regardless of the circumstances. They were quick to publicly recognize the skills and accomplishments of their opponents and just as quick to defer the credit for their success to their teammates. We were especially proud that they embodied the responsibility of being a role model and representative of our University community.

We have received countless messages from the citizens of Omaha who were continually impressed with the team's public demeanor, thoughtful gestures and genuine good nature—especially with children. It is these characteristics that we hope will help to define what it means to be a student-athlete at Fresno State well into the future. Clearly the extraordinary accomplishments of these men—and the manner in which they achieved them—will serve as an inspiration for many years to come. And for that they have our heartfelt respect and gratitude.

— *Thomas Boeh, Director of Athletics, Fresno State*

Fresno State football coach Pat Hill tips his cap to the Diamond Dogs. To Hill's left in that Bulldog cheering section are WAC Commissioner Karl Benson and Fresno State president Dr. John Welty, accompanied by his wife, Sharon.

Eric Sorenson

Our Bulldogs' journey to the NCAA baseball national championship is a story for the ages! It's about an outstanding coaching staff that guided extraordinary student-athletes to great accomplishments on the field by working together as a team to overcome obstacles. Throughout the season, these Bulldogs faced must-win situations and came through every time, maturing as players and teammates. They were characterized as underdogs, but Coach Mike Batesole and his assistants had taught these student-athletes well, instilling the confidence and pride that distinguishes champions.

Our community showed its support, too, with the Red Wave traveling to Omaha and cheering throughout the Central Valley. Our university and, indeed, the entire community won't soon forget this special group. They represent the best in intercollegiate athletics and made a powerful statement about the danger in underestimating Fresno State or the New California region that we're powering into the future.

— *Dr. John Welty, University President, Fresno State*

The Bulldog baseball team winning the national championship took me back to the old saying, "Why not us?" Why should a supposedly "mid-major" school not have a chance to contend at the highest level? They didn't have an easy road, by any stretch of the imagination, but their playoff system gave them a way to do it, and they did it. That's inspiring to any coach, anywhere, and it just leaves the dream open for our football team. Why not us someday, too?

— *Pat Hill, Head Football Coach, Fresno State*

National championships don't come around very often and for the Bulldogs to have two in the last ten years (softball in 1998) is very impressive. But not half as impressive as their 2008 post season run—from Ruston to Long Beach to Tempe to Omaha—what an incredible performance.

While the championship game was thrilling—what great performances by Wilson and Detwiler—the game I thought was the most thrilling was the second game of the finals against Georgia. Facing elimination once again and after such a tough loss on Monday night, and to go down by five runs in the 1st three innings, and then to score fifteen in the next three innings, was absolutely amazing!

I was in Omaha in 2003 when Rice won the CWS. But to be there with the Bulldogs and to be on the field for the post game celebration was much more special. And it will go down as one of the two most memorable experiences in my fourteen years as WAC commissioner, Boise State's Fiesta Bowl win being the other. And to top it off, by being nominated for an ESPY brought even more attention to the great job by Coach Batesole and his Bulldogs. Only bad thing about that is that the Bulldogs were put in the wrong category—rather than being in the "biggest upset" category they belonged in a special category all by themselves: "greatest performance ever by a team over a thirty day period." Yes, what a thrilling performance by the "underdogs to wonderdogs." Go Dogs!

— *Karl Benson, WAC Commissioner*

The Bulldogs had a magical month. They turned that magical month into a magical season. Thoughout the season Susdorf, Wetzel and Ahmady hit with amazing consistency and continued that consistency until the final out of the season. Their efforts set the stage for the strong finish. Their consistency held the team together through the rough times, which allowed the team to gain the confidence they showed in the playoff and in Omaha. The playoff and the World Series saw a total team effort.

In my opinion, Hedstrom's grand slam at Arizona State was the turning point. That home run seemed to lift the Bulldogs and completely deflate Arizona State. However, there were several other special moments and contributions. The outstanding relief pitching, headed by Burke, and the clutch pitching of the starters, led by Allison and Wilson, are examples. Of course, the outstanding offensive and defensive play of third baseman Tom Mendonca was a vital factor, as was the hitting of shortstop Danny Muno. Detwiler's determination and 6 RBIs in the final game will never be forgotten. Both catchers contributed greatly and Ribera grew as a hitter. They pulled together and everybody played as a team.

It was a special thing to watch how everyone on the team contributed, from first to last on the pitching staff, and from top to bottom in the batting order. Without trust, there is no teamwork, and these guys had trust. I was there in Omaha, watched them play the first game, and was impressed by how they played with confidence. I turned to my wife, Jane, in the middle of that win over Rice, and told her "they're gonna win the whole thing." I watched the championship game at home and was very proud of the 2008 World Series Champion Bulldogs.

— Bob Bennett, head coach,
Fresno State 1967, 1970–2002

As the owner of 580 KMJ it was an incredible feeling to hear history being made on the station that has been the voice of the Valley for over eighty years. When you think of all the major events that KMJ has covered for the Valley over the past eight decades, none may have been more impactful than the 2008 Bulldogs baseball team. The improbable run that the Bulldogs put together really united the Valley and gave the residents the ultimate sense of pride. The phone calls the KMJ on-air personalities received for the days and weeks after the series continued to emulate the excitement, pride and the fact that Fresno was in the spotlight instead of our neighbors in the Bay Area or Southern California.

I remember immediately following the celebration at Beiden Field that we hung a 20-foot by 40-foot banner off the side of our building at Palm and Shaw that read "Love them Dogs," and everyone driving by the station was honking their horn and stopping to take pictures of the banner. It was definitely a highlight of my broadcast career to be connected to this wonderful event. GO DOGS!

— Todd Lawley, CEO of Peak Broadcasting

"Love them Dogs" banner outside the KMJ Radio studios.
Robert Foshee

I had been away from the baseball broadcast booth for fifteen years when I was told I would be needed to broadcast Fresno State's appearance in the NCAA regional at Long Beach State. With Long Beach, San Diego and Cal in the field, I knew the Bulldogs had an uphill battle on their hands, and with Paul away in Washington, D.C., I had to rely on Ray O'Canto to carry me. He knew the players and I didn't. I have known Ray since his playing days with the Bulldogs, when I was calling the games on a regular basis, and he made it a wonderful experience for me again.

As the Regional unfolded and I had a chance to meet some of the players, it brought back memories of bygone days when I used to spend a lot of time at the ballpark. It was especially enjoyable to see how the fellows interacted with each other. From my point of view, there was a real bond between the players. No one seemed to take themselves too seriously and they appeared to really enjoy each other's company. I think that's what makes a winner. They got through the Long Beach Regional and were off to Tempe, where Paul and Ray carried them through to Omaha.

Again, I was told I would be needed to fill in for a game. I think the Omaha experience is something you have to live. I know the young men really enjoyed it and right away they became the crowd darlings of the series. Rosenblatt Stadium has changed since I did the Bulldogs games in the 1991 CWS, but the excitement is just as great. To go on and win it all? Well, it couldn't happen to a greater bunch of guys. I was fortunate of be a very small part of it. It's something I shall never forget, nor will that group of Bulldogs. Thanks, fellows, for the memories.

— Bill Woodward,
KMJ's "Voice of the Bulldogs" since 1971

◆ ◆ ◆

The story of the Fresno State baseball team's amazing run to win the College World Series is the ultimate tale of self-belief. The Bulldogs reached the unreachable star because they never allowed the word "failure" to become part of their vocabulary. Plus, they had a heck of a time pulling it all off, reminding so many of us why we love to play and follow sports. What a ride!

— *Chris Berman, ESPN*

Left to right: Steve Susdorf, Justin Wilson, Media Relations Director Steve Weakland, Jim Wilson, ESPN's Chris Berman, Mike Batesole, and Steve Detwiler on the red carpet at the ESPY Awards. *Fresno State Media Relations*

◆ ◆ ◆

Fresno State gave us one of those feel good stories that is all too rare in sports. We're familiar with underdogs springing upsets in individual games or early rounds of a tournament, but to continue the run all the way to a National Championship was incredible. The Bulldogs' ability to stay composed regardless of the score or situation served them very well in their title run. Coach Batesole established the tone for this team, and his players did a great job of staying composed when faced with enormous pressure.

— *Dave Miller, Senior Coordinating Producer, ESPN*

◆ ◆ ◆

The national championship won by Fresno State is one of the great stories in the history of the College World Series. Not only did the Bulldogs make history, but they did it with a grit that earned admiration from baseball fans all over the country. I was so impressed by the players' unshakeable belief in themselves, and by Coach Batesole's faith in them, too. I honestly believed they were down and out when they were facing elimination against North Carolina...everything seemed to be working in the Tar Heels' favor...yet the Bulldogs overcame the odds again on their way to the title.

The lasting memory I have is of so many players playing through injury, particularly outfielder Steve Detwiler, who was clearly in agony several times with a thumb injury that would require surgery. I was so impressed by how loose the players were when I visited with them at the team hotel. The "free-spirit" nature of the players served them well in the pressure of the CWS spotlight and in front of the national television audience. The rankings, and the history of teams with a similar seed in the NCAA tournament, would suggest that Fresno State had no chance. But their national championship was not a fluke. This was a talented, determined, and well-coached team that earned the title while overcoming the odds. I left Omaha with one question: How did that team lose 31 games during the season?

— *Sean McDonough, announcer who*
called Fresno State's three battles
with North Carolina for ESPN

◆ ◆ ◆

In Fresno State's victory, college baseball now has its Douglas beats Tyson, its George Mason. These guys didn't just make the Final Four, though, they went all the way, gleefully ignoring the seedings and predictions of so-called experts. The Bulldogs' story is unparalleled, not only in college baseball history, but in *baseball* history. Even in the majors, never has a club been as big an underdog as the Bulldogs were and managed to win the title. It's a feat we'll still be discussing in wonderment decades from now.

— *Eric Enders, author of*
The Fall Classic: The Definitive
History of the World Series

◆ ◆ ◆

If you've ever been to a game at Fresno State, be it at Beiden Field or even a football or basketball game, you understand how big this is for the San Joaquin Valley. They don't just love their Bulldogs, they live and die by them. They might not get 100,000 for their football games or 7,000 for their baseball games, but it's just as intense of a fan base as anywhere else. And I'm not saying I was pulling for them in Omaha. But I will say, you gotta like Fresno State winning the national title.

I'd put it on the same scale as a local rock band with loads of talent that has busted their butt for years, finally breaking through and making it big, bypassing all those over-hyped, over-produced Top 40 acts with all their big money and business suits behind them. To me, Fresno didn't "come out of nowhere" to win it all. They had some big-time talents. I think they just got the hammer-and-tong attitude that is kind of innate in the Fresno athletic program and rolled on from there. Nothing against the big boys here. But a "mid-major" taking the big prize? That is cool.

— *Eric Sorenson, National Baseball Writer,*
CBS College Sports

◆ ◆ ◆

When I decided to write a behind-the-scenes book at the 2008 CWS, I wanted to make sure I spent time with all eight teams. So naturally I decided to spend a lot time with Fresno State up front because, like my fellow so-called experts, I figured they'd be gone after two games, right? Now here I sit, writing my book while wearing a "Fresno State National Champions" ballcap and T-shirt. Who knew? What an honor to have experienced it all firsthand.

— *Ryan McGee,*
Senior Writer, **ESPN The Magazine,**
and author of the forthcoming book,
The Road to Omaha

◆ ◆ ◆

In the prognostication business, you take satisfaction wherever you can get it. So I'm proud to say that here at *Baseball America* we were onto Fresno State early. We ranked the Bulldogs 18th in our preseason top 25, the only rankings that gave Fresno any love. On paper, this was supposed to be a very good team, with key returnees on the mound and in the infield. So long before the Bulldogs became the Wonderdogs—Omaha's darlings—they were one of the biggest disappointments of the year in the halls of *Baseball America*. A month into the season, Fresno sat just 8–12. Some sleeper, we thought. Better luck next year.

I wish I could say that I believed in Fresno State all season long, that I had a feeling the Bulldogs would rally to win the WAC; that they would lose Tanner Scheppers and then emerge from the nation's most cut-throat Regional (we had nicknamed it the "Regional of Death" immediately upon seeing the brackets); that they would somehow shock high-powered Arizona State in Tempe, of all places; that they would cruise past Rice and hold off pitching-rich North Carolina; that they would cough up a three-run lead in the opener of the CWS finals against Georgia, then fall behind 5–0 in Game Two, yet bounce back to magically outscore UGa. 25–6 over the next 15 innings and be crowned national champions.

It was such a predictable sequence of events—of course we saw it coming. Didn't you?

— *Aaron Fitt, National Writer,* **Baseball America**

◆ ◆ ◆

It was one of the most significant wins in college baseball World Series history. They became the miracle team. It was like the U.S. hockey team beating the Russians, on a different scale of course, but just as improbable, impossible, unlikely, any word you like. What it showed is teamwork, the spirit of competition. Georgia was big and strong, but the Bulldogs had the fight. The coaches got out of the way and let the players play. I saw it and enjoyed every minute as a Fresno State alumnus.

— *Augie Garrido, NCAA's all-time winningest coach*
and four-time NCAA champ who played in the
1959 CWS for Fresno State

Mike Batesole and David Perno shaking hands in Omaha.
Minorwhite Studios/Fresno State athletics

❖ ❖ ❖

As tough as it is to get over finishing runner-up, you have to respect what Fresno did and how they did it! Their achievement didn't start in Omaha, it started in Ruston, Louisiana, when they won their conference tournament and got in the NCAAs as a four seed! They advanced through a challenging Regional and a very tough Super Regional and the rest was history! They did it against great odds and should be very proud because they made believers out of many other programs! My congrats to their players, coaches and staff.

— *David Perno, Georgia head coach*

❖ ❖ ❖

Fresno State did what all National Champions must do. They played their best baseball at the most important time of the year. Their kids played with confidence and poise on the biggest stage and in the biggest games. They received contributions from everyone in their lineup. It appeared to me that they used their so called "depleted" pitching staff and injuries to strengthen their resolve and take them to another level. That is one of the greatest things about baseball and it was fun to watch.

— *Mike Fox, North Carolina head coach*

❖ ❖ ❖

After the final game of the Long Beach Regional, I watched as my players hugged and cried for about an hour. Parents and fans were doing the same outside. I thought we had the mojo going into that game and were set up well with Griffin and Matusz waiting. I'm not a big destiny guy, Fresno flat out beat us. There are two sides of this story. Ours along with ASU and Georgia is one of heartbreak.

— *Rich Hill, San Diego head coach*

❖ ❖ ❖

I liked watching the team chemistry that was created during the run. A team can win, individuals cannot. If you are going to be eliminated, no one better than by the National Champions. Congratulations on being where we all want to be.

— *Mike Weathers, Long Beach State head coach*

❖ ❖ ❖

Coach Batesole has always done a great job. When we were in the WAC, I was always impressed with how well prepared his teams were. Mike has proven how vastly underrated the WAC is. Theirs was a great TEAM effort.

— *Wayne Graham, Rice head coach,*
who won the 2003 NCAA championship

❖ ❖ ❖

Fresno State's run to the National Championship was built on talent, toughness, character and grit. I, as a coach for nearly 35 years, greatly admired the way Fresno State competed—single-minded in purpose—determined to succeed and get the job done. The Western Athletic Conference is proud of this accomplishment, and it surely will inspire all of those who compete.

— *Sam Piraro, San Jose State head coach,*
who led the Spartans to the CWS in 2000

◆ ◆ ◆

Hawaii and Fresno State have been rivals in the WAC for many years and you don't generally find a lot of folks in the islands cheering for the Dogs in any sport. But the Diamond Dogs were a wonderful exception. What a magnificent accomplishment! Fresno State has raised the bar for the entire conference. Hold the trophy high and enjoy this special time.

— *Don Robbs, voice of Rainbow baseball*

◆ ◆ ◆

What Fresno State did during the 2008 baseball season was phenomenal. They remind me of the stories I heard my father tell about the Stanford football players (Class of 1936) that vowed never to lose to USC while they were in school, and they never did. They became known as the "Vow Boys." Maybe the 2008 Fresno State baseball team, called by many the "Diamond Dogs," could proudly be referred to as the "Wow Boys," because every time I heard them come up in conversation, people started by saying, "Wow, did you see what Fresno did?"

— *Dan Gustin, longtime voice of Nevada Wolf Pack sports, who played in the CWS for Santa Clara in 1962*

◆ ◆ ◆

I have been watching Bulldog baseball since 1940 when Stan Borleske was the coach, and nothing in all those years came close to what was accomplished by the Wonderdogs. Everyone contributed and that was the beautiful part. When they needed a hit, a great catch, an out, a double play, someone stepped up. The coaches made the right moves, players ignored injuries, they were never intimidated by the names on the opponents' uniforms. It was just a total package. After seeing the games in Tempe I figured they had a good shot. When they lost that first game to North Carolina I told several people they would win it. They proved me right.

— *Bruce Farris, longtime* **Fresno Bee** *sportswriter and member of Fresno State Baseball Wall of Fame*

◆ ◆ ◆

The 2008 College World Series was the most exciting I have ever watched. The first half of the season for Fresno State was not great, but the second half was fantastic. When they took on all the regions to make the finals, we all sat up to take notice. Truly the underdogs all the way, the Dogs came away with the championship, and it was deserved. They came together late and it was truly a good thing for the school and the San Joaquin Valley. Coach Mike Batesole did a great job and you could tell by the way they played the game that they were well coached.

Congratulations!

— *Gus Zernial, 1951 A.L. HR champ, 1953 A.L. All-star, and longtime sportscaster who announced Fresno State games on radio, 1963–1968*

◆ ◆ ◆

To call what happened a miracle would imply this bunch never had a chance. To call it unbelievable would suggest they did not believe in themselves. This is simply a return to old values that still work. What happened in Omaha, Nebraska in the summer of 2008 is what happens when talent meets team. No one would have guessed the Fresno State Bulldog baseball team with 31 losses would become a National Champion. The only ones who knew the possibilities were the team and its coaching staff. This team knew it had the talent but did not have the success-formula perfected.

So, twenty-five individuals dumped the selfish, statistics-driven, me-me-me concept in favor of "team," and the magic revealed itself. No miracle, just a reality check: team. Not unbelievable, just a smart decision at the right time: team work. A team that believed in itself and trusted each other enough to raise the National Championship trophy in college baseball for the first time ever in Fresno State history. Quite a concept, this unselfish, team thing. It works wonders in sports and life—just ask the Wonderdogs.

— *Marc Cotta, longtime Fresno broadcaster*

◆ ◆ ◆

There undoubtedly are many more milestone moments to come, but as a Bulldog fan/follower/supporter for 40 years I will compartmentalize this achievement in a separate time capsule. And my personal joy came from one Bulldog in particular: Steve Detwiler. Please indulge me.

I introduced myself to Steve in the batting cage at Beiden Field during his freshman year. I had heard that he was, like me, a graduate of San Rafael High School in the Bay Area. Not only that, I figured he just might have some hardware in the ol' SRHS trophy case, just like my brother ('57) and I ('63) do. An e-mail to Steve's former Athletics Director confirmed that he did, since "he won every award in several sports" for the red and white Bulldogs.

So I have lived vicariously through the exploits of that young man. I had a hunch he would be a hero of the post-season, but with his bazooka arm, not his bat. Even though we both enjoyed schoolboy success in Marin County (a mere 45 years apart), the similarities obviously ended there. My legacy is that I had deceptive speed. I was slower than I looked. We all have childhood memories that resurface from time to time, don't we? And as our Bulldog Foundation continues to assist in meeting the needs of a growing and increasingly successful athletics program, the young men and women reaching for their dreams should never be far from our thoughts.

— *John Wallace, Bulldog Foundation Chair*

San Rafael Bulldog alumni Steve Detwiler and John Wallace. *Wallace Family*

◆ ◆ ◆

As this month-long, keep-your-heart-paddles-handy, Bulldog post-season thrill ride started to garner coast-to-coast attention, predictable phraseology began to spill from the national media: "Cinderella Story," "Team of Destiny," etc. And while the authors of those buzzwords most certainly intended them as praise in describing Fresno State's astounding national championship run, they inadvertently, by falling back on cliché, minimized the magnitude of the team's accomplishment by failing to delineate the real reasons the Bulldogs were able to hoist the trophy on that Wednesday night in Omaha.

Namely, no matter who or where they played, no matter which teammate was playing in pain or out of the lineup altogether, these Bulldogs out-pitched, out-hit, out-defended and out-coached every team in their path. It wasn't smoke and mirrors, it wasn't destiny, it wasn't some veil of good fortune propelling these self-described "goofballs." Rather, it was, simply put, a group of very talented individuals coming together as one, performing to the optimum, at the absolute perfect moment in time—and becoming as deserving a champion as any sport, at any level, has ever seen.

— *Tony D'addato, longtime Fresno radio sportscaster*

◆ ◆ ◆

Forty-nine years have passed since the 1959 team became the first California State College team to play in the College World Series in Omaha. The stadium now has outfield bleachers, the fences are closer, and the left and right field stands have been extended. College baseball is still the most exciting game in town. What a great atmosphere! The hardest thing for me to believe is that it has taken Fresno State this long to win a national baseball championship. We've had great coaches with Beiden and Bennett and a highly respected program. But finally, the 2008 team has done it. With Coach Batesole pushing all the right buttons, hot hitting, great defense, solid pitching, Wilson's best control ever, and Detwiler's unbelievably hot bat, this miracle team won the title game. Finally a National Championship in baseball!

— *Merv Carter, outfielder on 1959 Bulldog team that went to Omaha, returned to Omaha for 2008 CWS*

Having been a former Bulldog during the '50s, I have been a die-hard fan of the baseball program at Fresno State for many years, and I can say, without the slightest doubt, the winning of the 2008 College World Series by the Fresno State Bulldogs eclipses any and all athletic feats I have witnessed in my lifetime. The mystery at which I marvel is what caused a team that looked destined to peter-out after winning the WAC become the best team in collegiate baseball? I don't know for sure, but this I do know: I saw a group of individuals transform themselves into an irresistible force, assume an indomitable will and epitomize the cliché "Never say die."

It became the most marvelous athletic scenario imaginable. I have never seen a team in serious pursuit of a major goal having so much fun and playing with such reckless abandon. Coach Mike Batesole reminded me of the Rock of Gibraltar, displaying a calm demeanor and a resolve that was the epitome of poise. Belief was written all over his face. Clichés like "rising to the occasion," "wouldn't be denied," and "doing the impossible" overwhelmed me as I watched each conquest unfold against what seemed like insurmountable odds. I must admit when I heard some one say "It was a miracle," I said (and meant it) that it was no miracle; it was a team that finally realized how good they were. As I look back at the teams of the past, I believe the 2008 team is the best of a long line of great baseball teams.

— Jack Hannah, pitched for Fresno State 1953–1955, member of the Fresno State Baseball Wall of Fame, as well as the Western Music Hall of Fame as lead singer of the Sons of the San Joaquin

◆ ◆ ◆

"Are you kidding me?" Those words, those magical glorious words that echoed in my mind hour after hour and day after day in Omaha, Nebraska. Beautiful, wonderful Omaha, the destination that all college baseball players yearn to vacation in for the month of June. I was sitting in the airport in San Francisco and grabbed a sandwich with my 11-year-old daughter, Diane. She slowly looked at the monitor in the restaurant, and tapped me on the shoulder as she shouted out, "Dad, look!" Slowly, I glanced up to see what seemed like the first time all over again, ESPN replaying the sweetest sight I have ever witnessed in Fresno State baseball history: Steve Detwiler stuffing a baseball in his back pocket moments before jumping on the biggest, greatest, most fantastic dogpile in the history of the school.

Ray O'Canto and his daughter, Diane, in Omaha. *O'Canto family*

Are you kidding me? If you would have told me in February, that on Fathers Day 2008 I would be in Omaha with my youngest daughter, that I would be doing color commentary next to my friend Paul, watching Fresno State win a national championship in front of 17,000 fans, I would have said, "Are you kidding me?" I haven't stopped flying since. Simply a blessing. Divine intervention! College baseball, in my humble opinion, is the most marvelous all of games. The crack of the bat, the smell of the grass, the sweet chatter in the dugout; all the sounds you have heard a thousand times: "It's all right, baby." "You can do it, Danny!" "Tommy, settle down, big guy." "You'll be OK, just hang in there, Clayton!" "We need you, Gavin!" "We need a spark, Jordan!" "Be the igniter, Erik!" "Don't make the last out, Steve!" "Never say never, Justin!"

Take it from this old Bulldog: those miraculous sounds... sound so much better in Omaha, Nebraska!

— Ray O'Canto, color commentator for 580 KMJ, played at Fresno State 1980–1981

◆ ◆ ◆

Since I stepped on the Fresno State campus in 1962 with the desire to play baseball, I have thought about what it must be like for those teams and their supporters who win the College World Series. Throughout my adult life, I have watched the Fresno State teams just try to get to the series, let alone compete and win. In 2008 it seemed impossible, especially as the year ended with significant losses in both games and players. I watched in amazement and awe as the team played through incredible adversity in Long Beach, then Tempe, and finally Omaha. My wife and I just hugged each other and cried as Steve Detwiler caught the ball for the final out, and then we wondered what we should do next. I was numb. Who do I call? What do I say? I called my grandson Drew, who spent six glorious days with me (and the team) in Omaha, cheering on the Bulldogs as he had all season. He even brought a new jersey to Omaha and had everyone on the team sign it after the first win against Rice. He believed the Bulldogs were going to win it all and he wanted to have a piece of the team to remember. I should have believed him.

As president of the Dugout Club I have received calls from coaches all over the country that have been to Fresno State for non-league games and the Pepsi-Johnny Quik Classic. All of them wanted to congratulate the team and the Dugout Club because they know the passion and caring hearts that many of the club members have for baseball and their Bulldogs.

It has been an incredible month. My goal is to remember that feeling I had the night they won for as long as I can, and always believe, because this year proved to all of us: you can never count out the Dogs!

— *Hal Froese, president, Fresno State Dugout Club*

◆ ◆ ◆

The 2008 CWS team at Fresno State is a tremendous compliment to Mike Batesole, Matt Curtis, Mike Mayne and Pat Waer. To lead a ball club to play its best baseball of the season from the regional playoffs through the final game against Georgia. The great baseball tradition of Pete Beiden, Bob Bennett and now the "Batesole Boys of Summer" brings great pride to every player who ever wore a Fresno State uniform. I personally have never seen a group of young men be so complimentary of one another. So unselfish. So team oriented. Applauding the heroics of one another. A true team effort!

— *Tom Sommers, played at Fresno State, 1962–1964, member of Fresno State Baseball Wall of Fame*

◆ ◆ ◆

The championship brought wonderful, positive recognition to Fresno State and to the community in general. Their win exemplified true heart and determination by a team who played together, each player making significant contributions to the win. They weren't even ranked going into the championship in Omaha, yet they overcame so many obstacles to produce a tremendous series and, ultimately, winning the entire CWS title. Coach Batesole will benefit because more young players will take a serious look at Fresno State to complete their college baseball careers.

Personally, I can relate to their sense of accomplishment and sheer joy in being able to participate in the College World Series. I was only 21 years old and was privileged to play for Cincinnati in the World Series against the Yankees, an experience I will carry with me the rest of my days. Hundreds of collegiate teams and players play ball their entire college career and never get the opportunity to compete in Omaha, let alone come home as national champs. I was so proud of my grandson, Jordan Ribera, a freshman designated hitter, and of the entire team of exceptional young men who will remember this CWS for the rest of their lives!

— *Jim Maloney, 1965 N.L. All-Star who threw three no-hitters for the Cincinnati Reds*

◆ ◆ ◆

Just as I was planning on a night with no baseball on June 25th, you guys had to play in some championship game, which forced me to watch. CONGRATULATIONS on the title, looking forward to the sequel.

— *Doug Greenwald, radio voice of the Fresno Grizzlies, AAA affiliate of the San Francisco Giants*

◆ ◆ ◆

The college experience of all participants who reach the College World Series in Omaha is a phenomenal feat. Then, if you are a member of the championship team, the joy derived in winning the crown will be forever instilled in the player's mind, and helpful to him in performing well again in other championship situations in the future.

— *Roland Hemond, Arizona Diamondbacks (former White Sox and Orioles GM)*

I've never been a part of covering the Final Four, so I've never been a part of a "Cinderella" ride. Being able to experience and cover this Fresno State team was a once in a lifetime opportunity. Once the team started showing some life in the championship series, we really started promoting what a great story this team was. As I was doing radio interviews and talking to newspapers, it finally hit me how special they really were.

Then the Dogs come out and do the unthinkable...they win it all! I don't think my goosebumps went away for a whole 24 hours.

— *Erin Andrews, ESPN Sideline Reporter*

ESPN's Erin Andrews exchanges a congratulatory fist bump with Mike Batesole. *Eric Sorenson*

The victory by Fresno State in Omaha in 2008 shocked the world of college baseball and was a huge win for the school, the Western Athletic Conference, and for Easton Sports. More than that, it was a resounding triumph for a coach who, ten years before, had almost had the rug pulled out from under his own spikes. Mike Batesole, then the head coach at Cal State Northridge, was told by the administration that the baseball program was being dropped due to budget cuts.

Not giving up, Batesole was able to convince the athletic director and school president to reinstate the program—and within a couple of years was able to take the Matadors to postseason play. It was through his tenacious leadership that the program was able to thrive. Coach Batesole was hired to take over the fabled baseball program at Fresno State in 2002, and his second recruiting class just won a national championship. One thing that Coach Batesole never forgot was the company that had been supporting his program at Cal State Northridge—and went on with him to Fresno State. That company was Easton Sports. In the dog-eat-dog competitive world of college baseball, Coach Batesole never wavered in his loyalty to the company that had been true to him. In June, 2008, that loyalty was paid off—in a big way!

— *Jim Darby, Vice President,*
Corporate Affairs, Easton Sports

ADDENDUM

CALIFORNIA GOLD

Mike Batesole mined every single one of his 25 players out of the Golden State. Fresno State was the only team in the 2008 College World Series that could boast a roster made up exclusively of players from its home state.

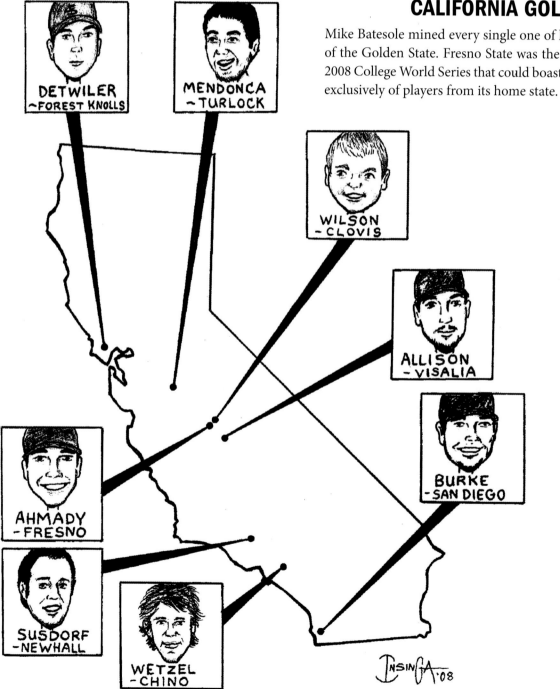

Alan Ahmady, #9

5'11" 195 lbs.
Sophomore
First Base
Fresno, CA (Clovis West HS)

- First team All-WAC
- WAC All-Tournament Team
- NCBWA National Player of the
  Week (4/1/08)

2008 Stats

	Avg.	R	H	2B	3B	HR	RBI	SB
Overall:	.382	60	110	17	1	13	92*	3-5
WAC:	.420	29	50	8	1	8	48	0-0

2nd in NCAA, 2nd in school history

CWS Highlight

Sliding catch in foul ground to start 3-5 double play against North Carolina.

Clayton Allison, #40

6'5" 215 lbs.
Senior
Right-handed Pitcher
Visalia, CA (Golden West HS/
College of the Sequoias)

- Academic All-WAC
- All-NCAA Regional Team
  (Long Beach)
- Drafted by L.A. Dodgers in 29th round

2008 Stats

	W-L	IP	K	BB	ERA	SV	Opp. Avg.
Overall:	4-5	96.2	57	23	3.91	1	.285
NCAA:	2-0	19	13	6	2.84	0	.270

CWS Highlight

6 innings, just 1 run in win over North Carolina to propel Bulldogs to championship series.

Blake Amador, #30

6'0" 190 lbs.
Senior
Outfield
Turlock, CA (Turlock HS/
Modesto JC/UNLV)

2008 Stats

	Avg.	R	H	2B	3B	HR	RBI	SB
Overall:	.167	5	2	1	0	0	0	0-0

Perfect 8-for-8 in defensive chances

CWS Highlight

Pinch-running and being on base at the same time as fellow Turlock HS graduate Tom Mendonca.

Sean Bonesteele, #37

6'5" 210 lbs.
Sophomore
Right-handed Pitcher
Santa Ana, CA (Foothill HS)

2008 Stats

	W-L	IP	K	BB	ERA	SV	Opp. Avg.
Overall:	2-2	25.2	10	13	6.31	0	.301
CWS:	0-0	5	0	0	5.40	0	.200

CWS Highlight

Starting championship series opener vs. Georgia, and allowing just 1 run on 2 hits in 3 innings.

Jason Breckley, #10

6'1" 220 lbs.
Senior
Right-handed Pitcher
Moorpark, CA (Moorpark HS)

- WAC Pitcher of the Week
  (May 12)

2008 Stats

	W-L	IP	K	BB	ERA	SV	Opp. Avg.
Overall:	3-2	24.2	28	13	7.66	2	.304
Last 20:	2-0	8.2	5	2	5.19	0	.258

CWS Highlight

Earning victory on 6/17 against North Carolina by retiring Tar Heels' all-time hits leader Chad Flack.

Brandon Burke, #25

6'3" 200 lbs.
Senior
Right-handed Pitcher
San Diego, CA
(Rancho Bernardo HS)

- 1st-team All-WAC
- Signed as free agent by Arizona
  Diamondbacks

2008 Stats

	W-L	IP	K	BB	ERA	SV	Opp. Avg.
Overall:	4-6	74	43	25	3.28	13*	.242
Last 20:	0-1	21	11	8	2.57	8	.205

*Fresno State single-season record, also holds career record with 24 saves. Famed pickoff move has claimed 20 baserunners since start of high school career.

CWS Highlight

Pitching the ninth inning of the final game and throwing the pitch that sealed the championship.

Steve Detwiler, #15

6'1" 220 lbs.
Sophomore
Outfield
Forest Knolls, CA (San Rafael HS)

- CWS All-Tournament Team

2008 Stats

	Avg.	R	H	2B	3B	HR	RBI	SB
Overall:	.269	48	65	12	0	12	59	5-5
CWS:	.333	7	10	3	0	3	11	1-1

Also led team with 8 outfield assists

CWS Highlight

4-for-4, 2 HR, 6 RBI performance in championship game, capping things off by catching the final out in right field.

Gene Escat, #42

6'5" 190 lbs.
Freshman
Right-handed Pitcher
Hanford, CA (Hanford HS)

2008 Stats

	W-L	IP	K	BB	ERA	SV	Opp. Avg.
Overall:	0-0	15	14	14	10.20	0	.302
WAC:	0-0	5.2	6	2	6.35	0	.227

CWS Highlight

Foot injury relegated him to the bench but didn't stop him from joining the dogpile.

Jake Floethe, #38

6'3" 195 lbs.
Freshman
Right-handed Pitcher
Lafayette, CA (Acalanes HS)

2008 Stats

	W-L	IP	K	BB	ERA	SV	Opp. Avg.
Overall:	1-1	25	20	16	8.64	0	.339
Last 20:	0-0	4	3	4	2.25	0	.316

CWS Highlight

Pitching in championship series opener vs. Georgia, and retiring stars Gordon Beckham and Rich Poythress back-to-back.

Danny Grubb, #4

5'11" 185 lbs.
Junior
Catcher
Orange, CA (Orange Lutheran HS)

2008 Stats

	Avg.	R	H	2B	3B	HR	RBI	SB
Overall:	.176	13	25	5	0	0	12	1-1
NCAA:	.263	3	5	0	0	0	2	0-0

Also threw out 8 would-be base stealers

CWS Highlight

Catching all nine innings of championship game.

Gavin Hedstrom, #29

6'1" 190 lbs.
Junior
Outfield
Irvine, CA (Woodbridge HS)

2008 Stats

	Avg.	R	H	2B	3B	HR	RBI	SB
Overall:	.303	51	76	10	0	7	35	5-7
Last 20:	.329	20	25	3	0	1	13	1-3

Had 18 sacrifice bunts in 2008, a new school record

CWS Highlight

2-for-5 with a double, RBI, and 3 runs scored in 19-10 win over Georgia.

Nick Hom, #7

6'0" 180 lbs.
Freshman
Infield
Benicia, CA (De La Salle HS)

2008 Stats

	Avg.	R	H	2B	3B	HR	RBI	SB
Overall:	.214	4	6	3	0	0	4	0-0

CWS Highlight

Single in only CWS at bat, in ninth inning of championship game.

Jake Hower, #50

6'4" 190 lbs.
Senior
Right-handed pitcher
Roseville, CA
(American River College)

2008 Stats

	W-L	IP	K	BB	ERA	SV	Opp. Avg.
Overall:	2-1	15	14	15	6.12	1	.253
Last 20:	1-0	6	3	2	0.00	1	.095

First American River College grad to win an NCAA Division I championship

CWS Highlight

Pitching 3 scoreless innings, allowing just 1 hit, to earn his first career save in a 19-10 win over Georgia.

Jake Johnson, #34

6'2" 205 lbs.
Freshman
Catcher
La Mirada, CA (La Mirada HS)

2008 Stats

	Avg.	R	H	2B	3B	HR	RBI	SB
Overall:	.224	4	13	3	0	1	5	0-0
WAC:	.375	1	6	1	0	0	1	0-0

CWS Highlight

Pinch-hit single in 19-10 victory over Georgia.

Tom Mendonca, #32

6'1" 200 lbs.
Sophomore
Third Base
Turlock, CA (Turlock HS)

- All-NCAA Regional Team (Long Beach)
- CWS Most Outstanding Player
- USA Collegiate Team

2008 Stats

	Avg.	R	H	2B	3B	HR	RBI	SB
Overall:	.281	48	83	8	1	19*	70	6-11
Last 20:	.333	11	24	4	0	5	23	2-3

led Bulldogs, 5th best in school history

CWS Highlight

Tied CWS record with 4 home runs, including pivotal 3-run blast to give the Bulldogs a 6-5 lead against Georgia. Fresno State never trailed again.

Justin Miller, #33

6'5" 195 lbs.
Junior
Right-handed Pitcher
Bakersfield, CA (Ridgeview HS/ Bakersfield College)

- WAC Pitcher of the Week (April 14)
- Drafted by Texas Rangers in 16th round

2008 Stats

	W-L	IP	K	BB	ERA	SV	Opp. Avg.
Overall:	6-4	87.1	81	50	5.46	0	.283

CWS Highlight

Started 5-3 win over North Carolina and went 4 innings, including the first 3 scoreless.

Danny Muno, #16
5'11" 170 lbs.
Freshman
Shortstop
Thousand Oaks, CA (Loyola HS)

- WAC Freshman of the Year

2008 Stats

	Avg.	R	H	2B	3B	HR	RBI	SB
Overall:	.330	62	95	13	2	3	30	10-13
CWS:	.357	7	10	0	1	1	8	0-0

Led team with 55 walks, 2nd in school history

CWS Highlight
2-for-6 with a home run and career-high 5 RBI in opening 17-5 win over Rice.

Ryan Overland, #24
6'2" 200 lbs.
Senior
Catcher
Atascadero, CA (Atascadero HS)

2008 Stats

	Avg.	R	H	2B	3B	HR	RBI	SB
Overall:	.291	23	46	3	0	4	24	0-0
WAC:	.307	10	23	1	0	1	14	0-0

Also threw out 9 would-be base stealers

CWS Highlight
2-for-2 with a home run in 5-3 victory over North Carolina.

Jordan Ribera, #19
6'0" 220 lbs.
Freshman
Designated Hitter
Fresno, CA (Clovis West HS)

2008 Stats

	Avg.	R	H	2B	3B	HR	RBI	SB
Overall:	.215	14	20	1	0	5	16	0-0
CWS:	.353	6	6	0	0	2	4	0-0

CWS Highlight
Home runs in CWS opener vs. Rice and championship series opener vs. Georgia.

Tanner Scheppers, #14
6'4" 200 lbs.
Junior
Right-handed Pitcher
Laguna Niguel, CA (Dana Hills HS)

- WAC Pitcher of the Year
- Drafted by Pittsburgh Pirates in 2nd round (did not sign)

2008 Stats

	W-L	IP	K	BB	ERA	SV	Opp. Avg.
Overall:	8-2	70.2	109	34	2.93	1	.202
WAC:	5-1	38.2	65	26	3.96	1	.197

13.88 strikeouts per nine innings (school record)

Shoulder injury kept him out of postseason play.

Trent Soares, #5

6'1" 195 lbs.
Freshman
Outfield
Fresno, CA
(San Joaquin Memorial HS)

2008 Stats

	Avg.	R	H	2B	3B	HR	RBI	SB
Overall:	.190	23	20	1	0	1	12	7-10
Last 20:	.250	4	3	0	0	0	2	1-1

CWS Highlight

Stealing second base against Georgia in the championship game.

Holden Sprague, #47

6'2" 210 lbs.
Junior
Right-handed Pitcher
Fresno, CA (Bullard HS)

2008 Stats

	W-L	IP	K	BB	ERA	SV	Opp. Avg.
Overall:	6-2	87.2	55	20	3.59	1	.287
Last 20:	4-0	30	15	9	3.60	0	.309

CWS Highlight

Retiring 7 North Carolina hitters in a row, 3 via the strikeout, in 2.2 innings of scoreless relief in a 5-3 victory.

Steve Susdorf, #27

6'1" 195 lbs., Senior, Outfield
Newhall, CA (Hart HS)

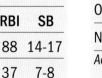

- WAC Player of the Year
- WAC Tournament MVP
- WAC Joe Kearney Award
- All-NCAA Regional Team
- CWS All-Tournament Team
- 2nd-team All-American (Collegiate Baseball)
- Academic All-American
- Drafted by Philadelphia Phillies in 19th Round

2008 Stats

	Avg.	R	H	2B	3B	HR	RBI	SB
Overall:	.344	80	104	33*	3	13	88	14-17
WAC:	.398	36	49	15	1	7	37	7-8

Led nation and set new school record
School record-holder for career RBI and career doubles

CWS Highlight

Sharing trophy with parents Katie and Bill after keying a Bulldog offense that tied a CWS record with 62 runs.

Kris Tomlinson, #43

6'0" 180 lbs.
Senior
Left-handed pitcher
Visalia, CA (Golden West HS)

2008 Stats

	W-L	IP	K	BB	ERA	SV	Opp. Avg.
Overall:	2-1	20	25	9	6.30	0	.263
NCAA:	1-0	3.1	4	2	0.00	0	.000

Academic All-WAC

CWS Highlight

Coming in with runners at first and third, no one out, and North Carolina's 3-4-5 hitters coming up, he got Tim Fedroff and Kyle Seager out to hold UNC scoreless in the inning.

Erik Wetzel, #3

6'1" 180 lbs.
Junior
Second Base
Chino, CA (Don Lugo HS)

- First-team All-WAC
- Academic All-WAC
- CWS All-Tournament Team
- Drafted by Colorado Rockies in 13th Round

2008 Stats

	Avg.	R	H	2B	3B	HR	RBI	SB
Overall:	.360	99*	112#	20	1	6	41	12-18
WAC:	.376	49	47	5	0	5	20	4-8

*led nation and set new school record
#tied school record

CWS Highlight

Pirouetting play in shallow right field to rob
North Carolina's Kyle Seager of a hit.

Justin Wilson, #21

6'3" 210 lbs.
Junior
Left-handed Pitcher
Clovis, CA (Buchanan HS)

- WAC All-Tournament Team
- All-NCAA Regional Team
  (Long Beach)
- CWS All-Tournament Team
- Drafted by Pittsburgh Pirates in 5th round

2008 Stats

	W-L	IP	K	BB	ERA	SV	Opp. Avg.
Overall:	9-5	124*	108	66	4.14	0	.263
CWS:	2-0	20.1	20	11	2.21	0	.234

*led nation

CWS Highlight

Striking out 9 Georgia Bulldogs in 8 innings in the
championship game, pitching on 3 days rest.

Mike Batesole, #44
Head Coach, 6th Season

- National Coach of the Year, NCBWA
- National Coach of the Year, Collegiate Baseball
- WAC Co-Coach of the Year
- Record at Fresno State: 219-165 (.570)
- Career Record (13 years): 475-323-1 (.595)
- NCAA Record at Fresno State (3 app.): 14-8 (.637)

Playing Experience
Garden Grove HS, Oral Roberts Univ., Minor Leagues with L.A. Dodgers system

Family
Wife, Susie; 4 children: Kassy, Kally, Kody, and Korby

Matt Curtis, #12
Assistant Coach, 6th Season
Third Base Coach
Recruiting Coordinator
Defensive instructor for catchers
Calls pitches

- 3 years (2000-2002) as volunteer assistant under Bob Bennett, and 1 (1998) as student assistant

Playing experience
Golden West HS (Visalia), Fresno State, Minor Leagues with Angels and Indians systems.

Family
Wife, Kim; 2 children: Lauren and Jacob

Mike Mayne, #36
Assistant Coach, 1st year
Pitching Coach

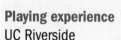

- Head Coach at Orange Coast College, 1977-1992
- Oakland A's catching instructor, 1996
- Also coached HS baseball and JC football

Playing experience
UC Riverside

Family
Wife, Patty; 2 children, Brent and Kevin; 5 grandchildren

Pat Waer, #6
Volunteer Assistant Coach, 2nd year
First Base Coach
Outfield Instructor

- Head Coach, Central HS (Fresno) 2002-2005
- Head Coach, Dinuba HS 1998-2002

Playing Experience
Clovis West HS, Mead HS (Spokane, WA), Bakersfield College, Washington State

Family
Wife, Natalie; son, Jackson

2008 NCAA Division I
Baseball Championship

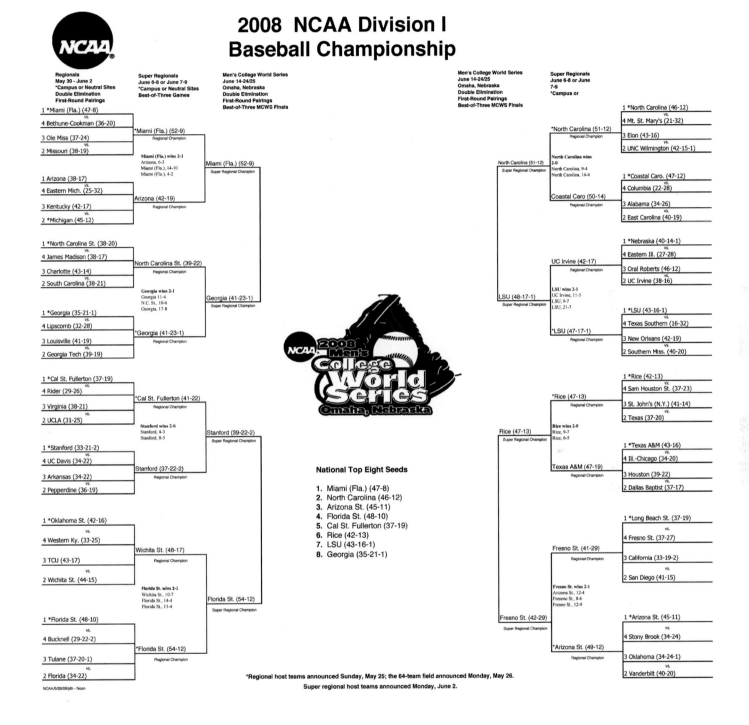

Regionals
May 30 - June 2
*Campus or Neutral Sites
Double Elimination
First-Round Pairings

Super Regionals
June 6-8 or June 7-9
*Campus or Neutral Sites
Best-of-Three Games

Men's College World Series
June 14-24/25
Omaha, Nebraska
Double Elimination
First-Round Pairings
Best-of-Three MCWS Finals

Men's College World Series
June 14-24/25
Omaha, Nebraska
Double Elimination
First-Round Pairings
Best-of-Three MCWS Finals

Super Regionals
June 6-8 or June
7-9
*Campus or

1 *Miami (Fla.) (47-8)
vs.
4 Bethune-Cookman (36-20)
*Miami (Fla.) (52-9)
Regional Champion
3 Ole Miss (37-24)
vs.
2 Missouri (38-19)

Miami (Fla.) wins 2-1
Arizona, 6-3
Miami (Fla.), 14-10
Miami (Fla.), 4-2

Miami (Fla.) (52-9)
Super Regional Champion

1 Arizona (38-17)
vs.
4 Eastern Mich. (25-32)
Arizona (42-19)
Regional Champion
3 Kentucky (42-17)
vs.
2 *Michigan (45-12)

1 *North Carolina St. (38-20)
vs.
4 James Madison (38-17)
North Carolina St. (39-22)
Regional Champion
3 Charlotte (43-14)
vs.
2 South Carolina (38-21)

Georgia wins 2-1
Georgia 11-4
N.C. St., 10-6
Georgia, 17-8

Georgia (41-23-1)
Super Regional Champion

1 *Georgia (35-21-1)
vs.
4 Lipscomb (32-28)
*Georgia (41-23-1)
Regional Champion
3 Louisville (41-19)
vs.
2 Georgia Tech (39-19)

1 *Cal St. Fullerton (37-19)
vs.
4 Rider (29-26)
*Cal St. Fullerton (41-22)
Regional Champion
3 Virginia (38-21)
vs.
2 UCLA (31-25)

Stanford wins 2-0
Stanford, 4-3
Stanford, 8-5

Stanford (39-22-2)
Super Regional Champion

1 *Stanford (33-21-2)
vs.
4 UC Davis (34-22)
Stanford (37-22-2)
Regional Champion
3 Arkansas (34-22)
vs.
2 Pepperdine (36-19)

1 *Oklahoma St. (42-16)
vs.
4 Western Ky. (33-25)
Wichita St. (48-17)
Regional Champion
3 TCU (43-17)
vs.
2 Wichita St. (44-15)

Florida St. wins 2-1
Wichita St., 10-7
Florida St., 14-4
Florida St., 11-4

Florida St. (54-12)
Super Regional Champion

1 *Florida St. (48-10)
vs.
4 Bucknell (29-22-2)
*Florida St. (54-12)
Regional Champion
3 Tulane (37-20-1)
vs.
2 Florida (34-22)

NCAA/5/26/06/jdh - Noon

1 *North Carolina (46-12)
vs.
4 Mt. St. Mary's (21-32)
*North Carolina (51-12)
Regional Champion
3 Elon (43-16)
vs.
2 UNC Wilmington (42-15-1)

North Carolina (51-12)
Super Regional Champion

North Carolina wins
2-0
North Carolina, 9-4
North Carolina, 14-4

1 *Coastal Caro. (47-12)
vs.
4 Columbia (22-28)
Coastal Caro (50-14)
Regional Champion
3 Alabama (34-26)
vs.
2 East Carolina (40-19)

1 *Nebraska (40-14-1)
vs.
4 Eastern Ill. (27-28)
UC Irvine (42-17)
Regional Champion
3 Oral Roberts (46-12)
vs.
2 UC Irvine (38-16)

LSU (48-17-1)
Super Regional Champion

LSU wins 2-1
UC Irvine, 11-5
LSU, 9-7
LSU, 21-7

1 *LSU (43-16-1)
vs.
4 Texas Southern (16-32)
*LSU (47-17-1)
Regional Champion
3 New Orleans (42-19)
vs.
2 Southern Miss. (40-20)

1 *Rice (42-13)
vs.
4 Sam Houston St. (37-23)
*Rice (47-13)
Regional Champion
3 St. John's (N.Y.) (41-14)
vs.
2 Texas (37-20)

Rice (47-13)
Super Regional Champion

Rice wins 2-0
Rice, 9-7
Rice, 6-5

1 *Texas A&M (43-16)
vs.
4 Ill.-Chicago (34-20)
Texas A&M (47-19)
Regional Champion
3 Houston (39-22)
vs.
2 Dallas Baptist (37-17)

1 *Long Beach St. (37-19)
vs.
4 Fresno St. (37-27)
Fresno St. (41-29)
Regional Champion
3 California (33-19-2)
vs.
2 San Diego (41-15)

Fresno St. (42-29)
Super Regional Champion

Fresno St. wins 2-1
Arizona St., 12-4
Fresno St., 8-6
Fresno St., 12-9

1 *Arizona St. (45-11)
vs.
4 Stony Brook (34-24)
*Arizona St. (49-12)
Regional Champion
3 Oklahoma (34-24-1)
vs.
2 Vanderbilt (40-20)

National Top Eight Seeds

1. Miami (Fla.) (47-8)
2. North Carolina (46-12)
3. Arizona St. (45-11)
4. Florida St. (48-10)
5. Cal St. Fullerton (37-19)
6. Rice (42-13)
7. LSU (43-16-1)
8. Georgia (35-21-1)

*Regional host teams announced Sunday, May 25; the 64-team field announced Monday, May 26.
Super regional host teams announced Monday, June 2.

2008 National Collegiate Division I
BASEBALL CHAMPIONSHIP

Johnny Rosenblatt Stadium, Omaha, Nebraska
June 14 - 24/25

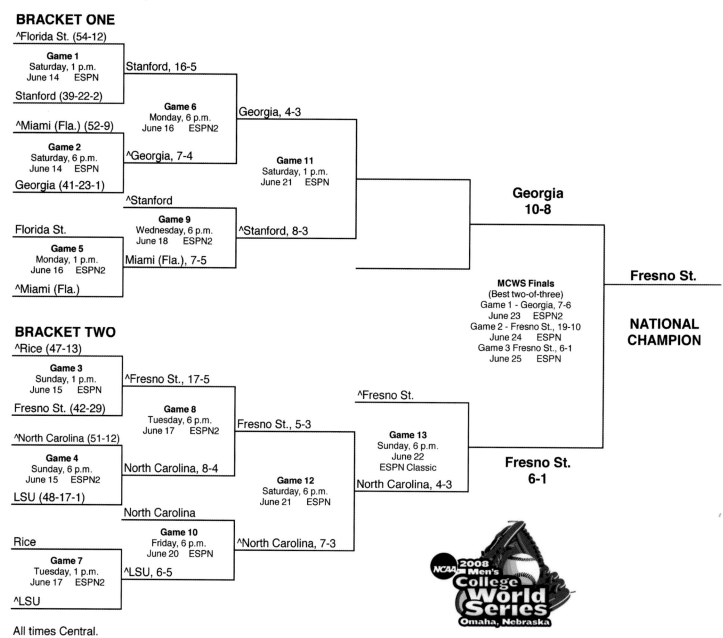

BRACKET ONE

^Florida St. (54-12)

Game 1
Saturday, 1 p.m.
June 14   ESPN   Stanford, 16-5

Stanford (39-22-2)

                          Game 6
                          Monday, 6 p.m.
^Miami (Fla.) (52-9)   June 16   ESPN2   Georgia, 4-3

Game 2
Saturday, 6 p.m.
June 14   ESPN   ^Georgia, 7-4

Georgia (41-23-1)   **Game 11**
                                               Saturday, 1 p.m.
                         ^Stanford   June 21   ESPN

Florida St.   ^Stanford, 8-3

Game 5   **Game 9**
Monday, 1 p.m.   Wednesday, 6 p.m.
June 16   ESPN2   June 18   ESPN2
                      Miami (Fla.), 7-5

^Miami (Fla.)

                                                                    **Georgia
                                                                    10-8**

BRACKET TWO

^Rice (47-13)
                                                                               Fresno St.
Game 3
Sunday, 1 p.m.
June 15   ESPN   ^Fresno St., 17-5   **NATIONAL
                                                                               CHAMPION**
Fresno St. (42-29)

                        Game 8   **MCWS Finals**
                        Tuesday, 6 p.m.   (Best two-of-three)
^North Carolina (51-12) June 17   ESPN2   Game 1 - Georgia, 7-6
                                                June 23   ESPN2
Game 4   North Carolina, 8-4   Game 2 - Fresno St., 19-10
Sunday, 6 p.m.   Fresno St., 5-3   June 24   ESPN
June 15   ESPN2   Game 3 Fresno St., 6-1
                                                June 25   ESPN
LSU (48-17-1)   ^Fresno St.

                                  Game 13
North Carolina   Sunday, 6 p.m.
                                  June 22
Game 10   ESPN Classic
Rice   Friday, 6 p.m.   North Carolina, 4-3
                June 20   ESPN
Game 7   **Fresno St.
Tuesday, 1 p.m.   6-1**
June 17   ESPN2   ^LSU, 6-5
                  Game 12
^LSU   Saturday, 6 p.m.
                  June 21   ESPN

                  ^North Carolina, 7-3

All times Central.

^ - Home Team

NCAA/6/20/08/DJL:JDH

ADDENDUM

2008 College World Series (Game 3)
FRESNO STATE vs. RICE
June 15, 2008 at Omaha (Rosenblatt Stadium)

Fresno State 17 (43-29)

Player	AB	R	H	RBI	BB	SO	PO	A	LOB	Avg.
Danny Muno ss............	6	2	2	5	0	2	2	3	0	.327
Gavin Hedstrom cf.......	4	1	1	2	1	0	7	0	0	.311
Erik Wetzel 2b..........	5	2	3	1	1	0	4	4	1	.365
Steve Susdorf lf........	4	1	0	0	0	1	0	0	1	.341
Alan Ahmady 1b..........	4	3	2	3	1	1	6	1	1	.386
Tommy Mendonca 3b.......	5	1	1	1	0	1	0	2	0	.280
Ryan Overland c.........	2	3	1	0	3	1	6	0	0	.294
Danny Grubb c...........	0	0	0	0	0	0	0	0	0	.185
Steve Detwiler rf.......	5	2	1	2	0	1	1	0	1	.258
Jordan Ribera dh........	4	2	2	3	0	1	0	0	0	.200
Trent Soares ph/dh......	1	0	0	0	0	1	0	0	0	.192
Justin Wilson p.........	0	0	0	0	0	0	0	1	0	.294
Sean Bonesteele p.......	0	0	0	0	0	0	1	0	0	-
Totals..................	40	17	13	17	6	9	27	11	4	

Rice 5 (47-14)

Player	AB	R	H	RBI	BB	SO	PO	A	LOB	Avg.
Jared Gayhart cf.........	4	0	2	1	0	0	0	0	3	.312
Rick Hague ss...........	5	0	1	0	0	1	0	3	1	.343
J.P. Padron 1b..........	4	0	0	0	1	1	12	0	0	.356
Aaron Luna lf...........	5	0	0	0	0	1	1	0	2	.309
Adam Zornes c...........	1	1	0	0	2	1	8	0	0	.307
Derek Myers pr..........	0	1	0	0	0	0	0	0	0	.234
John Hale c.............	1	0	0	0	0	0	1	0	0	.235
Jimmy Comerota 2b.......	4	1	2	0	0	0	1	8	0	.290
Diego Seastrunk 3b......	4	1	2	3	0	0	0	1	3	.356
Chad Mozingo rf........	3	1	1	0	1	0	3	0	0	.298
Jordan Dodson dh........	3	0	2	1	0	1	0	0	0	.202
Jess Buenger ph/dh......	1	0	0	0	0	0	0	0	0	.262
Ryan Berry p...........	0	0	0	0	0	0	1	2	0	-
Matt Evers p...........	0	0	0	0	0	0	0	0	0	-
Bryan Price p..........	0	0	0	0	0	0	0	0	0	-
Lucas Luetge p.........	0	0	0	0	0	0	0	0	0	-
Matt Langwell p........	0	0	0	0	0	0	0	0	0	-
Bobby Bell p...........	0	0	0	0	0	0	0	0	0	-
Cole St.Clair p........	0	0	0	0	0	0	0	0	0	-
Totals..................	35	5	10	5	4	5	27	14	9	

Score by Innings

```
                       R  H  E
Fresno State........ 040 705 010 - 17 13  2
Rice................ 000 011 030 -  5 10  1
```

E - Muno(25); Mendonca(11); Comerota(9). DP - Fresno State 3; Rice 1. LOB - Fresno State 4; Rice 9. 2B - Hedstrom(9); Wetzel(19); Dodson(8). HR - Muno(3); Ahmady(13); Mendonca(16); Ribera(4); Seastrunk(6). HBP - Hedstrom; Susdorf; Zornes. SF - Gayhart(4). SB - Ahmady(2).

Fresno State	IP	H	R	ER	BB	SO	AB	BF	NP	ERA
Justin Wilson.......	7.0	8	2	2	4	5	26	31	105	4.39
Sean Bonesteele.....	2.0	2	3	2	0	0	9	10	22	6.75

Rice	IP	H	R	ER	BB	SO	AB	BF	NP	ERA
Ryan Berry..........	3.1	7	9	5	3	1	18	21	73	3.63
Matt Evers..........	0.0	1	2	2	0	0	1	2	9	3.00
Bryan Price.........	1.2	0	1	1	2	1	5	7	34	3.72
Lucas Luetge........	0.2	1	2	2	1	2	3	4	18	6.16
Matt Langwell.......	1.1	3	2	2	0	1	7	7	27	4.52
Bobby Bell..........	1.0	1	1	1	0	3	4	4	14	1.31
Cole St.Clair.......	1.0	0	0	0	0	1	2	3	9	2.56

Win - Wilson (8-5). Loss - Berry (8-5). Save - None.
WP - Bonesteele(3); Price(11); Luetge(6). HBP - by Evers (Susdorf); by Bonesteele (Zornes); by St.Clair (Hedstrom). Inherited runners/scored: Evers 1/1; Luetge 1/0; Langwell 3/3. Pitches/strikes: Wilson 105/61; Bonesteele 22/13; Berry 73/46; Evers 9/4; Price 34/19; Luetge 18/10; Langwell 27/19; Bell 14/10; St.Clair 9/6.
Umpires - HP: Frank Sylvester 1B: Tony Walsh 2B: Mitch Mele 3B: Bill Speck
Start: 1:09 pm Time: 3:02 Attendance: 18108
Weather: 78 degrees, Mostly Sunny
Game notes:
Weather: 78 degrees, mostly sunny, wind SE at 8 mph.
Fresno State's 17 runs most at MCWS since Tennessee's 19 (6/11/01)
Evers faced 2 batters in the 4th.
Price faced 1 batter in the 6th.
Game: GAME03

145

2008 College World Series (Game 8)
NORTH CAROLINA vs. FRESNO STATE
June 17, 2008 at Omaha (Rosenblatt Stadium)

North Carolina 3 (52-13)

Player	AB	R	H	RBI	BB	SO	PO	A	LOB	Avg.
Dustin Ackley 1b.........	5	0	1	0	0	1	13	2	2	.404
Kyle Shelton lf..........	4	1	2	0	0	2	1	0	0	.333
Tim Fedroff rf...........	5	1	2	1	0	0	1	0	0	.401
Tim Federowicz c.........	4	0	0	0	1	0	6	1	1	.307
Kyle Seager 2b...........	4	1	1	1	0	1	0	1	0	.359
Chad Flack 3b............	4	0	2	1	0	0	0	4	3	.275
Mark Fleury dh...........	3	0	1	0	1	0	0	0	0	.279
Seth Williams cf.........	4	0	2	0	0	2	0	0	0	.326
Ryan Graepel ss..........	3	0	0	0	0	1	1	1	2	.256
Garrett Gore ph/ss......	1	0	0	0	0	0	0	0	2	.276
Adam Warren p............	0	0	0	0	0	0	2	1	0	-
Brian Moran p...........	0	0	0	0	0	0	0	0	0	-
Rob Wooten p............	0	0	0	0	0	0	2	0	0	-
Totals..................	37	3	11	3	2	7	24	12	10	

Fresno State 5 (44-29)

Player	AB	R	H	RBI	BB	SO	PO	A	LOB	Avg.
Danny Muno ss............	3	1	3	0	1	0	0	2	0	.335
Gavin Hedstrom cf........	4	1	2	0	0	1	1	0	0	.314
Erik Wetzel 2b...........	5	1	3	1	0	1	1	1	1	.369
Steve Susdorf lf.........	5	1	1	1	0	0	2	0	4	.338
Alan Ahmady 1b...........	5	0	2	2	0	0	11	1	1	.386
Tommy Mendonca 3b........	3	0	0	0	1	2	2	4	0	.277
Ryan Overland c..........	2	1	2	1	0	0	3	0	0	.303
Danny Grubb ph/c........	2	0	0	0	0	1	4	0	2	.182
Steve Detwiler rf.......	3	0	0	0	1	0	2	0	0	.255
Jordan Ribera dh........	3	0	0	0	1	0	0	0	4	.193
Justin Miller p..........	0	0	0	0	0	0	0	2	0	-
Kris Tomlinson p........	0	0	0	0	0	0	1	0	0	-
Jason Breckley p........	0	0	0	0	0	0	0	0	0	-
Holden Sprague p........	0	0	0	0	0	0	0	0	0	-
Brandon Burke p.........	0	0	0	0	0	0	0	0	0	-
Totals..................	35	5	13	5	4	5	27	10	12	

Score by Innings

```
                          R  H  E
-------------------------------------------
North Carolina...... 000 300 000 - 3 11  1
Fresno State........ 010 120 01X - 5 13  1
-------------------------------------------
```

E - Graepel(7); Overland(7). DP - N. Carolina 1; Fresno State 1. LOB - N. Carolina 10; Fresno State 12. 2B - Seager(29); Fleury(8); Wetzel(20). 3B - Fedroff(5). HR - Susdorf(12); Overland(4). HBP - Shelton; Muno. SH - Hedstrom(17). SB - Wetzel(12); Susdorf(14); Ahmady(3).

North Carolina	IP	H	R	ER	BB	SO	AB	BF	NP	ERA
Adam Warren.........	4.0	9	4	4	2	2	19	21	76	4.32
Brian Moran.........	0.2	1	0	0	0	1	3	3	13	2.14
Rob Wooten..........	3.1	3	1	1	2	2	13	17	58	1.80

Fresno State	IP	H	R	ER	BB	SO	AB	BF	NP	ERA
Justin Miller.......	4.0	7	3	3	1	2	18	20	66	4.97
Kris Tomlinson......	0.2	0	0	0	1	1	2	3	9	6.87
Jason Breckley......	0.1	0	0	0	0	0	1	1	3	7.54
Holden Sprague......	2.2	3	0	0	3	11	11	48	3.50
Brandon Burke.......	1.1	1	0	0	1	5	5	19	3.09

Win - Breckley (3-2). Loss - Warren (9-2). Save - Burke (13).
WP - Wooten(3). HBP - by Miller (Shelton); by Wooten (Muno). Inherited runners/scored: Moran 3/2; Wooten 2/0; Tomlinson 2/0; Breckley 3/0; Burke 2/0. Pitches/strikes: Warren 76/44; Moran 13/7; Wooten 58/34; Miller 66/40; Tomlinson 9/4; Breckley 3/2; Sprague 48/31; Burke 19/11.
Umpires - HP: Jim Garman 1B: David Wiley 2B: Mike Conlin 3B: Jack Cox
Start: 6:09 pm   Time: 3:06   Attendance: 23314
Game notes:
Weather: 80 degrees, hazy skies, winds calm.
Frank Sylvester (3B ump) enters game in bottom of 4th inning. Cox moves to 2nd base. Conlin to 1st base. David Wiley leaves game due to injury.
Miller faced 2 batters in the 5th.
Warren faced 3 batters in the 5th.
Game: GAME08

2008 College World Series (Game 12)
FRESNO STATE vs. NORTH CAROLINA
June 21, 2008 at Omaha (Rosenblatt Stadium)

Fresno State 3 (44-30)

Player	AB	R	H	RBI	BB	SO	PO	A	LOB
Danny Muno ss............	2	0	0	0	2	0	1	3	0
Gavin Hedstrom cf........	4	1	0	0	0	1	0	0	0
Erik Wetzel 2b...........	4	0	1	0	0	1	4	2	3
Steve Susdorf lf.........	3	0	1	1	1	1	1	0	0
Alan Ahmady 1b...........	4	1	2	0	0	0	7	1	1
Tommy Mendonca 3b........	4	1	1	2	0	2	1	3	2
Ryan Overland c..........	4	0	1	0	0	1	9	0	0
Steve Detwiler rf........	4	0	1	0	0	3	1	0	0
Jordan Ribera dh.........	2	0	0	0	1	1	0	0	0
Trent Soares pr/dh......	1	0	0	0	0	1	0	0	0
Justin Wilson p.........	0	0	0	0	0	0	0	0	0
Holden Sprague p........	0	0	0	0	0	0	0	1	0
Kris Tomlinson p........	0	0	0	0	0	0	0	0	0
Justin Miller p.........	0	0	0	0	0	0	0	1	0
Totals..................	32	3	7	3	4	11	24	11	6

North Carolina 4 (54-13)

Player	AB	R	H	RBI	BB	SO	PO	A	LOB
Dustin Ackley 1b.........	4	0	2	1	0	0	7	0	0
Kyle Shelton lf..........	2	0	0	0	1	2	2	0	2
Tim Fedroff rf...........	4	0	1	0	0	2	1	0	0
Tim Federowicz c.........	3	0	0	0	1	2	11	2	2
Kyle Seager 2b...........	4	1	1	0	0	2	5	3	2
Chad Flack 3b............	3	2	2	2	1	0	0	2	0
Garrett Gore dh..........	3	1	1	0	1	0	0	0	0
Seth Williams cf.........	3	0	1	1	1	0	1	0	0
Ryan Graepel ss..........	3	0	0	0	1	1	0	2	2
Matt Harvey p............	0	0	0	0	0	0	0	1	0
Rob Wooten p............	0	0	0	0	0	0	0	0	0
Brian Moran p...........	0	0	0	0	0	0	0	0	0
Alex White p............	0	0	0	0	0	0	0	0	0
Totals..................	29	4	8	4	6	9	27	10	8

Score by Innings		R	H	E
Fresno State.......	100 200 000 -	3	7	0
North Carolina......	000 200 02X -	4	8	0

DP - FSU 2. LOB - FSU 6; UNC 8. 2B - Detwiler(10); Seager, K(30); Flack, C(18). HR - Mendonca(17); Flack, C(7). SH - Shelton, K(13). CS - Susdorf(3).

Fresno State	IP	H	R	ER	BB	SO	AB	BF	NP
Justin Wilson.......	5.1	5	2	2	6	6	19	25	112
Holden Sprague......	1.0	1	0	0	0	1	3	4	16
Kris Tomlinson......	0.1	0	0	0	0	1	1	1	6
Justin Miller.......	1.1	2	2	2	0	1	6	6	21

North Carolina	IP	H	R	ER	BB	SO	AB	BF	NP
Matt Harvey.........	5.0	5	3	3	1	5	18	19	82
Rob Wooten..........	1.1	2	0	0	3	1	6	9	31
Brian Moran.........	0.0	0	0	0	0	0	0	0	2
Alex White..........	2.2	0	0	0	0	5	8	8	34

Win - White, A (13-3). Loss - Miller (6-4). Save - None.
WP - Wilson(8). PB - Federowicz,T(8). Pitches/strikes: Wilson 112/60; Sprague 16/12; Tomlinson 6/3; Miller 21/13; Harvey, M 82/53; Wooten, R 33/16; Moran, B 2/0; White, A 34/26.
Umpires - HP: Tony Walsh 1B: Mike Conlin 2B: Jack Cox 3B: Mitch Mele
Start: 6:56 pm   Time: 3:03   Attendance: 18611
Game: NC67

2008 College World Series (Game 13)
NORTH CAROLINA vs. FRESNO STATE
June 22, 2008 at Omaha (Rosenblatt Stadium)

North Carolina 1 (54-14)   Fresno State 6 (45-30)

Player	AB	R	H	RBI	BB	SO	PO	A	LOB	Avg.
Dustin Ackley 1b........	5	0	3	0	0	0	9	0	0	.417
Garrett Gore dh.........	5	0	0	0	0	0	0	0	0	.275
Tim Fedroff rf..........	4	1	3	0	0	0	0	0	0	.404
Chad Flack 3b...........	3	0	1	0	1	0	2	3	3	.277
Kyle Seager 2b..........	4	0	0	0	0	2	2	2	2	.347
Tim Federowicz c........	3	0	1	0	1	1	6	2	0	.303
Kyle Shelton lf.........	3	0	1	1	1	0	2	0	0	.326
Seth Williams cf........	4	0	0	0	0	3	1	0	2	.315
Ryan Graepel ss.........	3	0	1	0	0	1	2	3	3	.253
Mark Fleury ph..........	1	0	0	0	0	0	0	0	0	.275
Adam Warren p...........	0	0	0	0	0	0	0	2	0	-
Brian Moran p...........	0	0	0	0	0	0	0	0	0	-
Colin Bates p...........	0	0	0	0	0	0	0	0	0	-
Rob Wooten p............	0	0	0	0	0	0	0	1	0	-
Alex White p............	0	0	0	0	0	0	0	2	0	.000
Rob Catapano p..........	0	0	0	0	0	0	0	0	0	-
Tyler Trice p...........	0	0	0	0	0	0	0	0	0	-
Totals..................	35	1	10	1	3	7	24	15	10	

Player	AB	R	H	RBI	BB	SO	PO	A	LOB	Avg.
Danny Muno ss...........	4	0	1	1	1	1	1	3	5	.331
Gavin Hedstrom cf.......	3	0	1	0	0	0	2	0	0	.309
Erik Wetzel 2b..........	5	2	2	0	0	2	5	5	1	.368
Steve Susdorf lf........	4	2	2	0	0	1	1	0	3	.340
Alan Ahmady 1b..........	1	1	0	1	4	0	8	0	0	.386
Tommy Mendonca 3b.......	4	0	3	4	1	0	0	5	0	.284
Ryan Overland c.........	4	0	0	0	0	0	6	1	1	.294
Steve Detwiler rf.......	5	0	0	0	0	2	3	0	4	.249
Jordan Ribera dh........	1	1	1	0	2	0	0	0	0	.198
Jake Johnson ph.........	1	0	0	0	0	1	0	0	0	.218
Clayton Allison p.......	0	0	0	0	0	0	0	0	0	-
Holden Sprague p........	0	0	0	0	0	0	0	0	0	-
Brandon Burke p.........	0	0	0	0	0	0	1	0	0	-
Totals..................	32	6	10	6	8	7	27	14	14	

Score by Innings   R H E

North Carolina...... 000 100 000 - 1 10 1
Fresno State........ 002 112 00X - 6 10 0

E - Bates(2). DP - N. Carolina 1; Fresno State 2. LOB - N. Carolina 10; Fresno State 14. 2B - Ackley(21); Susdorf 2(31); Mendonca(8). HBP - Hedstrom; Susdorf; Overland. SH - Hedstrom(18). SB - Hedstrom(5).

North Carolina	IP	H	R	ER	BB	SO	AB	BF	NP	ERA
Adam Warren.........	1.2	0	0	0	4	3	4	9	43	4.23
Brian Moran.........	1.1	3	2	2	1	0	6	7	35	2.76
Colin Bates.........	1.0	3	1	0	0	1	6	6	24	2.78
Rob Wooten..........	0.1	1	1	1	2	0	2	5	18	1.87
Alex White..........	1.2	3	2	2	0	0	8	8	19	2.83
Rob Catapano........	1.0	0	0	0	0	2	3	5	21	3.03
Tyler Trice.........	1.0	0	0	0	1	1	3	4	19	2.04

Fresno State	IP	H	R	ER	BB	SO	AB	BF	NP	ERA
Clayton Allison.....	6.0	6	1	1	3	6	23	26	90	3.91
Holden Sprague......	1.0	2	0	0	0	0	5	5	20	3.42
Brandon Burke.......	2.0	2	0	0	0	1	7	7	18	3.00

Win - Allison (4-5). Loss - Moran (1-2). Save - None.

WP - Warren(7); Allison 2(7). HBP - by Wooten (Overland); by Catapano (Hedstrom); by Catapano (Susdorf). Inherited runners/scored: Moran 3/0; White 3/0; Trice 1/0. Pitches/strikes: Warren 43/20; Moran 35/23; Bates 24/15; Wooten 18/7; White 19/11; Catapano 21/11; Trice 19/14; Allison 90/53; Sprague 20/12; Burke 18/12.

Umpires - HP: Mitch Mele 1B: Bill Speck 2B: Jim Garman 3B: Mike Conlin

Start: 6:09 pm   Time: 3:08   Attendance: 15125

Game notes:

Weather: 83 degrees, clear skies, wind ENE at 5 mph, humidty 33%

North Carolina eliminated.

Fresno State advances to Championship Finals vs. Georgia (starts Monday)

Catapano faced 1 batter in the 8th.

Game: GAME13

2008 College World Series (Game 14)
FRESNO STATE vs. GEORGIA
June 23, 2008 at Omaha (Rosenblatt Stadium)

Fresno State 6 (45-31)   Georgia 7 (45-23-1)

Player	AB	R	H	RBI	BB	SO	PO	A	LOB	Avg.
Danny Muno ss............	4	0	0	0	1	0	1	4	0	.326
Gavin Hedstrom cf........	5	0	0	0	0	2	2	0	1	.303
Erik Wetzel 2b...........	4	1	0	0	1	1	3	3	0	.363
Steve Susdorf lf.........	4	0	2	1	0	1	5	0	1	.342
Alan Ahmady 1b...........	3	0	1	0	1	0	11	0	0	.386
Tommy Mendonca 3b........	4	1	1	1	0	1	1	3	0	.283
Ryan Overland c..........	2	2	0	0	1	0	1	0	2	.290
Steve Detwiler rf........	4	1	2	3	0	0	0	0	1	.253
Jordan Ribera dh.........	3	1	1	1	0	0	0	0	0	.202
Jake Johnson ph.........	0	0	0	0	0	0	0	0	0	.218
Justin Wilson ph........	1	0	0	0	0	0	0	0	1	.278
Sean Bonesteele p........	0	0	0	0	0	0	0	0	0	-
Jake Floethe p..........	0	0	0	0	0	0	0	0	0	-
Kris Tomlinson p........	0	0	0	0	0	0	0	0	0	-
Jason Breckley p........	0	0	0	0	0	0	1	0	0	-
Brandon Burke p.........	0	0	0	0	0	0	0	0	0	-
Totals..................	34	6	7	6	4	5	24	11	6	

Player	AB	R	H	RBI	BB	SO	PO	A	LOB	Avg.
Ryan Peisel 3b...........	4	1	1	0	0	1	1	3	0	.341
Matt Olson rf............	4	1	1	0	0	0	1	0	0	.317
Gordon Beckham ss........	4	1	2	2	0	0	3	1	0	.404
Rich Poythress 1b........	3	2	1	1	1	0	9	1	0	.374
Bryce Massanari c........	4	1	1	0	0	0	4	0	1	.335
Jake Crane c.............	0	0	0	0	0	0	1	0	0	.321
Matt Cerione cf..........	3	1	2	2	1	0	5	0	0	.307
Joey Lewis dh............	4	0	2	2	0	0	0	0	1	.258
Adam Fuller pr...........	0	0	0	0	0	0	0	0	0	.173
Lyle Allen lf............	4	0	0	0	0	0	1	0	2	.280
David Thoms 2b...........	4	0	0	0	0	0	2	3	1	.197
Trevor Holder p..........	0	0	0	0	0	0	0	1	0	-
Alex McRee p.............	0	0	0	0	0	0	0	0	0	-
Justin Earls p..........	0	0	0	0	0	0	0	0	0	-
Will Harvil p...........	0	0	0	0	0	0	0	0	0	-
Joshua Fields p.........	0	0	0	0	0	0	0	0	0	.194
Totals..................	34	7	10	7	2	1	27	9	5	

Score by Innings   R   H   E

Fresno State........ 001 020 030 - 6   7   0
Georgia............. 100 101 04X - 7 10   1

E - Holder(1). DP - Georgia 1. LOB - Fresno State 6; Georgia 5. 2B - Susdorf(32); Detwiler(11); Peisel(22); Cerione(15);
Lewis(7). 3B - Susdorf(3). HR - Mendonca(18); Detwiler(10); Ribera(5); Beckham(27). HBP - Overland.

Fresno State	IP	H	R	ER	BB	SO	AB	BF	NP	ERA
Sean Bonesteele.....	3.0	2	1	1	0	0	11	11	28	6.31
Jake Floethe........	0.2	2	1	1	1	0	4	5	18	8.64
Kris Tomlinson......	1.1	0	0	0	0	0	4	4	11	6.30
Jason Breckley......	2.0	3	2	2	0	1	9	9	34	7.66
Brandon Burke.......	1.0	3	3	3	1	0	6	7	23	3.33

Georgia	IP	H	R	ER	BB	SO	AB	BF	NP	ERA
Trevor Holder.......	7.0	4	3	3	3	4	26	29	106	4.41
Alex McRee..........	0.2	2	3	3	1	0	3	5	17	4.05
Justin Earls........	0.0	1	0	0	0	0	1	1	2	6.14
Will Harvil.........	0.1	0	0	0	0	0	1	1	6	3.64
Joshua Fields.......	1.0	0	0	0	0	1	3	3	12	3.41

Win - Harvil (2-1). Loss - Burke (4-6). Save - Fields (18).
WP - Holder(8). HBP - by McRee (Overland). Inherited runners/scored: Tomlinson 2/0; Burke 1/1; Earls 1/1; Harvil 1/0.
Pitches/strikes: Bonesteele 28/18; Floethe 18/7; Tomlinson 11/8; Breckley 34/19; Burke 23/14; Holder 106/64; McRee 17/9; Earls
2/1; Harvil 6/4; Fields 12/7.
Umpires - HP: Jim Garman 1B: David Wiley 2B: Frank Sylvester 3B: Tony Walsh
Start: 6:12 pm   Time: 2:55   Attendance: 19559
Game notes:
Additional Umpires: LF: Jack Cox RF: Mitch Mele
Weather: 78 degrees, overcast, winds E at 10 mph
Georgia leads best-of-3 CWS Finals, 1-0
Earls faced 1 batter in the 8th.
Breckley faced 1 batter in the 8th.
Game: GAME14

2008 College World Series (Game 15)
GEORGIA vs. FRESNO STATE
June 24, 2008 at Omaha (Rosenblatt Stadium)

Georgia 10 (45-24-1)

Player	ab	r	h	rbi	bb	so	po	a	lob
Ryan Peisel 3b	6	2	3	0	0	3	1	0	2
Matt Olson rf	6	1	1	1	0	1	2	0	2
Gordon Beckham ss	4	1	3	2	2	0	3	3	0
Rich Poythress 1b	4	1	2	3	0	0	9	1	1
Bryce Massanari c	3	1	0	0	1	0	3	0	0
Jake Crane c	1	0	0	0	0	0	3	1	2
Matt Cerione cf	2	1	0	0	2	1	2	0	1
Joey Lewis dh	3	0	1	2	0	2	0	0	0
Robbie O'Bryan ph/dh	2	1	1	0	0	1	0	0	0
Lyle Allen lf	2	0	0	0	0	0	0	0	0
Adam Fuller ph/lf	2	1	2	1	0	0	0	0	0
David Thoms 2b	5	1	3	1	0	1	1	2	4
Nick Montgomery p	0	0	0	0	0	0	0	0	0
Stephen Dodson p	0	0	0	0	0	0	0	0	0
Will Harvil p	0	0	0	0	0	0	0	0	0
Justin Grimm p	0	0	0	0	0	0	0	0	0
Justin Earls p	0	0	0	0	0	0	0	0	0
Steve Esmonde p	0	0	0	0	0	0	0	0	0
Jason Leaver p	0	0	0	0	0	0	0	0	0
Totals	40	10	16	10	5	9	24	7	12

Fresno St. 19 (46-31)

Player	ab	r	h	rbi	bb	so	po	a	lob
Danny Muno ss	4	4	3	2	2	0	0	2	1
Gavin Hedstrom cf	5	3	2	1	0	0	4	0	0
Erik Wetzel 2b	4	3	2	3	2	0	3	1	0
Steve Susdorf lf	5	3	2	4	1	1	1	0	0
Alan Ahmady 1b	5	1	2	2	1	0	5	1	0
Tommy Mendonca 3b	5	1	2	3	1	1	1	2	3
Ryan Overland c	3	0	1	2	0	0	6	2	1
Blake Amador pr	0	0	0	0	0	0	0	0	0
Danny Grubb c	1	0	0	1	0	1	4	0	0
Steve Detwiler rf	5	2	2	0	0	3	2	0	3
Jordan Ribera dh	3	2	2	0	1	1	0	0	0
Jake Johnson ph	1	0	1	0	0	0	0	0	0
Trent Soares pr	0	0	0	0	0	0	0	0	0
Justin Miller p	0	0	0	0	0	0	0	0	0
Holden Sprague p	0	0	0	0	0	0	0	0	0
Jake Hower p	0	0	0	0	0	0	1	0	0
Totals	41	19	19	18	8	7	27	8	8

Score by Innings

	1	2	3	4	5	6	7	8	9	R	H	E
Georgia	3	1	1	1	0	0	4	0	0	10	16	0
Fresno St.	0	0	6	5	4	0	3	1	X	19	19	2

E - Ahmady(6); Overland(8). DP - Georgia 1; Fresno State 2. LOB - Georgia 12; Fresno State 8. 2B - Olson(14); Hedstrom(10); Ahmady(17). 3B - Muno(2). HR - Susdorf(13); Mendonca(19). HBP - Cerione; Allen; Hedstrom. SF - Poythress 2(6); Grubb(2). SB - Peisel(14); Detwiler(5). CS - Beckham 2(4).

Georgia

	ip	h	r	er	bb	so	ab	bf
Nick Montgomery	2.1	4	5	5	3	1	10	13
Stephen Dodson	1.0	5	5	5	0	0	8	8
Will Harvil	1.2	5	5	5	2	2	10	12
Justin Grimm	1.0	2	3	3	2	2	5	8
Justin Earls	1.0	2	1	1	0	2	4	5
Steve Esmonde	0.2	1	0	0	0	0	3	3
Jason Leaver	0.1	0	0	0	1	0	1	2

Fresno St.

	ip	h	r	er	bb	so	ab	bf
Justin Miller	2.2	6	5	5	4	3	12	18
Holden Sprague	3.1	8	5	3	0	3	17	18
Jake Hower	3.0	2	0	0	1	3	11	13

Win - Sprague (6-2). Loss - Dodson (5-5). Save - Hower (1).
WP - Montgomery(5). HBP - by Miller (Allen); by Sprague (Cerione); by Grimm (Hedstrom).

Umpires - HP: Mike Conlin 1B: Frank Sylvester 2B: Tony Walsh 3B: Bill Speck
Start: 6:36 pm Time: 3:55 Attendance: 17223
Game notes:
Additional Umpires: LF: Mitch Mele; RF: Jim Garman
Weather: 68 degrees, overcast, winds SE at 9 mph. Game start delayed 26 min
Fresno State and Georgia tied 1-1, in best-of-3 CWS Finals.
Sprague faced 4 batters in the 7th.
Grimm faced 4 batters in the 7th.
Earls faced 2 batters in the 8th.

2008 College World Series (Game 16)
FRESNO STATE vs. GEORGIA
June 25, 2008 at Omaha (Rosenblatt Stadium)

Fresno State 6 (47-31)

Player	AB	R	H	RBI	BB	SO	PO	A	LOB	Avg.
Danny Muno ss............	5	0	1	0	0	1	0	1	0	.330
Gavin Hedstrom cf.......	5	0	1	0	0	0	7	0	2	.303
Erik Wetzel 2b..........	4	0	0	0	0	1	1	2	0	.360
Steve Susdorf lf........	2	3	1	0	1	0	0	0	0	.344
Alan Ahmady 1b..........	3	1	0	0	1	1	7	0	0	.382
Steve Detwiler rf.......	4	2	4	6	0	0	3	0	0	.269
Tommy Mendonca 3b.......	4	0	0	0	0	2	0	3	3	.281
Jake Johnson dh.........	2	0	0	0	0	0	0	0	0	.224
Jordan Ribera ph.......	1	0	0	0	0	0	0	0	0	.215
Nick Hom ph............	1	0	1	0	0	0	0	0	0	.214
Trent Soares pr........	0	0	0	0	0	0	0	0	0	.190
Danny Grubb c...........	4	0	0	0	0	0	9	0	0	.176
Justin Wilson p.........	0	0	0	0	0	0	0	0	0	.278
Clayton Allison p.......	0	0	0	0	0	0	0	0	0	-
Brandon Burke p........	0	0	0	0	0	0	0	0	0	-
Totals..................	35	6	8	6	2	5	27	6	5	

Georgia 1 (45-25-1)

Player	AB	R	H	RBI	BB	SO	PO	A	LOB
Ryan Peisel 3b...........	3	0	0	0	2	1	0	2	3
Matt Olson rf...........	5	0	0	0	0	1	5	0	4
Gordon Beckham ss........	4	1	2	1	0	0	2	0	0
Rich Poythress 1b........	4	0	1	0	0	0	10	1	1
Bryce Massanari dh.......	4	0	0	0	0	1	0	0	1
Matt Cerione cf..........	4	0	1	0	0	2	2	0	0
Joey Lewis c.............	4	0	2	0	0	1	5	1	0
Lyle Allen lf...........	3	0	0	0	0	2	2	0	0
Robbie O'Bryan ph.......	0	0	0	0	1	0	0	0	0
Adam Fuller pr.........	0	0	0	0	0	0	0	0	0
Miles Starr 2b.........	3	0	0	0	0	1	0	4	1
David Thoms ph.........	1	0	0	0	0	0	0	0	0
Nathan Moreau p.........	0	0	0	0	0	0	0	0	0
Dean Weaver p..........	0	0	0	0	0	0	0	3	0
Alex McRee p...........	0	0	0	0	0	0	1	0	0
Joshua Fields p........	0	0	0	0	0	0	0	0	0
Totals..................	35	1	6	1	3	9	27	11	10

Score by Innings

	R	H	E
Fresno State....... 020 103 000 -	6	8	4
Georgia............. 000 000 010 -	1	6	2

E - Muno 3(28); Detwiler(2); Poythress(3); Lewis(5). DP - Fresno State 1. LOB - Fresno State 5; Georgia 10. 2B - Susdorf(33); Detwiler(12). 3B - Lewis(1). HR - Detwiler 2(12); Beckham(28). HBP - Susdorf. SB - Soares(7). CS - Hedstrom

Fresno State	IP	H	R	ER	BB	SO	AB	BF	NP	ERA
Justin Wilson.......	8.0	5	1	1	1	9	32	33	129	4.14
Clayton Allison.....	0.0	1	0	0	1	0	1	2	7	3.91
Brandon Burke.......	1.0	0	0	0	1	0	2	3	10	3.28

Georgia	IP	H	R	ER	BB	SO	AB	BF	NP	ER
Nathan Moreau.......	5.0	3	3	2	1	4	18	19	88	5.1
Dean Weaver.........	2.2	4	3	3	1	0	12	14	47	4.2
Alex McRee..........	1.0	1	0	0	0	1	4	4	17	3.9
Joshua Fields.......	0.1	0	0	0	0	0	1	1	3	3.3

Win - Wilson (9-5). Loss - Moreau (4-4). Save - None.
WP - Wilson(9); Moreau(5). HBP - by Weaver (Susdorf). Inherited runners/scored: Burke 2/0; McRee 2/0; Fields 1/0.
Pitches/strikes: Wilson 129/87; Allison 7/2; Burke 10/5; Moreau 88/54; Weaver 47/27; McRee 17/11; Fields 3/3.
Umpires - HP: David Wiley 1B: Tony Walsh 2B: Bill Speck 3B: Jim Garman
Start: 6:11 pm   Time: 2:56   Attendance: 18932
Game notes:
Additional Umpires: LF: Frank Sylvester RF: Mike Conlin
Weather: 87 degrees, mostly sunny, wind S at 7 mph.
Total attendance of 330,099 for 2008 is all-time record for CWS.
Fresno State wins first MCWS title, winning CWS Finals 2-1.
Allison faced 2 batters in the 9th.
Game: GAME16

Here's a look at Fresno State's side of my scorebook for the 19-10 win over Georgia, with a little more graphite on the page than usual. You can see how Mike Batesole made an effort to get everyone involved offensively.